Advance Praise for
CARE Packages for the Home

"In CARE *Packages for the Home*, Barbara Glanz has created a most special 'silver box'—a whole book full of encouraging ways to make our homes the spiritual touchstones of our lives."

—Florence Littauer, author of *Silver Boxes* and *Dare to Dream*

"For all of use who 'CARE' deeply about our extended families, multiple copies of CARE *Packages for the Home* will be on our gift list! Creative, exhaustive, loving . . . and a powerful help for those who love and care for families."

—Naomi Rhode, past president, National Speakers Association

"My soul needed to receive this CARE package that Barbara Glanz has wrapped so tenderly with love, humor, great suggestions, and much passion. My heart rejoiced as I read it because she was giving a voice to my deepest feelings."

—Rosita Perez, professional speaker, Cavett Award
Winner, and Council of Peer's Speaker of
the Year and Award of Excellence Winner

"Families need inspiration today because of their busy work schedules. This book is ideal for inspiration and practical ideas. Barbara has integrated her wisdom with others to create an endearing *spirit* in her book that is packed full of great ideas to keep families renewed. Thank you, Barbara!"

—Bonnie Michaels, coauthor of *Solving the Work/Family Puzzle*

"Barbara Glanz has provided transformational ideas that are guaranteed to create an atmosphere in your home that will provide the peace and joy that home should represent for all of us."

—Glenna Salsbury, CSP, CPAE, 1997–98 president,
National Speakers Association, professional
speaker, and author of *The Art of the Fresh Start*

"Barbara's book brought back fond memories of just how much my parents loved us. It raised my awareness of how to be the husband and father I truly want to be. Perhaps most of all, it reaffirmed the importance of acknowledging the power greater than us. None of us can truly go it alone. Open your heart and mind to what is shared in this book. Life really does begin in the home."

—Larry Ray, Pacific Northwest State Office, Nationwide Insurance

"Barbara Glanz doesn't just recharge people's batteries. She points you in a whole new direction. Use this book again and again and again."

—W. Mitchell, CSP, CPAE, author, speaker, and television host

"Whether it is in the workplace or in the home, Barbara Glanz has captured the true spirit of a caring world. A positive attitude, a smile, a hug, a few words of encouragement . . . all go a long way in making our personal and business lives more meaningful and fun. Thanks, Barbara, for making these messages so clear."

—Ted A. Beattie, president/CEO, John G. Shedd Aquarium

"This book will make a big difference . . . where you live! This delightful gold mine is filled with engaging ideas and practical tips you can use immediately. CARE *Packages for the Home* will leave you feeling regenerated, renewed, and refreshed . . . what a great CARE package for you and your family!"

—Dr. Joel Goodman, The HUMOR Project,
Saratoga Springs, New York

CARE
PACKAGES
FOR • THE • HOME

Other Books by Barbara Glanz

CARE Packages for the Workplace:
Dozens of Little Things You Can Do to Regenerate Spirit at Work

The Creative Communicator:
399 Tools to Communicate Without Boring People to Death!

Building Customer Loyalty:
How YOU Can Help Keep Customers Returning

CARE PACKAGES

FOR • THE • HOME

Dozens of Ways
to Regenerate Spirit
Where You Live

BARBARA A. GLANZ

**Andrews McMeel
Publishing**

Kansas City

www.andrewsmcmeel.com

98 99 00 01 02 RDH 10 9 8 7 6 5 4 3 2 1

Library of Congress Cataloging-in-Publication Data

Glanz, Barbara A.
   Care packages for the home : dozens of ways you can regenerate spirit
where you live / by Barbara A. Glanz.
      p. cm.
   Includes bibliographical references.
   ISBN 0-8362-6834-2 (pbk.)
   1. Family. 2. Home. 3. Conduct of life. I. Title.
HQ734.G54   1998
306.85—dc21   98-23044
                                                                          CIP

The author has donated a portion of all the royalties to CARE,
the international relief and development agency.

Designed and composed by Kelly & Company, Lee's Summit, Missouri

ATTENTION: SCHOOLS AND BUSINESSES
Andrews McMeel books are available at quantity discounts with bulk purchase for educational, business, or sales promotional use. For information,
please write to: Special Sales Department, Andrews McMeel Publishing,
4520 Main Street, Kansas City, Missouri 64111.

*To my dear family members on Earth as well as those in Heaven,
to all families everywhere, and to our loving Heavenly Father, who
created families to shield us, to challenge us, to teach us, to love us,
and to help us grow more like Him.*

Permissions

Close to Home cartoons appear courtesy of John McPherson. *Close to Home* © 1995, 1996. Universal Press Syndicate. All rights reserved. Reprinted with permission.

Excerpts taken from "Dear Abby" columns by Abigail Van Buren © 1996, 1997. Universal Press Syndicate. All rights reserved. Reprinted with permission.

All occurrences of songs by David Roth © David Roth. All rights reserved. Reprinted with permission.

Dr. James Dobson's *Focus on the Family* bulletin, November 1997 © Tyndale House Periodicals. All rights reserved. Reprinted with permission.

"Looking for a Way of Life That Is Clean and Exact," article by Bob Greene © Tribune Media Services, Inc. All rights reserved. Reprinted with permission.

"The Sound of Two Hands Clapping" article, May 1, 1995 © *Newsweek* magazine. All rights reserved. Reprinted with permission.

Behavior Self Chart by G. Snyder and T. Keever © Performance Management Publications/Aubrey Daniels and Assoc. All rights reserved. Reprinted with permission.

Note: Every effort has been made to locate the copyright owners of the material used in this book. If an error or omission has been made, please notify the publisher and necessary changes will be made in subsequent printings.

Contents

Preface   xvi

Acknowledgments   xix

Introduction—My Story   1

Chapter One: How to CARE for Your Home and Family   9
"A Framework for Understanding Spirit in the Home"

Chapter Two: C = Creative Communication   13
"Get Your Messages Across in Creative and CARE-ing Ways"

Use Creative Slogans and Signs to Focus on Family Goals
   and Values   14
Share a "Piece" of Yourself   18
Develop a Personal Newsletter   18
Find Special Ways to Remember Your Family When You Travel   19
Begin the Day in Meaningful Ways   21
Foster Family Communication   25
Create Treasure Maps   27
Add a Personal Signature to Your E-mail Messages   28
Find Special Ways to Regenerate Everyone's Imagination   30
Create a "Baby Log" for Working Mothers   33
Find Ways to Communicate That Make Others Smile   34
Use Special Signals to Communicate   36
Try "Leftover Lotto"   37
Give Handmade Gifts   39
Plan Special Get-Togethers with Other Families   42
Find Creative Ways to Keep in Touch with Family and Friends   43
Write a Poem Just for That Person   44
The Three Ts of Great Relationships   48
"Nine Gold Medals" —David Roth   50

Chapter Three: A = Atmosphere 51
"What Does It Feel Like to Be in Your Home?"

Let Your Values Show 52
Have an Annual Blessing for Your House 53
Make Your Home a Place of Welcome 54
Make Your School a Courteous Place 55
Become a Reading Family 56
Choose an Object in Your Home That Demonstrates Love
   and Support 59
Find Fun Ways to Keep in Touch Even When Family Members
   Are Far Away 60
Plan Special Activities for Travel 63
Encourage Your Children to Play "Dress-up" 64
Use Calendars to Help Focus on Your Blessings 66
Create an Inviting Atmosphere—No Matter Where You Are 67
Approach Your Day with Humor 68
Encourage Laughter in Your Home 71
Banish Boredom in Your Home 72
Make a Family Fun Box 75
Create an Extended Family 77
Do Kind Things for Others 80
Give Your Children the Gift of Music 81
"More Alvins in the World" —David Roth 83

Chapter Four: A = Appreciation for All 84
"Become a Thankful Family"

Send an Anonymous Gift of Cheer 85
Make a Thanksgiving Tree 87
Write Thank-You Notes 88
Discover the Healing Power of Praise 88
Find Creative Ways to Appreciate People 89
Celebrate Your Pets 92
Share Your Appreciation in Words 95
Surprise Others with Little Treats 98
Every Family Needs a "Red Plate" 100
Find Fun Ways to Be More Thankful People 102
Give Fun Thank-You Gifts 104
Nurture Your Spouse 106
Hug Your Child with Your Words 107

Give Five Compliments a Day   108
Never Underestimate the Power of Your Smile   110
Send Thanksgiving Cards   111
Gift Ideas When the Budget Is Tight   112
Share an Amish Friendship Cake   113
"Pass It On™" Cards   114
"Thank You, Mr. Ryan" —David Roth   117

Chapter Five: R = Respect   118
"Value People"

Have Family Meetings   119
Share Your Passion and Involve Your Kids   121
Be Creative in the Ways You Discipline   123
Teach Your Children Fun Ways to Set Goals   125
Involve the Whole Family in Doing Things for Others   127
Find Ways to Spend More Time with Family   128
Schedule Special Family Time   129
Begin an Intergenerational Sharing Program   130
Use the Power of Positive Talking   133
Make People Feel Uniquely Valuable   135
Celebrate "Brothers' (or Sisters') Day"   139
Provide Opportunities for Young People to Learn a Better Way of Life   140
Give with Respect   141
Share What You've Learned from Others   142
Share Ways for Senior Citizens to Be Involved   144
Caring for a Blended Family   145
Discover Your Child's/Mate's/Parent's Love Language   149
Get Involved in a Family Literacy Program   151
Respect Yourself—Be Self-Fulfilled   153
"Dragon to Butterfly" —David Roth   155

Chapter Six: R = Reason for Being   157
"Create a Feeling of Purpose and Belonging"

Have Family Secrets   159
Have Fun Family Dinners   160
Create Precious Memories   164
Find Special Ways to Keep Loved Ones' Memories Alive   166
Little Things Can Show Our Love the Most   169
Do Special "Dad" Things   171

Have a "Friday Night Campout"   173
Create a Collage of Family Values and Traditions   174
Find Your Own Personal Way to Make the World Better   177
Let Family Members Know in Writing How Much They Mean to You   179
Share Family Tasks   183
No Child Is an Island   184
Have a "My Family Is Special" Day   185
Create a Family Mission Statement   187
Find Ways to Take Care of Our World   191
Create a "Dream List"   192
Do Special "Grandma" Things   194
Give Gifts of Support and Hope   197
"John and Josie" —David Roth   200

Chapter Seven: E = Empathy   201
"CARE for the World Both Inside and Outside Your Doors"

Listen with Your Heart   203
Walk a Mile in the Other Person's Shoes   205
Do a Project to Help Others   206
Teach Your Children to CARE for Others   208
Use Your Skills to Help Others   210
Give "Angel Gifts"   214
Share Your Blessings with Others   217
Scatter Seeds of Joy Wherever You Go   218
Control Worry and Negative Thoughts   220
Remember Older People   223
Begin a "Kindness Campaign"   227
Find a Charitable Cause You Can Support as a Family   230
Create a Christmas Cheer Box for Someone   234
Start a S.O.U.L. Group   236
Help a Sick Mom   238
Have a Baby Shower for the "Big" Brother or Sister   241
Begin a Foundation for Educational Excellence in Your Community   242
"The Dream" —David Roth   244

Chapter Eight: E = Enthusiasm   245
"Create Traditions and Celebrate Those You Love"

Make Banners   246
Have a Family Guest Book   247

Create Special Christmas Traditions for the Family   248
Share Christmas with a Needy Child   252
Give a Holiday Gift of Food for the Body and the Soul   254
Give Holiday Gifts That Focus on the Human Being   257
Take Traditional Holiday Photos   259
Make Meaningful Holiday Ornaments   260
Special Holiday Recipes Become Traditions   262
Start Special Grandparent Holiday Traditions   264
Celebrate Other Holidays   266
Do Group Cooking   270
Do Silly Things Together   272
Find Fun Recipes That the Whole Family Can Enjoy   274
Celebrate Good Neighbor Day   276
Discover Special Ways to Celebrate the Seasons   277
Plan Theme Birthday Parties   278
Start Birthday Traditions in Your Family   282
Have a "Come-as-You-Are" Party   285
Give Gifts from Your Heart and Personal Passion   286
Find Romantic Things to Do for Those You Love   288
"A Little Something More" —David Roth   291

Afterword   293

Resources   295

Biography   299

More CARE Packages for the Home   301

Bibliography/Sources   303

Preface

I TRULY BELIEVE that the future of our world lies in the regeneration of the family as an institution. In the ideal family, home is the place where we can come with our hurts, our pain, our sorrows, and our joys, and be fully accepted and loved. Home is the haven from the rest of the world where we are often overwhelmed with the frantic pace of change, the disillusionment and cynicism of today's workforce, and the fear of failure and lack of purpose in many of our own lives.

My belief is that most people today are in survival mode, just trying to make it through each day. Thus, they don't have time for theory and concept—they need hands-on, "how-to" ideas that they can apply immediately in their lives. This book reaches each one of us exactly where we are and shares many, many ideas of what others in our world are doing to make their homes, neighborhoods, and communities better places to live. I decided to include neighborhoods, communities, and even schools because as we make a difference in our own homes, that spirit spreads to those who live around us.

The ideas are simple, many of them do not cost any money, and anyone can apply them wherever they may live. Most of them can be done by any member of the family, yet they all will add a new spirit to your family life—a spirit of caring, communication, creativity, and fun. They will provide you with family legends, traditions, and stories to pass down throughout the years. And best of all, they will make your home, no matter what your financial circumstances, a much more caring place to live.

In an earlier book, CARE Packages for the Workplace—Dozens of Little Things You Can Do to Regenerate Spirit at Work (McGraw-Hill, 1996), I wrote about many ways any individual can make his or her workplace more joyful, and the book was a tremendous success. However, as time went on and I began speaking on this topic throughout our country and abroad, it became apparent that it is very difficult for a person who is living in an unhappy home environment to come to work and completely change his or her attitude toward life. I also have been studying some of the current data on the need for the balance of work and family. The result is a deep desire to not only help workplaces but to also help families create a more joyful, caring environment, and that is the purpose of this book.

I have used the metaphor of CARE Packages since each of us at some time in our lives has probably received a surprise package that tells us that someone cares about us. Similarly, each family member has opportunities every day to give that same kind of creative caring to others in his or her home. I also use the acronym CARE as the elements of a spirited home, and one chapter in the book is devoted to each:

C = Creative Communication
A = Atmosphere and Appreciation for All
R = Respect and Reason for Being
E = Empathy and Enthusiasm

Keep an open mind as you read and don't discard ideas because they are "different." Rather focus on the element of surprise and what you CAN do. It is often the simple things that have the biggest impact. This book is a celebration of many very special people and families who are making a difference in this troubled world. My wish is that this book and the ideas within will help you to celebrate your own families and to create the havens of love and joy that we all so desperately crave. Only then will we find balance, acceptance, and the freedom to be our best selves.

Warmly,
Barbara Glanz
4047 Howard Avenue
Western Springs, IL 60558
708-246-8594
Fax 708-246-5123
e-mail: bglanz@barbaraglanz.com
web site: www.barbaraglanz.com

Keeping a family together is like keeping a bonfire going in a rainstorm.
—Charles Swindoll

The depth of love between a man and woman is most beautifully expressed in the happiness of their children.
—Marjorie Ames

This Is a Family

A place of warmth when the world is cold . . . a place of safety when the world is hostile . . . a place of light when the world is dark. This is a family.

A family shares things . . . like dreams and hopes and possessions and memories and smiles and frowns and gladness.

A family is a place of respect and understanding . . . a place where love and faith dwells. A family is a place where all members can enjoy the dignity of their own personalities.

No person is ever alone—who is a member of a family.

A family is a group of human beings who care about each other . . . and feel comfortable with each other . . . and who will stand up for each other.

This is a family.

Like all groups of human beings, families will taunt and fight and bicker among each other . . .

But when trouble threatens from outside the clan, there is an instant closing of the ranks against the outsiders.

This is a family.

—author unknown

Acknowledgments

I WANT TO THANK the many people who had a part in this book of the heart:

To my grandparents and great-grandparents, who laid the foundation for our family.

To my parents, Wayne and Lucille Bauerle, who gave me the gifts of music, of reading, of creativity, of caring for others, and most of all, the gift of believing in myself and the freedom and courage to follow my dreams.

To my own dear family, Charlie, Garrett, Gretchen, and Erin, for being my laboratory, for putting up with my undaunted enthusiasm for life, and for always keeping me humble.

To my trusted assistants, Laurie Trice and Leslie Seidel; to my head cheer-leaders and helpers, Karen Sivert, Marina Marino, Rita Emmett, Barbara McCauley, Cathy Norman, Rosita Perez, Beth Lewis, Cindy Zigmund, and Rita Blitt; and to my editor, Dorothy O'Brien, who has always had my best interest at heart.

To all the contributors to the book who are truly CARE-ing for their precious families.

And most of all, to my husband, Charlie, the "wind beneath my wings."

God bless you all.

CARE
PACKAGES

FOR • THE • HOME

Introduction:

My Story

A FAMILY CAN CONSIST of one person or many. It can be a single-parent family, a blended family, a retired family, an extended family, or a traditional family. There are ideas in this book for all of these.

This book has been in my heart for many years. It is important, I think, for you as readers to know my story, for it will help you to understand how many of the ideas I've shared came about. I was very blessed because I was able to stay home with my children for almost nineteen years. However, times were different then, so it is important that any of you who are working mothers do not feel guilty—that is certainly not my purpose in telling my story—but perhaps you can better understand my values and the importance of writing this book to me as you hear the events of my family life in an article I wrote recently:

YOU <u>CAN</u> HAVE IT ALL

A Message of Hope for Women Who Choose to Stay Home with Their Children

This is a true story. It is about the choices I have made over the last twenty-eight years and how those choices have affected my life and my career. It is also a message of hope and encouragement for those of you who have chosen to put your family first during the early years of their lives. I firmly believe that you CAN have it all—home, family, and successful career—*you just have it at different times in your life.*

In 1965 I graduated from college with a degree in English education. Because I had met my husband-to-be the preceding summer and he was employed by a Chicago newspaper, my job search was limited to the suburbs of Chicago. That spring I was thrilled to sign a contract to teach freshman and sophomore English at Lyons Township High School in La Grange, Illinois. My teaching career was everything I had dreamed of—exciting, challenging, and grounded with a deep sense of mission that I was helping young people learn to appreciate the power of the written and the spoken word and their own unique value as human beings.

Close to Home © John McPherson/Dist. by Universal Press Syndicate.

When I became pregnant with our first son, Garrett, in 1968, there was no question in my mind about what I would do. I taught until the end of January 1969; then I left to become a full-time mother. I still, however, kept up a regular contact with my friends who were teachers, and I corresponded with many of my former students. Although I missed the professional stimulation of my job, I was delighting in learning everything I could about being a parent.

Then came 1971—the worst year of my life! Early in that year my gentle mother-in-law died after an agonizingly long battle with cancer. In September my vigorous father at age sixty-two had a sudden heart attack in the night and was gone. And in December we lost our second son at birth with no warning whatsoever. Soon after that, I found a lump in my breast. For the next several years my focus was simply on survival, somehow learning to cope with the grief and the losses I had experienced.

During this time I made two deeply important choices in my life: One was to *live five minutes at a time.* There were many days when the grief was so overwhelming that I couldn't face even the next few hours; however, I could always make it through just five minutes! That choice has enabled me to be fully in the present, no matter what I am doing.

The other conscious choice I made was to *never again try to be something or someone I was not.* I was hurting so much that I knew I could never be hurt so deeply again; thus, I chose to take the risk of being totally authentic in my life.

Somehow, over time, I gradually began to rediscover that every day is a **gift** to be opened with courage and anticipation and joy. Finally I was again able to reach out to others and to feel a sense of purpose in my life. In 1973 we were blessed with our first daughter, Gretchen, and in 1976 our third child, Erin, completed our family.

During those years my focus, my primary "career," became my children. I made it my job to expose them to the widest variety of life experiences I could. Because of our close proximity to Chicago, I was able to take them to many special classes at the museums, the zoos, the Art Institute, and the Aquarium, most of which were free. We attended children's concerts, children's theater productions, and story hours at the library, and I was deeply committed to reading aloud to them for thirty minutes every day. As they grew older, they all took piano lessons (one of the two "nonnegotiables" in our home: They each had to take piano lessons until their twelfth birthday *and* they could not use a gift until they had written a thank-you note to the giver!)

I also invited people from all walks of life and all parts of the world to our home to help broaden our children's perspectives. We went to church and Sunday school, we had many picnics, we played many games, we did many crafts together, and we all loved the costume box which I constantly kept stocked from resale shops and garage sales! Although my budget was low, my motivation was high, and I felt successful in my chosen "career."

About 1974, I began to feel a need for my own *professional* growth. I had been volunteering in the community, my church, and the school system, and those activities not only taught me a great deal about organizational skills, people management, and fund-raising, but they were also deeply satisfying. However, it became more and more important to me to use my education and my teaching skills in a more professional way while at the same time keeping my primary focus on my children.

About that time I heard of an opening in the Adult Evening School to teach English as a Second Language, and I accepted the job of teaching five hours a week in the evenings. Since I had had no formal training in that area, I signed up for a weekend extension graduate class from Northern Illinois University. That class led to a commitment for the next five years of my life—I took one course every quarter until 1980, when I received my master's degree in Adult Continuing Education. As part of the graduation ceremony, the chancellor asked the family of each of the graduates to stand up as he or she received a diploma. My children nearly burst their buttons with pride for their help in accomplishing this feat! It certainly taught them a lot about the value of education while at the same time it fulfilled my own professional needs.

From that time on, I chose to do a variety of different things part time to keep current in my field: I taught both English as a Second Language and writing skills at Argonne National Laboratory (this became a wonderful source for new family friends from around the world); I taught classes in the Developmental Learning Lab of a local junior college; I presented programs and workshops around the Chicago area; and I edited a book for a friend. These were all activities that did not interfere with my primary career of being a mother.

When our oldest child was getting ready to go off to college, suddenly I had to become more serious about my career, and my focus gradually changed from doing what I could do part time to considering a full-time position. As a transition, in the spring of 1987 I read of a gentleman who did seminars on the English language all over the country. I felt I could do that, so I called him. He was so impressed with my confidence as well as my credentials that he hired me over the phone! That experience ultimately led to a full-time position as Manager of Training for Kaset International in 1988.

From 1988 to 1993 I was a full-time employee of Kaset International, first in a management position and later in an executive position as Director of Quality in Training. During those years I trained trainers all over North America, I developed a facilitator training process to certify trainers to do Kaset's programs as well as helping to develop a number of new training programs, I wrote several white papers, and I spoke to large groups of executives as far away as Hawaii and New Zealand. I wrote two books *The Creative Communicator* and *Building Customer Loyalty*, which were published by Irwin Professional Publishing Company, and I was selected for *Who's Who of American Women*, *Who's Who in the Midwest*, and, most recently, *Who's Who in Entertainment*.

At this writing I have had my own company, Barbara Glanz Communications, Inc., for three and a half years and during that time have spoken on three continents and in forty-four states on customer service, improving internal communication, team building, and regenerating spirit in the workplace, all topics that were applicable even during the time I was home with my children. My third book, *CARE Packages for the Workplace—Dozens of Little Things You Can Do to Regenerate Spirit at Work,* has sold thousands of copies and has been translated into both long and short form Chinese, and this success has led to the writing of my "heart" book, which you are reading, *CARE Packages for the Home—Dozens of Little Things You Can Do to Regenerate Spirit Where You Live.*

My children are now young adults, and I am deeply proud of the people they have become. While for many years my passion was to make a difference in my children's lives, today I am deeply committed to making a difference in other people's lives by helping them see the **choices** they have in each one-on-one interaction, no matter what their job or their life experiences may be.

As I look back on my experiences, here are some tips I can share:

- **MAKE THE MOST OF YOUR LIFE EXPERIENCES.** No matter what happens in your life, *grow* from those experiences. Don't allow difficult situations to diminish you or your dreams. Find positive ways you can *use* them. I made some extremely positive choices in my life as a result of my pain, and many of the most powerful stories and illustrations I use in my speaking and writing come from those life experiences.

- **CHOOSE A PRIMARY FOCUS FOR EACH STAGE OF YOUR LIFE AND BE INTENSELY COMMITTED TO IT.** If you have decided what your primary focus is at this point in time, it will help you to make hard choices a little easier. A primary focus gives you a FRAME for the way you approach the world. For example, if you have decided that your children are your primary focus at this point in time, then it will be easier to make decisions when you are offered a promotion in your part-time job. One of the things I used in my "self-talk" when I was confused and torn between a desire to be successful in my career and to stay home with my children was to remind myself that other jobs would always be out there if I kept my skills honed, while my children would be young only once. I was merely postponing one wonderful thing for another!

- **NO MATTER WHAT YOUR PRIMARY FOCUS IS, ALWAYS MAKE SURE THAT YOU ARE IN SOME WAY KEEPING YOUR PROFESSIONAL SKILLS ALIVE.** Read current writings in your field, rent tapes from the library, talk to others periodically who are still working full time in your area of expertise, attend conferences and workshops, and go back to school part time if you possibly can. Start a file system and collect clippings, articles, cartoons, and poems that interest you or relate to your professional area. I still use things today from the files I started many years ago at home.

- **REEVALUATE YOUR PRIORITIES AT LEAST ONCE A YEAR, ALWAYS KEEPING THE LONG TERM IN MIND.** When the time is right to change priorities and focus, communicate that clearly to others and make decisions that support that change. Be confident in yourself and your skills and *aim for the top.* When I was about two-thirds of the way through the manuscript of my first book, I decided to handwrite a note to all of my professional heroes and ask them if they would be willing to look at my manuscript and perhaps write an endorsement. Now, that was a pretty gutsy thing to do, especially for a first-time author! However, I *believed* in what I was doing and I decided that all they could do was say no and then I could ask someone else. Amazingly, *every single one* of them said yes, including Og Mandino, the wonderful Christian writer who has sold *35 million books in nineteen different languages.* In fact, we became friends as a result of that request, and before his death we wrote one another often.

- **BE CREATIVE.** Whatever your life situation may be, do the very best you can within the focus you've chosen. In the 1960s there was an expression I loved: "Bloom where you are planted."

Find fun, unusual, creative ways to approach tasks and experiences. Use all available resources, especially if your budget is limited. At one time I knew the "free day" of every public place in the Chicago area, and I planned our schedule accordingly! You can also be creative in ways to earn extra money while still staying at home or being with your children. One year I taught preschool and another I gave piano lessons in our home.

- **NETWORK CONSTANTLY.** Get to know people in your community, your church, the schools. Get involved wherever you feel you can make a difference. Let your skills and talents be known by others. Then, when your focus changes, you will already have a group of people who can recommend you.

- **BELIEVE IN YOURSELF AND YOUR DREAMS.** Even though you may have chosen to put your career "on the back burner" for a while, always approach each life task or experience like a professional: What did I do well? What do I need to work on? How can I get better at whatever my chosen focus is? What can I learn from this experience that will help me later? I strongly recommend keeping a personal journal to record your thoughts, ideas, and experiences during your time at home. As a speaker, author, and consultant, I find much of what I share with others comes from the experiences I had when I was home raising my children. Think of your years at home not only as your chosen career FOR THAT TIME—a temporary situation yet a vitally important one—but also as a *special gift of preparation* to truly make a difference in the world when you reenter the workforce.

For nineteen years I chose to stay home with my children, making their education, values, and experiences my primary focus. Even though I have only been back in the workforce full time for ten years, I feel I have accomplished a great deal, and I am making a difference in another realm. I have been blessed to "have it all"—special time with my children as well as a successful career. It just happened at different times in my life. With creativity, a definite focus, and a belief in yourself and your dreams, the same can happen for you!

That is my story, but there are many stories and many different choices, and none of them are right or wrong—they are simply what we choose at that time. Even though we may not have a choice about some of the things that happen in our lives, we always have a choice about the way we will respond to them.

If you are an "at-home" parent, I hope my story and this book will be an encouragement and help you to find even greater value in the life decision you've made. For those of you who are working parents, this book may have an even greater value in many ways because it will give you many quick and easy-to-implement ideas that add quality to the precious time you do have with your family.

My heart goes out to those of you in difficult family situations—my life has been easy in comparison; however, I celebrate your desire to create a caring family in whatever circumstances you find in your life, and my hope is that the ideas in the book can help you do this. My prayer is that you will find encouragement, hope, and love in these pages.

CHAPTER ONE:

How to CARE for Your Home and Family

"A Framework for Understanding Spirit in the Home"

THIS BOOK IS ALL ABOUT CHOICES—the choices you have to make a difference no matter where you live, what your family situation is, or what your family members are doing. In every individual interaction you have, you have some awesome choices, and only *you* can decide whether they will be positive or negative.

Joseph Epstein in *Ambition: The Secret Passion* writes:

> *We do not choose to be born. We do not choose our parents. We do not choose our historical epoch, or the country of our birth, or the immediate circumstances of our upbringing. We do not, most of us, choose to die; nor do we choose the time or conditions of our death. But within all the realm of choicelessness we do choose how we shall live: courageously or in cowardice, honorably or dishonorably, with purpose or in drift. We decide what is important and what is trivial in life. We decide that what makes us significant is either what we do or what we refuse to do. But no matter how indifferent the universe may be to our choices and decisions, these choices and decisions are ours to make. We decide. We choose. And as we decide and choose, so are our lives formed.**

---

*Epstein, Joseph. 1980. *Ambition: The Secret Passion.* New York: E.P. Dutton.

You Have a Choice in Your Interactions

Several years ago I created the following three-column chart to help me visually understand the choices I had in any interaction. No matter where I am, each time I interact with someone I have three choices: I can discount that person, making him or her feel less important than me; I can just take care of the "business" at hand—whatever his or her need is; or I can create a human-level connection, acknowledging him or her as a living, breathing human being with a story.

Discounts (-)	Business Only (0)	Human Level Connection (+)
CHOICE	CHOICE	

These are the powerful choices we have in any interaction, whether it is in our home, our workplace, or our social life. People all over the world are desperate to be recognized as human beings, not just numbers or workers. I have this model in my head when I go through the checkout line at the grocery store, for example. I try my hardest to create a plus for the person behind the cash register because no one else notices her. My greatest challenge is the tollbooth—but you can do it! When I stay in a hotel for several days, I make a point to get to know something personal about the person at the front desk and the bell person, and then I refer to that throughout my stay. When I leave, I find I have made many new friends, and I've made someone's life a little better as a result of my being there. This thought from Mother Teresa has become a philosophy of life for me:

*Be kind and merciful. Let no one ever come
to you without coming away better and happier.*

When you apply this model in your home, you will realize that there are many more choices to "go the extra mile" and make a difference than you've ever realized. Each time you have an interaction you can create a "-," a "0," or a "+" for that person. Whenever you create a "+" for someone in your family, you are helping to create a more caring place to live. Take a three-by-five-inch card and make a replica of this model and keep it with you in your home for a week. Each time you have an interaction with anyone in your family, make a little check mark in the appropriate column. At the end of the week see where you have the most check marks. That will tell you how well you are contributing to a positive, caring spirit in your home!

Remember the Two Levels of Any Interaction

Whenever you have an interaction with anyone, there are two levels of that interaction—the Business level of meeting that person's needs and the Human level of how he or she feels in the interaction. For example, have you ever been told "no" in a kind and caring way?

Think about how you can apply this model in your home. If you do what someone has asked you to do, but you do it in a way that is resentful and mean, you may have fulfilled the person's Business need, but you certainly haven't met his or her Human need. Many parents who simply take care of their children's physical needs for food, clothing, and shelter feel as if they are doing their job as parents (Business level); however, they never spend any time with their children and they do not know what they feel and value (Human level).

> **When love and skill work together, expect a masterpiece.**
>
> —C. Reade

Likewise, when a parent disciplines a child to teach him or her necessary values for life, the way the parent makes the child feel (Human level) is more important than the actual punishment (Business level). Is the discipline being done from a loving spirit or a spirit of power and control? Always try to meet both levels of need in any interaction—it is your CHOICE.

Keep Emotional Bank Accounts Full

I love the hands-on concept that each of us in a family has an Emotional Bank Account, and during the day we get deposits and withdrawals. Unfortunately, most of us in our lives get far more withdrawals than deposits. When we receive withdrawal after withdrawal, our Emotional Bank Accounts get overdrawn, and that is when most of us get into trouble.

If we are looking and listening with our hearts (Human level), we will easily notice when a family member's Emotional Bank Account is overdrawn, and that is when we can CHOOSE to make a difference and give them a deposit. This book is filled with many ways to make a deposit in someone else's account, especially in Chapter Four, "Appreciation." We can also become aware of our own Emotional Bank Accounts. When we are beginning to feel overdrawn, we must learn to give ourselves deposits. Think of things that make you feel good, make a list of them, and the next time your account is getting low, choose one of them and allow yourself the joy of doing something that makes *you* feel good.

Remember the CARE acronym

The rest of this book will focus on the elements of a caring, creative, fun, and loving home. Each chapter contains many ideas that are being implemented by people and families all over the world. The elements of a spirited home are:

C = *Creative Communication* (How well are you communicating—do you get your messages across in creative and caring ways?)

A = *Atmosphere* (What does it feel like to be in your home?)
Appreciation for All (How often are you appreciating one another?)

R = *Respect* (Are you spending time together and treating one another in respectful and caring ways?)
Reason for Being (Does your family have a purpose, a feeling of belonging and being a team?)

E = *Empathy* (Are you aware of the needs of one another as well as of your community and world?)
Enthusiasm (Do you celebrate one another and your family?)

Effective family life does not just happen. It's the result of deliberate intention, determination, and practice. This book is a tool to help you and to encourage you. Now, the choice is yours!

CHAPTER TWO:

C = Creative Communication

"Get Your Messages Across in Creative and CARE-ing Ways"

*Call it a clan, call it a network, call it a tribe, call it a family.
Whatever you call it, whoever you are, you need one.*

—Jane Howard

NOTHING IS MORE important in keeping a family together than communication. However, because most families today are so busy and everyone is so bombarded with communications, it is more important than ever to make your communications creative—to do things that get family members' and others' attention. I recently read that the average person in America receives 178 communications per day, so the only way we are going to get people to hear and heed our messages is to do something that surprises or delights them. This is especially true in busy families with many different schedules.

Here are three questions to consider whenever you have anything important to communicate:

1. Will it get the information across clearly and accurately? (Business level)

2. How will it make the receiver feel? (Human level)
3. Will it surprise or delight the receiver? (Creative Communication)

This chapter is filled with ideas of ways you can communicate creatively both to family members and to others. Use these ideas to generate creative ideas of your own. Let the whole family get involved in improving communication in your home.

"Apparently I have done something to upset you."

Use Creative Slogans and Signs to Focus on Family Goals and Values

The Idea:

Whenever you have something important going on in a family, it is fun to use creative slogans and signs as reminders that everyone is involved and important in the process. Signs can also become a way to quietly communicate your beliefs and values.

The Idea in Action:

When Ray and Linda Kraig of Western Springs, Illinois, decided to marry some years ago, they had a difficult assignment in blending two households and four children! Just two and a half weeks after their wedding, Linda found she had breast cancer and had to undergo major surgery. During that trying time, they posted a sign in the kitchen that said: EVERYBODY PADDLE! Linda said it helped everyone understand the need to cooperate and also gave a light touch to a pretty serious time.

A young man who is a friend of ours noticed this sign as he left a church he was visiting: NOW YOU'RE ENTERING THE MISSION FIELD. He decided that when he has his first home, he will hang that sign over his back door as the goal he wants to give his family.

When Bob Lewis was working for IBM, he volunteered his time as a leader in Junior Achievement. Whenever he worked with the children, he wore a badge that said **BIONIC**. When the children asked what it meant, he told them, "**B**elieve **I**t **O**r **N**ot, **I** **C**are!" At the party on the last day of the session, he gave each of them a badge as a lesson in how we can all make a difference.

My friend Greg Risberg, who speaks on the power of praise, has created bumper stickers that he gives to his audiences. They say: DON'T LEAVE HERE WITHOUT A HUG! Next to the bumper sticker, which peels off, there is a picture of Greg and this quote of his:

CAUTION: *Hugs can become habit-forming and lead to fits of euphoria as well as uncontrollable feelings of goodwill toward others.*

He tells me he has this bumper sticker pasted on his front door!

As I am writing this book, we are renting a condominium in Marco Island, Florida. When we walked in the door, this calligraphy sign was dramatically placed on top of the television: IF YOU'RE SMOKING IN HERE, YOU'D BETTER BE ON FIRE!

One of our family friends always posted a handmade WELCOME HOME sign on the front door when any of their children had been away. Years later the children expressed how much they appreciated those signs.

ED, TODAY IS YOUR 10TH ANNIVERSARY! YOU BETTER HAVE A GIFT AND FLOWERS WITH YOU OR YOU'RE DEAD MEAT!
* PAID FOR BY THE FRIENDS OF ED ZIMPLER.

Close to Home © John McPherson/Dist. by Universal Press Syndicate.

🎁 In a recent edition of *Focus on the Family* magazine, I read a beautiful story about the Van Wingerden family, a Colorado family with twenty-two children. They have opened their hearts and their home to ten orphans from Brazil and Haiti as well as having twelve children of their own. A sign in the Van Wingerden kitchen says: HELP WANTED. EVERYONE IN THIS HOUSE QUALIFIES.

🎁 Even corporations are communicating family values through signage. Hy-Vee Food Store Director Jim Lingo of Cedar Rapids, Iowa, has one parking spot near the store's entrance that is marked with a big pink sign saying RESERVED PARKING FOR NEW MOMS! The "Moms-only" parking space has won lots of compliments from women shoppers and not one gripe, and now the idea has spread throughout the national chain.

🎁 Cities, too, can communicate important values in creative ways. In Gainesville, Florida, a college town, there is a city ordinance against painting graffiti on walls. However, there is a one-block-long wall and sidewalk near the university that students are encouraged to paint, and the police will not give them a ticket. They continually paint over the preceding artwork except for one section, which is a memorial to the university students who were murdered there several years ago. What a creative way to encourage communication and offer an outlet! The wall is a delightful display of social statements with constantly changing messages ranging from the heartrending memorial to LET HE WHO IS WITHOUT BLAME CAST THE FIRST STONE to JOHNNY LOVES MARY (with "Tim" and "Glenn" scratched out!).

🎁 When our third child, Erin, was born, we realized we were outgrowing our little English cottage, so we began house hunting as a family. Because we wanted to stay in our community of Western Springs, Illinois, and real estate was booming (many houses did not even go on the market or were sold in one day!), we knew it would be difficult to find what we wanted, especially in our price range. We also wanted the children to be involved in the decision, so we decided to do a family project. I got the real estate sections of several different newspapers, and each of us cut out a picture of a house we liked. Then we mounted them on a large poster board with each person's name written above.

Each of us then wrote down on the poster two or three things we wanted in our new home. My dream was for a Tudor-type house, a bigger kitchen, and two bathrooms. Charlie, my husband, wanted a garage where we could park our car and a basement workroom. Our son, Garrett, who had a little paneled room over the garage, wanted a room "that was warm." And our daughter Gretchen, who was two and a half at the time, wanted a room "that Garrett couldn't come in." (Gretchen and Erin's room was connected to Garrett's, and you couldn't get to his room without going through theirs.) Erin was just a baby, but the children even helped her pick out a picture! We hung that poster in our breakfast nook, where we ate all our meals, and every night at dinner we'd pray that God would help us find the right house.

Several months after we did this, friends had come for dinner and noticed our poster. Nancy said, "I just heard that friends down the street from us are going to be transferred and their house will be for sale. Do you want me to call them?" We were thrilled. It turned out that the family who lived there had raised four children in the house and wanted it to go to another family who loved it. It had a huge backyard, was three blocks from the school, and had everything else each of us wanted—AND it was even an English Tudor! They agreed to our price, and no one else ever got to look at the house. We have lived in that special house for over twenty years.

Tips:

I have often thought that focusing on our goal as a family helped us in many ways. We were all a part of the project. We each had an opportunity to share our dreams. And each day we concentrated on our need through prayer. Just as the Kraig family focused on their goal of happily surviving a crisis by posting a slogan, we focused on our needs and dreams by creating and hanging up that poster. And a side benefit is that anyone who enters your home will understand what your family goal is and may even be able to help you!

Share a "Piece" of Yourself

The Idea:

Encourage your friends to share their appreciation of you in a creative way.

The Idea in Action:

🎁 When he was nearing a milestone birthday, Mark decided to do something different to celebrate. He took a large photograph of himself and cut it into thirty pieces, like a puzzle. Then he sent one piece to each of thirty friends along with a party invitation. In the invitation he asked them to take their "piece of Mark" and create a five-by-seven-inch representation of what he meant to them using any media they chose. The night of the party each person presented Mark with his or her representation, and they created a huge "Mosaic of Mark" as their gift to him. Mark says this is one of the greatest treasures of his life! He gave them a piece of himself, and they gave him back a gift he'll never ever forget.

Tips:

This could be done at a children's birthday party, for a special anniversary, or even as a significant way to let special people in your life "have a piece of you."

Develop a Personal Newsletter

The Idea:

Find ways to creatively keep in contact with your children, especially when you are away from them.

The Idea in Action:

🎁 Lisa Jimenez, a professional speaker from Coral Springs, Florida, suggests this:

Next time you tape your presentations, pop in a different tape and leave a personal message for your child. Read them their favorite story or share a favorite quote. It's your child's personal newsletter especially made for them. A good *friend of mine shared with me that he and his son enjoyed doing this so much they have over a dozen "books read by Dad" in their video library!*

🎁 A friend of mine sends a postcard to his children from each place he visits on business. The children have an album they put these cards in, and then when he comes home, he explains the card. Although he hates to be away from them, he feels he can still find value as he is teaching them about other cities, cultures, and parts of the world.

🎁 Another friend who has very young children records a short personal message on an audiotape to be played at breakfast, one message for each day she is gone. This reminds the children that she loves them and also helps them understand when she will be coming back, because each message ends with, "Only ____ more days until I can give you a hug!"

🎁 When Jeff Blackman was asked to speak for the first time in Australia and New Zealand, his first child was just three months old. Before he left, he prepared an audiotape for that child, telling Chad what he meant to him and also how special his mommy was and how he felt about her. That tape will be a special treasure for Chad one day.

Tips:

Find a creative way to keep personally in communication with your family that fits *your* style. When they are leaving on a trip, some people hide little "love" notes all over the house in places that will surprise the person or persons at home as they go through their routine. Sometimes those who will be staying at home slip special notes into the traveler's bags to remind the person that he or she is loved. Other people compose poems or cut little sayings out of magazines and make a personal collage for a family member. These communications create the bonds that help each family member feel special and loved.

Find Special Ways to Remember Your Family When You Travel

The Idea:

If you begin some family traditions that revolve around travel, you will find that they take some of the pain of separation away.

The Idea in Action:

🎁 When I began traveling in my speaking and consulting business, my sister gave each of my children a printer's drawer. (We call it a "shadow box.") I did not want to get in the habit of bringing them a big, expensive present every time I was gone, so I carried on a family tradition that my sister had started on her travels. Each time I travel, I bring each of my children some little thing that is a symbol of the city or country I visited—a miniature cable car from San Francisco, a little basket of tiny crabs from Maryland, a totem pole from British Columbia, a miniature bottle of Coke from Atlanta, a gavel from the U.S. Supreme Court in Washington, D.C., a little pineapple from Hawaii, a lighthouse from Rhode Island, a miniature jazz player from New Orleans, a tiny record from Nashville, a milk can from Wisconsin, a cowbell from Liechtenstein, a miniature St. Bernard from Switzerland, a panda bear from San Diego, a duck from Memphis, and a small container of Vegemite from New Zealand! These gifts are fun to find, inexpensive, and easy to tuck into the corner of a suitcase. Now my children are bringing souvenirs for the shadow box from their own trips!

🎁 Another thing I did to help keep in close touch with my children when I had to travel was to give them a "Things to Tell Mom" notebook. The kids were eleven, thirteen, and seventeen when I went back to work full time in a job that required some travel. I picked a special notebook for each of the girls, which I knew they would like (Garrett was away for his first year of college). Then I told them to keep that notebook with them every day and write down anything they wanted to tell me. Every night when I called home, they would have their notebook lists as a reminder of what had happened during the day. I think they told me more because of those notebooks than they would have if I had been at home!

🎁 Bonnie Michaels, the president of Managing Work and Family in Evanston, Illinois, shares a new family ritual she and her husband have created to help them feel close to each other even when traveling:

When I go away, I leave a special note for him under his pillow. When he goes away, I leave a special note for him in his suitcase. He does the same for me. In addition, he has left poems on my e-mail or special messages on my voice mail. All these little gestures help the traveler to feel special and connected, appreciated and cared for.

Tips:

Whether a trip is for business or pleasure, the more ways you can find to share it with your family, the closer you will be and the more you will learn and grow together. Here are some travel tips from an article called "Til Travel Do Us Part" in the May 1991 issue of *Training & Development* magazine to help minimize the stress of business travel on both traveler and family. These tips are from Richard Leider, a Minneapolis-based consultant on lifestyle management:

- Carefully analyze the purpose of each trip; say no to unnecessary ones.
- Draw travel "boundaries" as a family, deciding how much travel is excessive.
- Maintain reasonable intervals between trips.
- Don't travel on weekends.
- Don't travel on special occasions such as birthdays and anniversaries.
- Telephone home each day.
- Give your family your complete itinerary, phone numbers, maps, and other trip details.
- Take one hour off each day on the road to be alone, relax, exercise, or do something new and different.
- Schedule weekly relationship time on your calendar.
- Take loved ones on business trips occasionally.
- When you come home, listen before you share the details of your journey.
- Write down a master dream list. List all the things you want to do, be, have, or go to in your lifetime. Pick one dream to do each year.

Begin the Day in Meaningful Ways

The Idea:

Whether your family is composed of two or twenty people, find special ways to start the day out right.

Yesterday is history.
Tomorrow is a mystery.
Today is a gift.
That's why we call it "the present."

The Idea in Action:

🎁 Richard Narramore, my editor at McGraw-Hill, and his new wife, Kathryn, have a wonderful daily ritual they share. Every morning they do a one-page Lutheran liturgy together in German. They read a Bible passage, and then they ask each other four questions:

- What are you thankful for today?
- What do you want to confess today?
- What prayer requests do you have for today?
- What are you going to do today?

🎁 Richard says that it takes them only five to ten minutes, but they both find it very centering. I also remember being very impressed that for many months after they were married, he and Kathryn had candlelight breakfasts!

🎁 Several families shared with me that they begin the day with positive affirmations such as:

- I will find something good in someone I don't like today.
- I will tell the truth every day.
- I will remember to be kind to everyone I meet today.
- I will give five compliments today.
- I will appreciate my teacher/boss/friend today.

🎁 Some families start the day with the Scripture verse, "This is the day the Lord has made. I [we] will rejoice and be glad in it." Others begin each breakfast with a family prayer for the day, with each person praying for a good day for the person next to him or her. Other families begin the day with a short family devotion. Two of my favorite resources for daily devotions are *Our Daily Bread* published by RBC Ministries, Grand Rapids, Michigan, and *Living Juicy* by Sark. There are many other books of daily devotions available for younger children.

🎁 When I was teaching high school English, at the start of each day I always wrote a "Thought for the Day" on the blackboard. One day one of the custodians stopped by my room to tell me how much he always enjoyed cleaning my blackboards because he loved the "Thought for the Day!"

Frances Dornon of Sioux City, Iowa, shared a completely original family tradition they had at their house:

Before any of the children went to school, we started our day with a musical game. I would go to Mary's room and slowly pull the shade up and sing:

> **Creativity may express itself in one's dealings with children, in making love, in carrying on a business, in formulating physical theory, in painting a picture.**
>
> **—Jerome Bruner**

It's time to pull the shade up
And let the sun in,
For God's made a beautiful day.
It's time to pull the shade up
And let the sun in,
For God's made a beautiful day.
The sun is up
And the sky is blue.
The birds are up
And the squirrels are too,
It's time to pull the shade up
And let the sun in
For God's made a beautiful day.

By that time the room would be bright and Mary would be squirming out of bed. Then I would go to Johnny's and Bobby's rooms and do the same thing. Next I would go downstairs and wait for the children to appear. I would sit on a big chair in the kitchen and wait. As soon as I heard someone coming I would start singing:

I hear somebody coming down the stairs,
Coming down the stairs,
Coming down the stairs.
I hear somebody coming down the stairs,
Coming down the stairs,
Coming down the stairs.

Then as one of them peeked around the corner, I sang hurriedly:
There she is,
There she is,
It's Mary, Mary, Mary Dornon.

And then it was the boys' turns. Usually Bobby came first. Mary and I went through the same motions with him. So now I had two in my lap. And now it

was Johnny's turn. We all three sang and sang as we heard him coming down the stairs. As he peeked around the corner, we hurriedly sang:

> There he is,
> There he is,
> It's Johnny, Johnny, Johnny
> Dornon.

And boisterous Johnny would run and leap on top of the three of us, and we'd all laugh and giggle. I had all three of my children in my lap now. What a happy way to start a day!

🎁 A couple I met shared a special way that they always end their day. Just before they go to sleep, they tell each other one thing they really like about the other person. What a wonderful way to close the gift of a day.

Tips:

Think of special things you can do in your family to begin each day positively, from taking turns serving one another, making creative surprises to eat, reading a book together, or simply sharing a hope or prayer for the day. I remember my mother often made animal-shaped pancakes to delight us on days she knew would be difficult.

I have always loved this poem from *Yes, World: A Mosaic of Meditation* by Mary Jean Irion:

NORMAL DAY,
Let me be aware of the treasure you are.
Let me learn from you, love you, savor you, bless you,
before you depart.

Let me not pass you by in quest of some perfect tomorrow.
Let me hold you while I may,
for it will not always be so.

One day I shall dig my fingers into the earth,
or bury my face in the pillow,
or stretch myself taut,
or raise my hands to the sky,
and want more than all the world:
your return.

Foster Family Communication

The Idea:

Find unique ways to encourage each family member to share.

The Idea in Action:

A family with older children, many of them adults, found that when they were together, they were often just sitting in front of the TV, not talking and sometimes even sleeping. While they were "together" physically, they were not sharing with one another. As a family they decided that the next holiday time they were all together, they would discuss a book that they would all read ahead of time.

Several weeks before the holiday, they decided on the book *Into Thin Air*. Although the parents thought some of the children might balk at the "assignment," of the eleven family members, only one person did not read the book, and she did read the preface. However, each of them went about it in their own way—one read the condensed version, another rented the TV special, and several of them were scurrying into the bedroom the night before to finish their reading.

They determined a set time for the book discussion, but several of the family members were so excited that they even started to discuss it ahead of time. When they finally did all sit down together, the mother said it was amazing to see what happened. Not only did they thoroughly enjoy talking about the book, but also it broke the mold of the traditional roles each of them often played in the family. They even talked about what this "project" revealed about their own character. One of the daughters said it revealed her generous nature because she bought the book and then loaned it to several of the others. The father laughed because he said it brought out his stingy nature since he borrowed the book from the library! As a result of this experiment, they shared more in different ways than they ever had as a growing family group. They have decided to choose a book to discuss each time they are together in the future.

Diane Karnaze Clark, a former sorority sister of mine from Kansas City, tells how her family made communication fun:

Something that our family did when my children were little was that Dad would lightly tap on a glass after dinner to give Christy and Cara a chance to speak (about anything) to the whole family. We had a very large family, and after each family gathering, we would remain at the dining-room table and have political and other kinds of discussions, and everyone, no matter what their age, had a chance to share. Dad started the tradition, and we continue it today, whenever we gather. It was a real esteem builder for my children because it made them feel important, and it also gave them a chance to articulate their thoughts and opinions.

Tips:

What meaningful ways to allow true freedom of speech for all ages! Just be careful to be open and not judgmental, because this can be an important time for young people to try out new ideas and opinions in a safe haven. I know our kids often shock us with what they say, but sometimes that is the whole purpose!

Here is something I was given recently that really made me smile:

HOW TO RAISE YOUR PARENTS

1. Do not be afraid to speak their language. Try to use strange-sounding phrases like, "I'll help you with the dishes," and "yes."

2. Try to understand their music. Play Andy Williams' "Moon River" on the stereo until you are accustomed to the sound.

3. Be patient with the underachiever. When you catch your dieting mom sneaking salted peanuts, do not show your disapproval. Tell her you love fat mothers!

4. Encourage your parents to talk about their problems. Try to keep in mind that to them things like earning a living and paying off the mortgage seem important.

5. Be tolerant of their appearance. When your dad gets a haircut, don't feel personally humiliated. Remember it's important to him to look like his peers.

6. Most important of all, if they do something you consider wrong, let them know it's their behavior you dislike, not themselves.

Create Treasure Maps

The Idea:

One of the ways we can keep focused on what is really important to us either as a family or as individuals is to create treasure maps.

The Idea in Action:

Gail Howerton, the founder of Fun*cilitators in Fredericksburg, Virginia, writes about her treasure maps:

I have these in my office, in my garage, in a dream / idea / resource book, and in my medicine cabinet. They represent my dreams, aspirations, goals, places I want to travel, and the lifestyle I want to have. They help keep my radar active and focused on these things when I look through magazines and collect the photos. I have fun cutting and pasting, and they keep my goals in front of me in a fun way. I take a mental escape in them when I wait on "hold" or for my e-mail to come up. They are the right-brain way of listing my goals in addition to my left-brain list in my Daytimer. My friend and fellow speaker, Pat Moore, who is a Professional Organizer (the Queen of Clutter), told me that studies show that 39 percent of guests who visit your bathroom will look into your medicine cabinet. So I decided to give them a show!

Tips:

What a delightful way to teach children the fun of setting goals for themselves as well as to dream and plan as a family. Wouldn't this be a fun project on a cold winter Friday or Saturday night? Get lots of old magazines, poster board, scissors, and rubber cement. Let each person share what they chose and why, and then have a family powwow about where to hang them. I think I will have to be more creative with the inside of my medicine cabinet!

Add a Personal Signature to Your E-mail Messages

The Idea:

John Naisbitt said several years ago, "The more high technology around us, the more the need for human touch." Many people today have e-mail, both at work and at home. It can be a wonderful communication tool. However, most e-mail messages I read sound as if they come from a computer, not a real live person. Think about ways to humanize your e-mail messages.

The Idea in Action:

"Gene, e-mail the kids and tell them to come downstairs for dinner."

🎁 It is possible to add a personal signature to your e-mail messages, which lets your reader know something about you and your values. Emily Schulz, a freshman at Bradley University in Peoria, Illinois, always ends her e-mail messages with this thought:

Love and friendship are the greatest gifts of all.

Here are a few guidelines from an article by Sacha Cohen in *Training & Development*, October 1997, when creating a signature file for your PC:

- Signatures should be four lines or less.
- It's okay to include your name and e-mail address, but unless you are a business, don't include a phone number in a signature file.
- Be polite in your signature.

To create a text signature file, you can use Microsoft Word, Notepad, or MSDOS Editor. Whatever program you use, it must be able to produce a plain ASCII file. You can't use fonts or formatting in a signature file.

To begin, type in the information that you want included at the end of all your e-mail messages—your name, a quote, or a saying. Then save the file to a location on your hard drive. Last, you'll need to tell your browser (Netscape Navigator or Microsoft Explorer) where to find the file. Follow these steps:

- Select the Options menu.
- Choose Mail and News Preferences.
- Click on the Identity Tag to call up the identity dialog box.
- Locate the space provided for the signature file.
- Enter the complete path and name of the signature file. (For example, c:\mystuff\wkeep\sign.txt.)
- Close the dialog box by clicking on the "OK" button, then select Options again, and select Save Options.

Tips:

Because e-mail is one of the examples of how high tech has taken over high touch such as personal letter writing, it becomes even more important to add a human level to our messages. A signature message that shares a value of the sender or a personal philosophy of life is an easy and nonthreatening way to do this.

Find Special Ways to Regenerate Everyone's Imagination

The Idea:

So often family time is spent in front of the TV, being together but not interacting, that it is important to create family activities that foster creative thinking, interaction, and imagination.

The Idea in Action:

🎁 Margaret Rooney of Sycamore, Illinois, tells of an interactive activity that her family enjoys:

As an inexpensive creative family activity, we give each family member a marker and a stack of scratch paper. Each person makes a "scribble" on a piece of paper. Then we pass the paper to the next person who has the job of creatively turning the scribble into a picture of anything. It's fun to be creative together as a family. We draw pictures of anything you can imagine. This is especially great to do with school-age children, who love to use their imagination and take pride in their work (and it frees up the often dormant creative spirit in Mom and Dad, too!).

🎁 Mary Schulz tells of one way she found to encourage communication and creativity with both her family and others. She had special craft nights where everyone could create something. One of her favorites was with Sculpi dough, which comes in many different colors. The children and adults alike loved making tiny things for dollhouses—miniature toys, tiny food, animals, and holiday decorations. She found that this worked especially well for family gatherings when the children didn't know each other well. It was almost like a quilting bee! Everyone talked and had a good time while they created.

Jerry Pavloff of Ligonier, Pennsylvania, tells of a creative activity he does with his son Evan:

The other day I was playing a board game with Evan, my seven-year-old. He's very creative and has combined his Monopoly and Game of Life games to make a new game complete with rules, moves, etc. Because the two original game's operate with currencies, in the game he made up, players have lots of money. You still have to pay the other player when you land on a space owned by them, but it's usually something you can afford. I hit a run where I kept landing on his spaces, and I had to pay him millions of dollars, which depleted a lot of my resources. I remarked that old cliché, "Money goes to money." He said, "No, Dad, money goes to the generous."

Sue Foster and her children love to make up stories. Each of them records one line of a story—one person begins and then the next adds another line and on and on. Sue has decided that she will give the special tapes to her children at their first baby shower.

One of the most delightful and creative organizations I've ever encountered is The Scrap Exchange. The Scrap Exchange is an environmentally correct, non-profit organization, with locations throughout the United States, founded to reuse industrial scrap for educational and creative purposes. It is a huge warehouse filled with bins of all kinds of "stuff"—

pieces of foam rubber, tubes of all kinds, plastic parts, wire, ribbon, film canisters, various kinds of fabrics, funnels. Every child and child-at-heart will quickly catch the spirit of discovery and selection, as the ever-changing stock offers a bonanza of creative possibilities. You can fill a discount bag with goodies, add individually priced items, and all the while enjoy the atmosphere of fun finding things you didn't know you could get!

It is a great place to buy quite inexpensive materials for creative projects, it is a discard collection service for businesses to keep materials from literally going to waste, it is a great place to have a birthday party, and it is a resource for hands-on creative arts workshops for children, teachers, families, and adults either at your site, at the center, or at an "Events by the Truckload." Each year The Scrap Exchange sends truckloads of fabulous trash to events all over the states in which they're located for hands-on creative arts activities the whole family can enjoy together. The Scrap Exchange staff help children and adults have fun making wild scrap hats, crazy trash critters, and wonderful costumes from throwaway stuff from hundreds of different materials, and whatever they make, they can take home. "Events by the Truckload" is free to participants. Sponsors hire TSE to make an event, festival, or corporate picnic exciting and fun for families.

> *Many people would sooner die than think. In fact, they do.*
>
> **—Bertrand Russell**

These "stores" are a great resource for families, schools, and other groups who want a creative and different project that uses resources that would otherwise be wasted by industry, and just visiting one is an experience you'll never forget! I was first exposed to the group in Durham, North Carolina, but there are others throughout the country. See the Resources section at the end of this book for more information.

Tips:

Look for games and other activities that will challenge family members to think. For example, take the word "HALLOWEEN" and have the family see how many different words they can make using those letters. You might do this in teams if your family is big enough, and you can choose any word that has a number of vowels in it. Any time you can find an activity that both encourages communication as well as creative thinking you will be impacting your family in a long-lasting way.

Create a "Baby Log" for Working Mothers

The Idea:

When mothers need to work outside of the home, it is always a sacrifice to miss out on the daily happenings of their children's lives, particularly when they are babies. One of the ways to experience some of the activities is to ask the caregiver to keep a baby log.

The Idea in Action:

Brenda Adaire, who is the director of membership for the National Association of Independent Insurers, has two young children, Alexander and Connor, who stay with a nanny while she works. When her first child was born, she created a "baby log" that the nanny fills out each day so that she knows exactly what happened during her day at work. These are the different categories of the log, with one page for Alexander and another for Connor:

        DATE:
        WAKE UP:
        MORNING BM:
        BREAKFAST:
        MORNING ACTIVITIES:
        LUNCH:
        AFTERNOON NAP:
        AFTERNOON BM:
        AFTERNOON ACTIVITIES:
        DINNER:
        WHAT HAPPENED TODAY:
        EVENING ACTIVITIES/BEDTIME:

For Brenda, this baby log has been a wonderful comfort because she feels a part of her children's days, and she and her husband can build on the activities and talk about them with the children when she gets home.

Tips:

This same kind of log would work for elder care, day care, or even for occasional times that you use baby-sitters.

Find Ways to Communicate
That Make Others Smile

The Idea:

When I speak on Creative Communication, I suggest that most of us are bombarded with communications (and this includes children today, too), so we either ignore, delete, or toss out most of the communications we receive. My belief has become that if we truly want to get a communication heard or heeded, we need to do something to surprise our listeners. This gets their attention, and the communication is completed. Finding ways to surprise or delight your receivers will not only impact whether or not your communication is received, but it will also be more fun.

The Idea in Action:

A speaker friend of mine, Greg Risberg, always asks people if they'd like to see a picture of his "pride and joy." Of course, people expect another ordinary family picture. This, however, is the picture he pulls out of his wallet:

Then, after a good laugh, he shows them his real family picture. On the back of the first photo is the statement: *We all need twenty-four laughs a day for good health. Please share your "Pride and Joy" to help others!*

David Roth, a wonderful songwriter and friend from Seattle, Washington, uses a delightful surprise to celebrate his Jewish heritage during the holiday season. He gave me a pair of cardboard glasses that looked like the ones you used to wear for 3-D movies. Then he asked me to put them on and look at the Christmas lights in the restaurant where we were. Voila! All the little lights and candles became Stars of David! I was mesmerized as were others around who tried them. On the back of the glasses were the words: "See the Magic in the Holiday Lights!" What a beautiful way to share your faith.

Note: The glasses are called Gemini Hol*day Specs® from Gemini Kaleidoscopes, Zelienoople, PA 16063.

🎁 Another person I know asks everyone he meets "if they'd like a hug." When some of them look at him rather strangely, he pulls out a Hershey's Hug from his pocket and hands it to them! He always gets a big smile.

🎁 To encourage and sometimes even to discourage communication, at least for a while, the father of a large family keeps a number of hats in the hall closet. When he comes home from work, he immediately puts on one of the hats to communicate to his family what kind of mood he is in:

> Baseball cap—he is ready to "play"
> Stocking cap—leave him alone until he gets "warmed" up
> Army hat—it's been a battle today; stay far away!

🎁 Sally Winkler of Western Springs, Illinois, told me about Mr. Chefski, the fourth-grade teacher of her grandson at Yahara School in Stoughton, Wisconsin. In the summer before the start of school, he left each child a voice-mail message welcoming them to his class and letting them know how excited he was to be their teacher. Several of the things he does with the children really communicate his values of caring and humor. Sometimes they have "Laughing Contests" to see who can laugh the longest, the hardest, and who has the funniest laugh. When children have a messy desk, he writes their names on the blackboard, and when they aren't around, he puts old sandwiches and all kinds of other "junk" in their desks to tease them a bit. He seems to find that the best way to get the children to learn is through using humor, not strict discipline. Sally says the children love Mr. Chefski!

🎁 Mark Manrique of Lansing, Michigan, tells about a "zany" way he communicates:

One of my fondest possessions is a thing called an Intercom-edy box. It looks like a little intercom and comes equipped with five buttons that produce five different sounds: hysterical laughter; a "boingggg" sound; a rimshot (for those really corny jokes); a school bell (for when the conversation or meeting is dragging on much too long—class dismissed!); and "foxy" (which I'll leave to your imagination . . .). I originally gave the box to my brother for Christmas several years ago. He loved it and kept it close to his phone and would hit the appropriate button during the course of our conversations. When we realized how much fun it was, we began searching for Intercomedy boxes for my other brother and myself. Unfortunately, it appears the company that made them went out of busi-

ness. So we began rotating possession. If you can't share the wealth, you might as well share the laughter!

🎁 Barbara McCauley suggests starting a "laughter club" with a group of friends or family members. Get together once a week and each person share a funny experience from the week. The one with the funniest story gets a free lunch or an extra dessert. This will help you all focus on positive things that make you smile.

🎁 Send someone you love an important message on the back of a five-by-seven-inch postcard or picture. Then cut it into puzzle pieces and put the pieces in an envelope. Send this in the mail or leave it where the person will find it. They will have fun deciphering your message!

Tips:

It is important that you be comfortable with any new forms of communication you might use both with your family and in your community. However, finding ways to communicate that surprise people and make them smile will make a real difference in your interactions.

Use Special Signals to Communicate

Glenda reminds Ted not to leave his dirty laundry lying around the house.

Close to Home © John McPherson/Dist. by Universal Press Syndicate.

The Idea:

Sometimes it becomes important to have ways to indirectly or nonverbally communicate in order to save misunderstandings and pain later.

The Idea in Action:

🎁 Nancy Provenzano of Lake Geneva, Wisconsin, shared a way that she and her teenage daughter Martha learned to avoid embarrassment and conflict when they were in public talking to others. They had a signal clue when either of them used the words, "Okay, (Mom or Martha)." This signal meant to change the subject. Nancy says it was much better than "Shut up!" and helped them save face and not let everyone else know of the other's embarrassment. It doesn't matter what the words are, but the signal becomes important in understanding how the other person may be feeling. I suspect this might be a good idea with a marital partner too!

🎁 Avice Rodda, who is a teacher in Chicago, tells of an assistant principal who puts a beanie baby crab on his desk on those bad days when he is really at the end of his rope. This is a signal to teachers and students alike to be extra kind and gentle! Greg Paine at SMU has crab hats that he passes out to those in the office who need them that day, including himself.

Tips:

The more openly we can communicate with others, the better. Any signals or clues that will help us better understand the state of mind of another will help to avoid potential conflict and unnecessary pain. Think of signals you might use with those with whom you live and work.

> *Creativity is so delicate a flower that praise tends to make it bloom, while discouragement often nips it in the bud. Any of us will put out more and better ideas if our efforts are appreciated.*
>
> **—Alex F. Osborn**

Try "Leftover Lotto"

The Idea:

We all know that most children don't like leftovers, so here's a fun way to make them special.

The Idea in Action:

🎁 Allison Blankenship of Naples, Florida, married her husband when his children were five and eight. Because they had always eaten most of their meals out, the children weren't used to home-cooked meals. But to Allison, who grew up in the South, food means love, so she always cooked special things for them when they visited. However, when it came to leftovers, they, like most children, balked! So Allison created "Leftover Lotto," a fun game that not only cleaned out the fridge but also left the children begging for more leftovers.

To play "Leftover Lotto," print numbers for each member of the family on a small scrap of paper. Allison's family had four, so she had four slips of paper with the numbers 1 to 4. Each person then draws a number to establish who is the "winner," followed by the runners up in order.

Assemble the leftovers in a buffet line on the dining room table. The winner, the person who drew number 1, gets to fill his or her plate from the buffet first, taking whatever he or she chooses. Then number 2 goes through the line, followed by number 3 and then number 4. The last person gets whatever is left.

Allison says, "Whenever our family plays 'Leftover Lotto,' we are not limited to having a 'balanced' meal. Everyone selects what he or she feels like eating as long as it is a leftover, which makes the evening an extra special treat." Today the children are nine and thirteen, and they still ask for leftover dinners!

Tips:

If you can make a game out of something with your children, they are much more apt to do what you want them to! This works with some adults as well. . . .

Dinnertime for working parents is reduced to its most basic form.

Give Handmade Gifts

The Idea:

A handmade gift has always communicated to me someone's special caring. It is as if the giver puts a little bit of his or her own spirit into the gift, so the gift becomes a valued treasure.

The Idea in Action:

Laurie Trice tells how her mother, Doris Kunkel of Stratford, Wisconsin, made each of the grandchildren a special Christmas ornament:

It was a doll with buttons for arms and legs and a cute dress and hat. While the doll was darling, the story she put with it was even cuter. Mom's button box was always a treasure to all of us kids and grandchildren. Now each grandchild has some of those treasures in their ornament. The story includes the names of all of us kids, which makes it even more special to the grandchildren.

Laurie says, "You wouldn't believe what a treasure these dolls and the story is for the grandchildren. Most of them are in their teens so they can really appreciate the creativity."

Tips:

What a wonderful gift this grandmother gave of herself! Anyone can create a similar story and gift to give to family members as a special treasure that will communicate their love and live on forever and ever.

Cute as a Button

Many, many years ago we were big globs of plastic in a place called a factory. We were poured into molds, and we came into being in all shapes and sizes. They punched holes in us and called us "buttons." They put us on cards and then in boxes—my, it was dark in there! Then we were put on a truck and taken to a place called Marshfield, Wisconsin.

Some nice ladies put us on a rack, and we were able to watch all the people come and go. We were very sad when no one picked us. One day the store lady threw us in a bin and put up a sign: 10 CENTS A CARD. How humiliating! We were worth much more.

One day a very nice lady came in with two small children. She didn't have a lot of money and seemed very pleased to see us. We were so happy when she picked us and took us home with her.

She began to sing and sew, and soon some of us were on a dress for a girl named Sandy. Sandy was the oldest and looked out for the other two. She liked to play school, and maybe that is why she's a teacher today.

Then the lady made a shirt for Dale. It's a good thing we had a "spirit of adventure" because we walked beams, climbed trees, and crawled under barbed wire fences. Life sure wasn't dull for us!

The lady then made a dress for Theresa. Theresa liked to play with pill bottles and bandage up our broken arms and legs. I suppose that's why she is a nurse today.

Soon we were cut off all these garments and put in a box. It was sad to be in a dark place again, but one day the lady opened the box, and what was this—two new girls, one named Laurie and one named Susie.

The lady began to sing and sew, and pretty soon we were on a shirt for Susie and a shirt for Laurie. It was fun in the sun again. Laurie had a friend named Sara, and they liked to take a picnic lunch and go to the woods. They let Susie tag along because she had no one to play with. They did 4-H projects, and we all went to the fair. They did a lot of fun things, and we were all very happy. When Susie's brothers came along, she played ball with them, and we called her our "little tomboy."

Now, with three boys, the lady opened the box again and began to sing and sew, and pretty soon we were on shirts and pajamas for three boys, David, Mark, and Scott.

David liked to wrestle, and his favorite sport was to wrestle his brother Mark. He liked baseball, too, but we weren't too happy when he slid into base on his stomach and almost popped his buttons!

I guess the best word for Mark was "impulsive." He went out the door so fast he ripped off his buttons. He liked to step on nails, ride three-wheelers, and knock down football players and then help them up. Life was never dull for us, and those of us on pajamas were glad for a quiet night's sleep.

Then there was Scott. We felt sorry for him because he was so little and his brothers were so big. They liked to take him along to play football with the neighbors, and I think the only thing they didn't knock out of him was his music. He liked to go to his room and lock the door for some quiet time, and even the nice lady sometimes wished she could find a room where no one could find her.

Soon the house was quiet, and we were all back in the box again—and we still didn't like the dark. We were there a long time, but one day the nice lady opened the box and dumped us all out on the bed. She began to sort and line us all up. We were happy because we were going to have some fun again.

But what was she doing? She was stringing us up and laying us in piles. We watched while she made a doll with just a head and a body and then put a dress on it. To our surprise, WE were the arms and legs! She wasn't singing when she put the hair on because the glue gun and the hair were not cooperating. Soon she put on a hat and a flower, and then she smiled and said, "You're as cute as a button!"

Then she lined us all up and said, "You are going on a new adventure. You are going to granddaughters who will love and care for you. You will hang on their Christmas trees, and you will watch them grow up and graduate from high school and go off to college and marry and start a home of their own. As each granddaughter places you on her tree, she will remember she had a grandmother who prayed for her and who loved her very much.

Someday when the grandmother is in heaven, she will look down and see the granddaughters smile at their little boys or girls when they hang you on the Christmas tree, and she will know that love is passed on to future generations.

Plan Special Get-Togethers
with Other Families

The Idea:

One of the ways to build relationships and to encourage communication with others is to plan special ways to share time with other families.

The Idea in Action:

Reay and Julie Verner-Mackay of Brisbane, Australia, arrange special rendezvous at their local park with one or two other families. They take some pâté and maybe a nice bottle of wine. Reay says, "We are able to enjoy watching our children interact with children from other families and at the same time build stronger relationships with friends from our local community. It's a great way to enjoy our children, enjoy our friends, enjoy our neighbors' company, and enjoy getting out in a natural environment."

Tips:

I also love what Reay, the president of the Australian Customer Service Association, Queensland Division, wrote to me in a letter:

We still continue to enjoy reading your newsletter here in Brisbane. I am particularly interested in your new project on CARE Packages for the Home. I think it's so important, as most excellence in customer service begins at home. In addition, our most important customers, if you think about it, are our partners, family, and friends. So often we get caught up meeting our own needs or our career needs to the detriment of meeting the needs of our most important customers, our family.

Think of a special place where you might invite another family or two. Make it simple, and make sure there is ample time for interaction. This can become a regular tradition at a certain time, for example, every Sunday afternoon. If you met one new family a week, think of the network of support your family members would have!

Find Creative Ways to Keep in Touch with Family and Friends

The Idea:

When loved ones live far away, it is vital to your spirits to keep in touch. Find ways that are creative and fun and do not take a lot of time. That way you will not feel overburdened in communicating on a regular basis.

The Idea in Action:

Kathie Hightower, an author and professional speaker from Corvallis, Oregon, tells of ways she has found to communicate creatively with family and friends:

I've set a goal to keep in touch with family and friends (as someone who has moved with the military every few years, it takes a conscious effort since most live far away). When I send letters or cards, I use fun stickers on the outside. My favorite sticker says, "Think of this as an excuse for a cookie break." I buy fun postage stamps to always have some ready and often choose the stamp based on the person it is going to. For example, I might put the flower from the state of that person, a doll stamp to someone with that interest, Women in the Military to many of my military friends, a cartoon stamp for someone that needs a lift.

I also use fun rubber stamps to stamp across the back. For example, "You are simply amazing!" (a stamp by Mary Ann Hershey, a favorite artist from Cannon Beach, Oregon, 503-436-2854). I also bought a set of eighty stamps called the Rubber Stamp Poet from All Night Media so I can use fun words or sayings like "Wild Woman" or "Imagine Magic." It makes it fun for me in the creating and, hopefully, fun in the receiving.

I also took Alexandra Stoddard's idea to heart years ago—I'm ready for easy correspondence. I have hatboxes full of cards so I can always find an appropriate one for any occasion—no shopping trip necessary.

I automatically get doubles of my photos made when I send them in for developing. Then I send the copies to friends and family members who are either in them or might be interested in them. For example, my eighty-seven-year-old aunt lives in Canada, so she hasn't seen her grandnieces who live in Virginia. When I visited with my nieces, I sent photo copies to Aunt Kay. It's a great way to keep in touch. And if I had to go to the trouble of having copies made after the fact, I know me! I'd never get around to it—I'm great at sending the copies off to friends, but don't ask me about my photo albums. . . .

Tips:

Postcards are great ways to communicate quickly with family and friends. The length doesn't matter as much as the idea that you were thinking of them. I am a great "collector"—I am always clipping articles and ideas that remind me of someone or that I think they'd be interested in. After having piles of these on my desk for years, I have finally found a system. I keep a large 8½ × 11-inch envelope with each family member's name in a stack. Then, when I find something that applies to that person, I clip it and immediately put it into his or her envelope. About once a month or when I have several items in the envelope, I send them off and make new envelopes.

Write a Poem Just for That Person

The Idea:

If you have the gift of writing rhyme, you can celebrate a person or a situation in a wonderfully creative way. Some people write rhyming verse, others write free verse, and others may even write limericks.

The Idea in Action:

Jim Munroe from Moncks Corner, South Carolina, has used his gift of poetry to delight many hearts. We first met when he came to one of my workshops at a conference in Florida. This is the poem he wrote for me about that experience:

The Breeze

It happened so unexpectedly, the meeting was so brief,

but a breeze had blown through my heart and gave it

sweet relief.

For it had something locked inside and needed one

small key,   to open up the treasure there and finally

set it free.

Just like the small cocoon that hangs on flowers so

close by,   when kissed by rays of warm sunshine

becomes a butterfly.

  Such are the meetings in our life, nothing happens

just by chance,   so we can choose to trudge along

or we can learn to dance.

The breeze will blow most anytime, its touch can

move with gentle might,   then use the gift

    that's found within and be a shining light.

Jim often writes birthday poems and poems for special occasions for his friends:

Mary Amanda Modica

Angels were watching from their clouds up in heaven

for on the 28th day of the first month of the year 97',

Mary Amanda was born, a precious gift from above,

given to Mark and to Hazel to care for and love.

6 pounds and 3 ounces, a miracle wrought by God's hands,

who soon will wear perfume and makeup and pretty headbands.

19 and ½ inches was her length on that wonderful morn

as she drew in her first breath at 8:34.

Kaylee is her sister who is beaming with pride

because now she has Mandee to play by her side.

They will grow up so quickly and in the blink of an eye

will leave their warm home on 1533 Sterling Oaks Drive.

So guard each moment in time as a chest full of treasure

and may the faith, hope, and love in this home be the kind

that no one can measure.

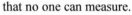

This is a very special poem Jim wrote about a little girl he met at a base-ball game:

Aden Jayne MacMillan

We met in Kansas City, a "Royal" meeting behind home plate.
Now some would call this coincidence and others may say fate.
But I believe each day we're given opportunities to share,
instead of aimless wandering without challenges and dares.
She walked up the stairs so cautiously from a couple rows below
and stopped beside my aisle seat with eyes that said "Hello!"
Children are a gift from God, their eyes will glow and dance,
if we would share some time with them and give them half a chance.
We didn't talk of baseball or the weather or business things,
just tater tots and Pepsi and if all the birdies sing.
Though words were few her actions spoke from a depth unknown,
a love for people, big and small, she'll bring peace to many homes.
Those few hours went by so fast, the last inning was at hand
but the memories will not fade like morning mist upon the land.
I said goodbye to my new friend, my heart felt a little pain.
May God who lights your face so bright, bless you always,

Aden Jayne

Tips:

You don't have to be a great poet to create a special verse for someone. Just get your creative juices going and really focus on that unique individual. You will be giving that person a priceless gift by communicating creatively what makes them special to you.

The Three Ts of Great Relationships

The Idea:

Maria Marino, a delightful speaker and trainer from North York, Ontario, says her secret to great relationships is practicing the three Ts:

> T-alk: open, creative communication and active listening
> T-ickle: bringing fun, laughter, and lightness
> T-ackle: the work and the energy that keeps things humming

The Idea in Action:

These are some of Maria's suggestions for when the human symphony is a little out of tune:

1. Bring out a tape of your favorite love songs, a video of happy times together, a scrapbook or photo album filled with treasured memories and success stories, a list of the twenty-five things you like best about each other, or balloons stuffed with love notes ready to be blown up and popped.
2. Have an old-fashioned pillow or water balloon fight. The anger and frustration will turn to laughter and fun in no time!
3. Hold a whisper argumentathon. Time yourself and see how impossible it is to sustain an argument when you speak softly.
4. Step on stage and dramatize your position (or better yet, the other person's position) using puppets or mimicking a well-known personality.
5. Tell and retell the other person's story in your own words.
6. Using an erasable marker on white board or a pencil and eraser on paper, have both of you draw a picture of what you want or wish to happen. Then take turns indicating what you'd like to keep in the other person's picture and erase what you would like changed. Eventually an agreement will be reached.
7. When angry or upset, bake cookies together, make a beautiful mess, and then feed the cookies to each other.
8. Have your loved ones keep a wish list and use this time to surprise them by granting one of their wishes.

9. Make or buy a pair of jumbo-sized ears, put them on, and hand over a card to a special loved one that reads, "I'm 'hear' for you." Then give at least half an hour of undivided attention to that person. Sometimes the gift of time and a listening ear are the best things you can give.

10. LIFT someone's spirit by personalizing a kite for them and then go kite-flying together.

11. Declare a national holiday in someone's honor and spoil them and celebrate lavishly all day. It will do wonders!

12. Start a tradition that is uniquely yours, such as choosing a different flower every year to be the "flower of the year." Then place it in unexpected spots throughout the year, especially when the going is tough as a reminder and celebration of the love that holds you together.

13. Walk hand in hand underneath the stars, look up at the heavens, and make a wish . . . for the other person.

Tips:

These ideas will work in any relationship. Whenever we communicate our caring in a creative way, we strengthen a relationship, even when that communication begins in anger. Remember to T-alk, T-ickle, and most important, T-ackle. It takes work and energy to keep a relationship strong.

One of the people I most admire is David Roth, a singer and songwriter from Seattle, Washington. His beautiful words and music reflect my message in a new and different medium, and all of his songs are based on true stories and real people. With his permission, I've decided to end each chapter of this book with one of his songs that expresses the theme of that chapter. This song is one of the most beautiful examples of creative and heartfelt communication I have ever heard:

Nine Gold Medals

The athletes had come from all over the country
To run for the gold, for the silver and bronze
Many the weeks and the months of their training
And all coming down to these games

The spectators gathered around the old field
For cheering on all the young women and men
The final event of the day was approaching
Excitement grew high to begin

The blocks were all lined up for those who would use them
The hundred-yard dash was the race to be run
There were nine resolved athletes in back of the starting line
Poised for the sound of the gun

The signal was given, the pistol exploded
And so did the runners all charging ahead
But the smallest among them, he stumbled and staggered
And fell to the asphalt instead

He gave out a cry in frustration and anguish
His dreams and his efforts all dashed in the dirt
But as sure as I'm standing here telling this story
The same goes for what next occurred

The eight other runners pulled up on their heels
The ones who had trained for so long to compete
One by one they all turned round and went back to help him
And brought the young boy to his feet

Then all the nine runners joined hands and continued
The hundred-yard dash now reduced to a walk
And a banner above that said SPECIAL OLYMPICS
Could not have been more on the mark

That's how the race ended, with nine gold medals
They came to the finish line holding hands still
And a standing ovation and nine beaming faces
Said more than these words ever will

That's how the race ended, with nine gold medals
They came to the finish line holding hands still
And a standing ovation and nine beaming faces
Said more than these words ever will

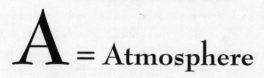

CHAPTER THREE

A = Atmosphere

"What Does It Feel Like to Be in Your Home?"

Laughter is the shortest distance between two people.

—Victor Borge

SO MANY THINGS are changing in our world today that making the atmosphere you create in your home or school a positive and caring one can change a person's life from one of defeat and despair to one of new dreams and hope. Dr. Myrle Vokey, the executive director of the Newfoundland and Labrador School Boards Association, shared this interesting comparison with me from a CBS news survey:

The Top Seven School Problems as Perceived by Students

1940s	*1990s*
1. Talking out of turn	1. Drug abuse
2. Chewing gum	2. Alcohol abuse
3. Making noise	3. Pregnancy
4. Running in the halls	4. Suicide
5. Cutting in line	5. Rape
6. Dress code infractions	6. Robbery
7. Littering	7. Assault

If we think of the magnitude of the changes in the lives of young people in the last fifty years, it becomes vitally important that the family provide the security, values, and stability that society can no longer provide. Whether a family is two or twelve people, the atmosphere created in the home can be one of love and support rather than one of criticism and pain, a haven and an anchor amidst the chaos of our world.

What does it feel like to be in your home? Haven't you been in homes that felt "bad," homes that were permeated with tension, competition, blaming, and pain? And then there are homes that are places of refuge and strength, founded on the values of respect and caring—they are happy homes, and we can feel it almost from the moment we enter. This chapter includes many ideas to help make your home exude an atmosphere of delight, caring, creativity, support, and fun, a place of hope and encouragement built on the bedrock of shared values in the midst of the storm.

Let Your Values Show

The Idea:

It is important to have roots and clear values as a family. Does your home show what is important to you?

The Idea in Action:

I wanted our children to know what we stand for as a family and to experience that every day in their surroundings. It is also important to me that guests in our home know what our values are. On the molding next to our front door, I have nailed a mezuzah that reads "Peace to all who enter here." On the back door is a plaque that says, "As for me and my house, we will serve the Lord."

Hanging in our entryway are three beautifully framed pieces. One is a handmade cross-stitch given to me by a dear friend: "A house is made of brick and stone. A home is made of love alone." Another has an etching of John 3:16, "For God so loved the world, that he gave his only begotten Son, that whosoever believeth in him should not perish, but have everlasting life." The third is a beautiful painting that reads, "In quietness and confidence shall be your strength."

In the kitchen is a framed copy of "Children Learn What They Live" as well as a little boy's blessing: "Thank you, God, for a hundred things:

The flower that blooms; the bird that sings; the sun that shines; the rain that drops; ice cream and gum and lollipops!" And in the hallway to the family room is the children's favorite, "The Mean Mother"! Throughout our home are family pictures, and the upstairs hall has framed copies of the front page of the *Chicago Tribune,* my husband's place of employment for thirty years, on the day of birth of each of our children.

Even my office sends special messages. I have a framed picture of Mother Teresa above my computer and a poster above my desk from a special artist friend that says, "Kindness Is Contagious. Catch it!" The rest of the walls are covered with huge collages, made by my daughter Erin as a gift for me, which contain dozens of cards, notes, letters, and pictures of people who have been in my sessions.

Tips:

What have you learned about our family as I've taken you on a mental tour of our home? What does your home say about your family? Do your surroundings reinforce the values that you hold dear as a family? I especially treasure handmade gifts because the giver is giving you a bit of his or her spirit. A home filled with spirit makes every guest feel welcome. For Christmas this year my daughter gave me a handmade ceramic plaque that reads, "Be not forgetful to entertain strangers for thereby some have entertained angels unawares. Hebrews 13:2."

> **Home is the definition of God.**
>
> **—Emily Dickinson**

Have an Annual Blessing for Your House

The Idea:

In her book *Shelter for the Spirit,* Victoria Moran suggests that each of us have an annual house blessing—a sort of spring cleaning for the atmosphere.

The Idea in Action:

A house blessing is a way to increase the positive energies of your home and can be done with a new residence or one in which you've lived for twenty years.

Victoria Moran suggests how to carry out such a blessing:

Invite people with whom you feel particularly in tune, friends whose qualities you would like to be reminded of when you enter your home. Ask each one to bring a prayer, poem, or ritual from his or her religious tradition or philosophical bent. Sit in a circle. You and those you live with speak first, thanking everyone for coming and expressing your hopes for your new home. Then each person shares what he or she brought to read or do or say.

> **Most folks are about as happy as they make up their minds to be.**
>
> **—Abraham Lincoln**

For pleasant feelings that linger, you might include in your ceremony a large pitcher of water placed in the center of your circle of seated guests. It symbolically catches the blessings as they are offered. As the water evaporates, it diffuses them into the air. One pitcher of aquatic blessings stayed on my mantle for nearly a month. Every time I glanced at it during those unsettling weeks of moving in, I thought of the people who had taken time from their lives to put some love into mine. In those moments I agreed completely with Emily Dickinson: "My friends are my estate."

Tips:

This can be a wonderful family project to plan. Invite friends of all ages to bless your home. Discuss whom to invite and why. I always loved reading John Ruskin, a nineteenth-century British writer. He was an architect and felt that each building had its own spirit. I think we can bring our special spirits into a house to create a home, no matter where we live, and when we bring into it the spirits of many people whom we love, we are adding their energy to our home as well.

Make Your Home a Place of Welcome

The Idea:

Does your home send a message of "welcome" to your visitors? Think of special ways you can make your guests feel valued.

The Idea in Action:

Kathie Hightower, an author and speaker from Corvallis, Oregon, tells of a delightful way she now welcomes guests into her home:

In 1991 we went to a wedding of friends. Although we weren't in the wedding party, we were close friends. Imagine our delight—and the feeling of being very special and appreciated—when we found a gift basket in our hotel room. I decided then to copy that idea for my houseguests. We have a basket that we put on the bed awaiting their arrival. It has ribbons tied to it and colorful tissue paper in the bottom. I fill it with things appropriate to where we live. At the coast of Oregon that meant seashells, Anne Morrow Lindbergh's wonderful book Gift from the Sea to read, local postcards, and local chocolates.

I include a card that says, "Welcome to our home. The book is for your reading pleasure while you are here. The postcards are for you to use . . ." In Germany, I included brochures on our little German town along with information on the area.

Kathie shares another idea we can all use:

As military spouses, my friend Holly and I had lots of company visiting us— especially in Germany. She "surveyed" all her company to find out what was important to have in a guest room. We then made sure to include the items mentioned most often: a mirror, a trash can, a chair to sit on. And we added what we enjoy—the gift basket, fresh flowers or one fresh flower, and a carafe of water for nighttime.

Tips:

Think of things that have made you feel especially welcome in another's home, and then try to implement those ideas for your guests. I love scented soap and easy access to an iron and ironing board. One of the loveliest treats I have ever experienced as a guest was upon going to my room at night and finding my bed pulled down and one single flower on my pillow!

Make Your School a Courteous Place

The Idea:

Start a school-wide initiative to make your school a kinder, more courteous place to be in the classroom, in the halls, in sports programs, at lunch, and even on the playground.

The Idea in Action:

📦 In Western Springs, Illinois, Laidlaw Elementary School students grades one to six are taking this year to become more familiar with the part courtesy plays in everyday interactions. Through a school-wide initiative, each classroom has brainstormed a list of courteous actions that the children will use as a focus for the year. By dropping a marble in a jar each time someone is courteous to them, they can rack up a whole jar full of courtesy! To record each classroom's success, streamers will be hung in the school vestibule each time a jar is filled. At the end of the year there will be a "courtesy" celebration for the whole school. The final outcome of this year-long activity should find students handling day-to-day interactions with greater kindness and courtesy. A further expectation is that, in some instances, courtesy skills will help children in their efforts to resolve problems with one another. This project is being funded by the Western Springs Foundation for Educational Excellence.

Tips:

This would also make a good project in a family. Whenever the jar is filled, have a family celebration—perhaps have dinner at a restaurant, go to a movie, or have a special picnic in front of the fireplace.

Become a Reading Family

The Idea:

Making reading a valued pastime in your family will lead to a lifetime of sharing and rewards. It is vitally important in our homes to turn off the TV. The average American will spend *one year of life* just watching the commercials! If you want more time to enjoy your family members, unleash your creativity, or ponder spiritual truths, turn off the TV and read together.

The Idea in Action:

📦 My father was a reader! My most lasting memory of my father is seeing him in the living room in his easy chair reading a book. He was a speed reader and read a book a night. He used to tell us that he had read every book in the library in our little town of Harlan, Iowa—and I do believe he had! Whenever we had a question about anything, we soon learned that Dad had the answer. (Many years later, he did admit to me that if he didn't know the answer, he made it up! However, I think that because of the vast amount of information he gained from his reading, his answers were probably pretty accurate.) From my earliest memory books have been a treasure to me, and I wanted to instill that value in my own children.

When I became pregnant with our first child, I immediately began reading to (him). I read Shake-speare and poetry and other writings that sounded beautiful, so that the baby would experi-ence the wonderful rhythm of words. I also played lots of clas-sical music during my preg-nancy. Today scientists have discovered that the child in the womb *can* hear sounds and particularly can recog-nize the mother's voice. That was of special comfort to me after our second son died soon after birth.

After the children were born, I committed thirty minutes every day to reading aloud to them. As babies, I would read Mother Goose rhymes and other poems, and I chose books with bright colors and ap-pealing illustrations. They particularly enjoyed interactive books such as *Pat the Bunny* and *Who Lives Here.* I have often wondered how many hun-dreds of times my husband and I read *Goodnight Moon!*

As the children grew older, it became a nightly ritual that we read to them for at least twenty to thirty minutes. A wonderful resource I found was Jim Trelease's *Read Aloud Handbook,* which gives suggestions of good literature to read aloud for each age group. On a trip to the Shakespeare festival in Stratford, Ontario, Canada, I purchased a book of prose stories for children of Shakespeare's most famous plays. As a result, my children, even at very young ages, have enjoyed Shakespeare because they already knew all the stories! We often read chapter books, a chapter a night, as they grew, and even when they were junior high age, we would often read a chapter of a special book such as A *Christmas Carol* at the dinner table.

When the children were quite young, I bought them each a bright-colored notebook that was their "Reading Record," and I gave them a special jar for "book money." Whenever they read a book on their own, they recorded the author, title, and one thing they liked about the book on a page. (As they grew older, I asked them one question for each book that they recorded such as: "Who was your favorite character? What made you laugh in the book? What is one lesson you learned from the story? Who in the story would you like to meet? Where did the story take place? What part was your favorite? Who didn't you like and why?") Then for each short book that they recorded, they got ten cents in their book money jar, and for every longer book, they got twenty-five cents. That way they always had money of their very own to buy new books!

> *A merry heart doeth good like a medicine but a broken spirit drieth the bones.*
>
> —Proverbs 17:22

Barbara McCauley, a very special teacher from Salt Lake City, Utah, shares these ideas about books:

1. Always carry a book with you to read aloud while you wait with family members.
2. Make both a family and a personal goal related to reading such as reading an hour a day, reading one book a month, etc.
3. When you find an author who speaks to you or your family, read all the books you can find by that author.
4. Buy your own copy so you can underline, star, write in the margins, etc. (This is especially fun for family reading so you can watch how the children's ideas change and grow as they grow.)
5. Share what you learned from a book with at least one other person—it will stick with you longer. (This is a wonderful idea for sharing at the dinner table—each person read one book a week or a month that he or she tells about.)
6. As a family, write to the authors of your favorite books and let them know what the book has meant to you. (This was the way I first

met Barbara. She wrote to me after she discovered my book CARE Packages for the Workplace.)

7. Send some bookplates to a favorite author to autograph so you can include one when you give a family gift of the book to someone else.
8. Share books with other families. You might want to have a one-week trade of special books.

Tips:

Even as very young children, my kids never tore a book. That was not because they were perfect children by any means, but I think it was because they grew up feeling that books were special, and they loved that sharing time with their parents. They all still love to read, and I think the value we placed on reading in our home greatly helped them in school as well. These are three quotations I have always loved about reading:

> The man who does not read good books has no advantage over the man who can't read them.
> —Mark Twain

> In a very real sense, people who have read good literature have lived more than people who cannot or will not read. . . . It is not true that we have only one life to live; if we can read, we can live as many more lives and as many kinds of lives as we wish.
> —S. I. Hayakawa

> A book is a mirror; if an ass peers into it, you can't expect an apostle to peer out!
> —George Christopher Lichtenberg

Choose an Object in Your Home That Demonstrates Love and Support

The Idea:

One special way to create an atmosphere of love and support in your home is to find an object that is a concrete expression of those feelings, and surprise other family members with it when they need encouragement.

The Idea in Action:

🎁 Jane Callahan of Scottsdale, Arizona, tells of a tradition her family had when her three daughters were growing up:

We had a pewter acorn that was about five inches in size. It had a removable top and a hollow center. I purchased it somewhere in my travels and enjoyed seeing it on our bookcase.

Once, when one of the girls had a test coming up the next day, I tucked a note inside the acorn that said, "Good luck with your test. We love you." Then I placed the acorn on her pillow so she would find it when she went to bed. She loved the note and told everyone about it at breakfast the next morning.

From that time on, the acorn was our means of offering support or love to anyone in the family at any time. The notes were never signed—and sometimes there wasn't even a note inside. The acorn itself was enough. It would sit on the bookshelf for weeks or months and then suddenly appear unexpectedly on a pillow, in a lunch box, in someone's pocket, etc. Once it was tucked in the refrigerator with a "Love you, Mom" note. Once it appeared in my husband's suitcase when he unpacked at a distant hotel while on business travel. It was always there, always ready for use, and always appreciated.

The girls are grown now, but I keep the acorn on my desk to remind me of them and the happy times we shared.

Tips:

Think about what you might choose as your family "acorn."

Find Fun Ways to Keep in Touch Even When Family Members Are Far Away

The Idea:

When family members are away from home, it takes creative thinking to keep that bond strong and to let them know they are loved even from afar.

The Idea in Action:

🎁 When my children were away at school or at camp, I used to send them CARE packages as many moms do. However, they weren't just filled with homemade things to eat. I decided that each box should be a reminder of all the fun and silly things we had done together as well as stress relievers for pressured times like final exams. So some of the things I put in their boxes were packages of little plastic ants to put in their roommates' beds: paint-with-water books; Silly Putty and Silly String; fake doggie doo and vomit to liven up the dorm; bottles of bubbles; paper dolls of all kinds for their imaginative time; party hats and poppers, confetti, and horns; all kinds of funny candies; card games like rummy and Authors, which they hadn't played for years; the game of Twister; paddle balls and jump ropes; little boxes of cereal; comic books; scientific things that "grow" when you put them in water; kites; and any other fun things I came across on my travels.

At Halloween I sent them trick-or-treat candy for their dormmates, door and room decorations for every holiday, and even sometimes practical things like rolls of quarters for their laundry. Each of my children told me that after they received the first package, whenever something came in the mail for them, a crowd always gathered round to see what their "crazy" mom had sent this time. Not only did they enjoy the packages, but they also became famous in their living quarters!

Mary Schulz shared a holiday tradition at Bradley University when her daughter Emily was a freshman there. In November all the parents received this letter:

Hello Parents! The holiday season is rapidly approaching, and unfortunately, so are finals here at Bradley. Your loved one is getting ready to go through her first round of finals here, and as her Resident and Assistant Resident Advisors, we are trying to do all that we can to help her though this. To relieve some of the stress, we are going to throw a holiday party during the week before finals. There will be games and goodies galore. We would also like to surprise the girls with a present from you! So, we're asking that you each send a present of fifteen dollars or less, gift-wrapped and labeled, to us. We will surprise them with a pile of presents from their folks at our party on December 10. You can just imagine the way their eyes will light up when they see the pile

Life isn't what you want, but it's what you got, so stick a geranium in your hat and be happy!

—Barbara Johnson,
Fresh Elastic for Stretched-Out Moms

and find one with their name on it. Please address the package to either one of us.

Hopefully, your loved one will have no idea about the presents until party time! If we receive the presents by Friday, December 5, we will have no problem delivering them at the party. Thank you in advance for your participation. We hope you have a safe and sane (at least as much as it can be) holiday season!

Mary got Emily a brand-new photograph album and filled it with pictures of various Christmases when Emily was little. On the top she tied an old Elmo doll, which was Emmy's favorite, with a note that read, "I miss you terribly. At last I found a way to come to Bradley for Christmas!" She gave Emily the gift of memories, and she had fun, too.

🎁 When one of my friend's husbands is on a business trip, she hides all kinds of little love notes in places where he will find them during the time he is away—in pockets of his suitcase, in his briefcase, in his shoes, in his shaving kit, and even sometimes in a pile of underwear!

🎁 A very special friend of ours from Western Springs, Illinois, gives her encouragement in quiet, often anonymous ways. Each year she compiles a list of names and addresses of the children of family friends who are away at school. Then during the spring and fall final times, she sends each of them a box of Frango mints, a very special chocolate candy that is available only at Marshall Fields, a Chicago-area department store. Not only is it a gift of special encouragement but it is also a reminder of something "from home"!

Tips:

It is such fun to imagine the surprise and delight of a loved one who is far away when they receive something from you—and the more unusual it is, the more tickled they are. I guarantee that you will enjoy creating the surprise as much as they enjoy getting it! And you are helping to re-create the atmosphere of home.

Plan Special Activities for Travel

The Idea:

Whenever you are traveling as a family, it is important to plan special things that will make the trip fun and will keep the children occupied. Creating an enjoyable atmosphere during the trip will help everything go more smoothly.

The Idea in Action:

When our children were little, we took lots of car trips to my parents' home in Iowa, an eight-hour drive away. One of the things they liked most was travel bingo, a game that can be purchased at a toy store (or you can make the cards yourself). For young children, put pictures of things on the cards that they might see, like a cow, a certain kind of gas-station sign, or a certain color car. Older children enjoy more challenging cards, perhaps with letters of the alphabet or with combinations of words such as those that appear on highway signs. One of the games our children loved most was looking for different license plates trying to get all the fifty states. These, too, could go on a bingo card. We also counted windmills and watched for letters of the alphabet in order on signs and buildings.

"When you take into account rest stops for me, Louise and the kids, I figure that towing the porta-john will save us about 50 minutes a day."

Close to Home © John McPherson
Dist. by Universal Press Syndicate.

Mary Schulz shares that when they drove the four hours to visit her parents or sister, she gave each of her children a Christmas stocking filled with tiny wrapped treasures such as matchbox cars and miniature books. They then got to open one present every thirty minutes. This made the car ride go faster because of the anticipation of opening another gift, and she said they were always "little angels" on those trips!

Nancy Provenzano says that on their trips to Kentucky to visit her parents, after they've gone one hundred miles down the road, they always stop and pray for a safe trip. She says they can feel the difference when they forget to do this.

Tips:

It is difficult for a whole family to be cooped up in a car or an airplane for several hours. However, with preplanning and a little creativity, those hours can be fun ones for all.

Encourage Your Children to Play "Dress-up"

The Idea:

Start a costume box for your children to encourage them to dress up and play make-believe games. This will help create an atmosphere of creativity and imagination in your home.

The Idea in Action:

When we were young, one of our favorite pastimes was playing make-believe and dress-up. My mother had collected many different kinds of costumes over the years. The ones I most remember were a small (about size six or seven) handmade tuxedo with a real collapsible top hat that she had found at an auction, a Chinese embroidered suit to which she added a black sock pigtail, a grass skirt someone had brought back from Hawaii, and adult-size pajamas with feet and a drop seat, on which I sewed pipe-cleaner ants to illustrate "Ants in my pants"!

Many of these things were passed on to my children, and I added to the costume collection. The girls loved my old negligees and especially babydoll pajamas because these could be party dresses, and the short ones just fit them. Colored

slips and half-slips can be sundresses and skirts. I made many trips to the resale shops and found old hats and purses and wigs and gloves and fur capes. We had three older nieces who gave the girls several of their used bridesmaid dresses and head-pieces, and I purchased more of these at thrift shops for very lit-tle money. We then cut them off, and they had beautiful "princess" dresses. I also used to watch for anyone at church or in our community who had tiny feet (size four to six), and I would ask them to save their old shoes for me. That way the little girls had high heels that fit them! We had piles of old jewelry from garage sales and grandmas and aunts, and for the boys I made Superman and Batman capes and collected various kinds of hats, bow ties, and even long red under-wear. I bought a hanging rack on wheels and a full-length mirror to have in the basement, and the children spent hours and hours dressing up with their friends.

They acted out stories and made up plays, and one of their most favorite things to do was to have a wedding. Connie Geppert, a special friend from church who used to make bridal gowns, made each of the girls a bridal outfit when they were about four and a half and seven years old. Gretchen was the bride, and Erin was the maid of honor. Then various friends were the bridesmaids, and the groom was any little boy whom they could talk into playing with them! I played "Here Comes the Bride" as they walked down the stairs, and Garrett was usually the preacher.

Tips:

It is amazing what you can find in thrift shops, at garage sales, and in friends' and relatives' attics or basements! And you're even luckier if you have friends who can sew. Playing dress-up was one of the best activities the children could have to develop their imaginations and to learn to put themselves in other people's shoes. They were learning about different cultures through costumes as well as experiencing being able to change their identity and become anyone they wished, from a prince or princess to a hobo or a wicked witch. Just keep your eyes open, and you'll discover all sorts of resources wherever you go.

Use Calendars to Help Focus on Your Blessings

The Idea:

Because there is so much negativity, violence, and pain in our world today, we need to make our homes positive places. One of the ways we can do this is to focus on our blessings.

The Idea in Action:

Dave opens up his birthday gift from Mamie.

🎁 Laurie Trice of Kenosha, Wisconsin, uses a daily calendar as more than just a way to keep track of time. At the end of each day when she tears off a page, she writes one or two blessings that occurred that day on the page and then she saves them in a special place. When she is having a particularly hard time, she often gets those pages out to see the special way God is working in every day of her life, even when she sometimes feels that He is very far away. On Thanksgiving Day she shares many of the blessings she has written down with her family.

Diane Pedersen shared with me that for the last six years either she or her mother purchases a tear-off calendar with a thought for each day or scripture verse and questions printed on each page for each of them. Then, even though they are hundreds of miles apart, they are each reading the same thought for that day and thinking about the same thing. They alternate years, with Diane choosing the calendars for one year and her mother the next. This special idea could be done with any family member who lives away from you, just to feel the closeness that you are both meditating on the same thought.

Tips:

A wonderful family activity to keep everyone focused on blessings would be to give each person in the family his or her own tear-off calendar and then each night at dinner share the blessings from that day. One family whose daughter is away at school sends their pages to her once a week, and she sends her pages back to them so that they can keep in touch in an especially positive way.

Create an Inviting Atmosphere— No Matter Where You Are

The Idea:

Whether it is in your home, your workplace, or your school, always try to create an atmosphere that is inviting, stress-free, and pleasant.

The Idea in Action:

 Sheila Huston teaches dental assisting in a small college in Carthage, Illinois. She writes about how she tries to create an atmosphere conducive to learning:

> **A great man is one who has not lost his Child's heart.**
> **—Mencius**

My goal is to inspire my students to be energetic, caring, empathetic, positive, and efficient. In a dental office the assistant can be the one person who gains the patient's trust by building a relationship with the patient. It is so rewarding to see a struggling student enter the program and exit full of confidence, pride, and commitment to the profession.

We just had finals week, which can be an awful drudge. So, to spark some enthusiasm, to get their "creative juices" flowing, to help students relax and show them I care, I do a few extras. There are all kinds of fresh flowers on our campus, so I pick a few and put them in a lovely vase. Candlelight makes everything more tolerable, so there is always a lightly scented candle in my classroom. Popcorn is a terrific inexpensive treat to nibble on during a test or a long lecture class. Light soft music helps a lot of students relax—Kenny G is my favorite! All students' birthdays are recognized by a class potluck—the birthday person brings a hefty appetite but nothing else.

Tracie Shafer works in a basement office with no windows. To create a more pleasing workspace, she purchased a large sheet of clear plastic, made window panes from it for a "fake" window, hung them on the walls, and created pictures of each of the four seasons. As the seasons change, she simply changes the pictures behind the window panes, and she has created her own atmosphere "with a view"!

Tips:

All the extras that Sheila does help create an atmosphere of caring and learning. Are there some of these things that might help make your home or school a warmer, more caring place to be? I tried to always have some kind of special decorations for each holiday, both for the front door and in several places in our home, like the kitchen table. The children loved getting these out each year and adding things they had made in school or Scouts. We were creating an atmosphere of celebration and warmth in our home.

Approach Your Day with Humor

The Idea:

Sister Anne Bryan Smollin, in her book *Jiggle Your Heart and Tickle Your Soul*, says, "There's nothing like a good laugh. It tickles our very souls. Laughter is an activity of the heart. We scrunch our souls with negativity and a lack of enthusiasm. Laughter smooths them out." She goes on to say, "Research indicates that an infant laughs when she is ten weeks old. At sixteen weeks, an infant laughs almost every hour. When a child is four years old, he laughs almost every four minutes—unless we interfere with the child experiencing joy!" How often do you laugh a day? The average child laughs *hundreds* of times a day. The average adult laughs a dozen times a day. We need to *find* those lost laughs.

Just as grief and anger can suppress the immune system, laughter can strengthen it. Laughter creates a unique physiological state, with changes in the immune system opposite to those caused by stress. It lowers blood pressure, wards off colds, stifles the flu, helps you sleep better, helps you lose weight, *and* it's good for the soul!

The Idea in Action:

So laugh early and laugh long. Send a quick and funny e-mail to a friend before heading to work, or catch a morning cartoon with the kids. Enjoying a few minutes of looniness in the morning can change your mood for the rest of the day.

My friend Brian Becker e-mailed this to me on a Monday morning:

TRUE THINGS I'VE LEARNED FROM MY KIDS
(Honest and No Kidding)

- There is no such thing as childproofing your house.
- If you spray hair spray on dust bunnies and run over them with roller blades, they can ignite.
- A four-year-old's voice is louder than two hundred adults in a crowded restaurant.
- If you hook a dog leash over a ceiling fan, the motor is not strong enough to rotate a forty-two-pound boy wearing underwear and a Superman cape.
- It is strong enough, however, to spread paint on all four walls of a 20 x 20-foot room.
- Baseballs make marks on the ceiling.
- You should not throw baseballs up when the ceiling fan is on.
- When using the ceiling fan as a bat, you have to throw the ball up a few times before you get a hit.
- A ceiling fan can hit a baseball a long way.
- The glass in windows (even double pane) doesn't stop a baseball hit by a ceiling fan.

- When you hear the toilet flush and the words, "Uh-oh," it's already too late.
- Brake fluid mixed with Clorox makes smoke, and lots of it.
- A six-year-old can start a fire with a flint rock even though a thirty-six-year-old man says they can only do it in the movies.
- A magnifying glass can start a fire on an overcast day.
- If you use the waterbed as home plate while wearing baseball shoes, it does not leak—it explodes.
- A king-size waterbed holds enough water to fill a 2,000-square-foot house four inches deep.
- Legos will pass through the digestive tract of a four-year-old.
- Duplos will not.
- "Play Doh" and "microwave" should never be used in the same sentence.
- Super Glue is forever.
- McGyver can teach us many things we don't want to know.
- Ditto Tarzan.
- No matter how much Jell-O you put in a swimming pool, you still can't walk on water.
- Pool filters do not like Jell-O.
- VCRs do not eject pb&j sandwiches even though TV commercials show they do.
- Garbage bags do not make good parachutes.
- Marbles in gas tanks make lots of noise when driving.
- You probably do not want to know what that odor is.
- Always look in the oven before you turn it on. Plastic toys do not like ovens.
- The fire department in San Diego has at least a five-minute response time.
- The spin cycle on the washing machine does not make earthworms dizzy.
- It will, however, make cats dizzy.
- Cats throw up twice their body weight when dizzy.
- Quiet does not necessarily mean, "Don't worry."
- A good sense of humor will get you through most problems in life (unfortunately, mostly in retrospect).

Thanks, Brian! You started my day out right. . . .

Tips:

Jeannie Robertson, a well-known professional speaker and humorist, keeps a daily humor diary where she records all sorts of funny things that happen each day. Then she uses this material in her presentations. Have you ever thought of keeping a record of funny things in your life? If you try it, I guarantee you'll find more things than you ever dreamed of *and* you'll laugh about them again and again.

Encourage Laughter in Your Home

The Idea:

Homes are very special places—filled with love and happy faces.
—Anonymous

"It took some getting used to, but the kids love it. Plus, I don't have to vacuum anymore."

A home filled with laughter will raise everyone's spirits and will help keep even the tough times in perspective. One of the greatest gifts we can give our children is the ability to laugh at themselves.

The Idea in Action:

One of the ways you can create an atmosphere of laughter and fun is to keep cartoons on your refrigerator. I have collected cartoons for years, and I have them filed by topic. Whenever I find one that exemplifies our family, it goes immediately on the refrigerator. I also had lots of fun sending these to my children when they were away at school.

Keep cartoon books around your home, especially in the bathroom! We love *Calvin and Hobbes*, *Close to Home*, *The Buckets*, and *For Better or For Worse* because these are all cartoons about families just like ours. You can purchase books of these cartoons at any bookstore in the humor section.

Have a joke night once a week. Everyone has the responsibility to bring a joke to dinner and then tell it to the rest of the family. Even very little children love this and often "make up" their jokes! You can use riddles, puzzles, limericks, poems (we love Shel Silverstein's books to trigger our imaginations), or knock-knock jokes. Our children went through different stages of what they thought was funny, but we always had fun doing this.

In a later chapter I will talk more about the importance of having dinner together as a family. One delightful idea for dinner conversation is for everyone to tell one funny thing that happened to them that day. Not only does this make a good sharing time but it also teaches children (and adults, too) to look for humor in their lives and to dwell on the things that make you smile rather than the difficult times. Oftentimes family legends and ongoing sagas can come from these stories!

> **Keep your face to the sunshine and you cannot see a shadow.**
>
> —Helen Keller

Tips:

We can't force anyone to look on the light side; however, it is an attitude that is contagious, and as families begin to share and talk about the fun things that have happened to them, an atmosphere is created that is positive and happy.

Banish Boredom in Your Home

The Idea:

Sometimes I hear people, and especially children, say they are bored. It never ceases to amaze me that with all the opportunities we have every day to learn and grow and all the technology we have available to communicate and to entertain ourselves that anyone could be bored. Help your children early in their lives develop habits and interests so that they will be plagued with not having enough time in their lives rather than being bored.

The Idea in Action:

In his book *Ten Secrets to Avoid Boredom*, Alan Caruba suggests these three tips:

1. Get the reading habit. *Never go anywhere without a book, magazine, or newspaper. It is reading, not watching TV, that will provide the real information and the entertainment you need to enrich your life.* [I have included many ideas to help you become a reading family in an earlier part of this chapter.]

I always have three books going at one time—one business book, one spiritual book, and one just for fun. Then, depending upon my stress level and the state of mind I'm in at any given time, I have something appropriate to read. I record the titles and authors of each book I read in my journal so that I have a record of what I've accomplished, and often I jot down a quotation or several ideas I liked from the book. Also I keep a basket in my office where I collect all the reading material that I want to read but don't have the time for currently, particularly magazines and professional papers. Then when I travel, my airplane time is my treasured reading time. I grab a large stack from that basket and that is what I read on the plane. I do the same when I go to an appointment if I know I'm going to have to wait—even finishing just a few pages from the basket makes me feel my time is not wasted. As you model these habits, your children, too, will learn the reading habit.

2. Develop hobbies. *Hobbies may be recreational, artistic, or intellectual, but whatever they are, they give a special dimension to life. No hobby is too silly or too serious to enjoy.*

Some people play a musical instrument or sing in a choir as a hobby. When I was growing up, I played the piano, and because I often practiced several hours a day in high school, it kept me focused and out of trouble. I was driven by all the wonderful music I wanted to play. Other people have sports hobbies. Several men I've met are trying to play as many golf courses as they can in their lifetime; others want to attend games with as many different baseball teams as they can. Perhaps your family loves zoos. You may decide to try to visit as many different zoos as you can and study how they are different. Other families love hobbies like woodworking and enjoy creating things together. I believe the very best gifts in the world are homemade gifts because they contain a little bit of the spirit of the giver!

I love collections! Do you have a collection as a family or as individuals? I have always loved dolls, so when I had my first little girl, I had an "excuse" to start a doll collection. When I was home with the children, one of the things I did part time was to teach English as a Second Language at Argonne National Laboratory. I had wonderful, interesting students there from all over the world, mostly scientists who were just in this country for six to twelve months to do research and wanted to learn to converse in our language. I tried to invite them all to our home at some time during their stay, and often when they'd leave to go back to their countries, they'd ask me what they could send me as a gift. I always asked for a little doll from their land, one that was authentic and not just "pretty." That was an easy and inexpensive thing for them to send, and both my children and I have learned so much from those gifts. As friends began to travel, they would bring me back dolls as gifts, and that is always the souvenir I purchase whenever I visit a new place. My collection has grown and grown, and each doll is a beautiful memory of a friend or of a place I've visited. Many of the dolls have stories behind them, so it is always a delight to share my collection with others. Through this collection, both my children and I have learned about different cultures, dress, and customs.

> *There is no day so dark that the gifts of sunshine, love, and friendly laughter cannot brighten it. Thank you for these gifts.*
>
> **—Gail Harano Cunningham**

Families who collect stamps can look for an unusual stamp whenever they go somewhere, and as they acquire new stamps, they, like me, are always learning about the place they came from. Some families collect matchbooks from various places they visit because this is a hobby that doesn't cost money. Others collect postcards. Encourage your children to start a collection of some kind—whatever they are interested in. It will bring them many hours of happiness and learning. Our son Garrett collects coin banks, and it is fun to look for one for him on our travels and for holidays, and through this collection, he has learned lots about how people value money in different cultures (many of them don't even have such a thing as a bank). A collection is a way to learn, to find a focus wherever you are, and it also becomes a representation of an individual or a family. Don't you know someone who collects cows or pigs or hats? You always think of that person and perhaps even buy the person something when you see one of those items!

3. Be a joiner. *There are thousands of organizations eager to have you as a member, whether at the local, state, national, or international level. Seek them out.*

As families, you may be involved with a church or a synagogue where there are many activities available. If you have a hobby or collection, there are interest groups you can join. There are family support groups for situations that have changed your life like a death in the family. Most communities have recreational groups and classes for families. And there are dozens of groups who need volunteer members, from Meals on Wheels to the American Red Cross. If you are not good at researching things and want to find a group for yourself or your family to join, go to the Research librarian at your local library for help. They are wonderful people, and that is part of their mission in being there!

Tips:

Helping your children to crystallize their interests and then to find ways to encourage and support those interests will give them a focus that is vitally important in their lives, both in understanding their own uniqueness and in helping them find a career path. And they will never be bored! I think we all should have both a vocation (the work for which we get paid) and an avocation (something we do just because we love doing it).

Make a Family Fun Box

The Idea:

It is important in any family that everyone gets to share in the planning of family activities. That way each person's interests are taken into account, and there is buy-in from each person since he or she has a say in the choices of activities.

The Idea in Action:

Tia Vaux of Coon Rapids, Iowa, sent me a copy of the newsletter called *Soul-o-Gram*, which is a publication of their sharing group, Stressed-Out Unified Ladies (SOUL). In the newsletter they suggested making a Family Fun Box to help plan regular family activities:

- Get a box; a shoebox or empty round oatmeal box is the best.
- Decorate the outside together, labeling the box "Family Fun Box."

- Have each family member write down on slips of paper some things to do as a family. These activities could include:

  Bowling
  Reading a book aloud
  Seeing a movie
  Playing a game
  Sending out for pizza
  Going for a bike ride
  Going to the mall for ice cream

- When the designated evening rolls around, pull a slip of paper from the fun box and do whatever it tells you.
- Replenish the slips of paper either by replacing the slip just drawn or by adding to the box as family members come up with additional ideas.

Tips:

This activity will work only if everyone in the family participates and if everyone AGREES to do whatever is written on the paper WITHOUT GRIPING. Interests for family members may be quite different; however, learning to share and learning tolerance and acceptance will be byproducts of using this process, besides having a good time as a family. At the end of each activity, you may want to have each family member share what they really liked about that activity, keeping the focus on the positive and how we can always find something good in everything.

Charlie and I love to go to the movies; however, we have very different tastes—he likes silly comedies and I like good tear-jerker dramas. One of the ways we have decided to handle our differences is that we

Close to Home © John McPherson/Dist. by Universal Press Syndicate.

"There. Now it's halftime. What do you say we all go to the table and have a nice, quiet Thanksgiving dinner."

alternate choices. One time it is his choice, and the next time it is mine. We try very hard not to complain about the other person's choice!

Create an Extended Family

The Idea:

Sometimes, whether you do not have any blood relatives, or they live far away, or you have become a widow or widower, or your family has been torn apart by divorce, you can create your own extended family.

The Idea in Action:

Linda Kraig writes about her experience as a divorced and then remarried mother:

Divorce destroys families. It breaks bonds and causes heartbreak that extends far beyond the immediate family. And noncustodial grandparents are much forgotten victims.

The divorce was easier for my parents. I depended upon them greatly, and they saw their grandchildren almost every day. The divorce was devastating, however, for my in-laws. I remember my mother-in-law expressing her profound grief over the loss of her son's family, and I made a very solemn promise to her that she would always share in my children's lives. Although it has meant breaking old rules and finding new ways, the promise has been kept, and my children's paternal grandparents have remained an integral part of our lives . . . even through remarriage.

The first few holidays after the separation were torture. My children would spend the holiday either with their father and his family or with me and mine. Someone was always left alone and hurting. I decided to "break the rules" for my oldest son's grammar school graduation. I hosted a party and invited everyone. Surprisingly, everyone accepted.

While the first ex-family gathering was a little awkward, we continued the tradition: first graduations, then birthdays, and then some holidays. At first, we would say we were "doing this for the kids." But each time we felt more comfortable, and eventually we established redefined relationships. The emphasis was not so much on what our relationship was, but just that we had one.

My ex-husband and I eventually met "significant others," and I found myself facing whole weekends of having to entrust my children to a woman I had never met—my ex-husband's girlfriend. I went through several of these weekends worrying myself sick, especially because one of my children was a toddler. Finally, when I could no longer endure the horrors of my imagination, I called my ex and asked him if I could meet his girlfriend. Needless to say, he was not crazy about the idea. But when I explained to him how anguished I was over the care of my children during visitation weekends, he finally agreed.

Nancy and I met for coffee on a Friday night. I was surprised to find that, even though she was thirteen years my junior and had never been married, she was very understanding about my concerns and soon I realized that she cared about my children and only wanted to do what was best for them. Nancy and I agreed to communicate about the kids before and after each visit, and ultimately, we became the best of friends . . . a relationship based on caring. She married my ex-husband, and they are now the proud parents of two beautiful children, ages seven and five.

> **When you enter a synagogue or a church, you know if it is one that is prayed in, because it has the odor of sanctity about it. You can also tell when you've entered a happy home—there's something in the atmosphere. If there has been continual fighting, even the smiles that are put on for you won't fool you.**
>
> **—Archbishop Desmond Tutu, winner of the 1984 Nobel Peace Prize**

Our relationship, while certainly not conventional (I call her my ex-wife!), has turned out to be incredibly healthy for all of us. My children do not have to harbor guilt about loving Nancy, because they know I do, too. She genuinely cares about my children, and her children are surrounded by lots of love and adoration from their ex-tended family—their half-brothers and -sisters (they don't use the word half when referring to each other), and from my husband and me—who babysit at every opportunity.

Thirteen years have passed since Nancy and I began making new rules to accommodate caring in our extended family. Today we share each of our children's triumphs and woes. The entire family—parents, grandparents, and *exes—gather comfortably for birthdays and holidays. We are always surprised at other people's disbelief in the success of our relationship. While we are very proud of what we have accomplished, we also admit that it was not that difficult for us to do . . . we simply cared.*

I read an article in the March 30, 1997, edition of Parade Magazine by Michael Ryan titled "How One Woman's Twelve Friends Became a Family." Susan Farrow knew she was dying of a rare form of cancer that originated in her salivary gland. In 1988 she asked a group of twelve of her friends, many of whom did not know one another, to a meeting. During that meeting Susan, a divorced mother of two girls, asked them to do something remarkable—to become the family she did not have near her but now desperately needed. They not only accepted the responsibility, but their lives were changed as a result of it. Sheila Warnock explained, "After a while, we began to call ourselves 'Susan's Funny Family,' and we really felt like a family, too."

Susan explained to them that first night that she would need help in every area of her life—caring for her seventeen-year-old daughter while she was in the hospital, cleaning and cooking while she was going through chemotherapy, getting her to appointments, and so on. The "Funny Family" divided themselves up into teams, and each week two would serve as captains to make sure everything got done. Sheila Warnock said, "People who are confronted with caregiving usually think, Oh, my God, what can I do? But they should know that you can just bake those great brownies that you bake, you can go shopping with her daughter for her college wardrobe. It's just a matter of uncovering what you're good at and doing it." As Susan's health worsened, the Funny Family even arranged her daughter's wedding, and they stayed together for the three and a half years that Susan lived.

Several years after the Funny Family began, an acquaintance of Susan's who had been diagnosed with cancer and needed a bone-marrow transplant approached the Funny Family members and asked if they would meet with her friends to try to set up a group like theirs to look after her and her family during the crisis. Since then, several members of the Funny Family have written a book called *Share the Care: How to Organize a Group to Care for Someone Who Is Seriously Ill* to pass on what they've learned to others, and Funny Families have been forming all over the country. Susan's Funny Family envision the day when thousands of groups like theirs will be supporting sick people across the country. One member said, "It gives you a chance to put something back in the universe. It gives people more to do with their lives."

Tips:

These examples show so beautifully ways we can care for others by creating an extended family. One powerful lesson I have learned from both Linda and Susan is that we have *choices* in any circumstance, and those choices impact not only us but those we love. Linda and Susan gave priceless gifts to all those around them by creating their own special extended families in an atmosphere of caring.

Do Kind Things for Others

The Idea:

We have all heard about "Random Acts of Kindness," and many individuals, organizations, and communities have adopted this as a philosophy of existence.

The Idea in Action:

Annetta Collman of St. Charles, Illinois, tells of a magical experience of kindness in her life:

One beautiful spring morning a few years ago, I set out on my daily walk and found myself at the supermarket (fourteen blocks from my home). Checking my small leather case with paper money, which I usually carry with me, I decided to stop and purchase a couple of "light" grocery items. When the cashier at the checkout counter informed me the amount of my purchases, I immediately realized I did not have that much cash with me and embarrassingly asked her if she would deduct the cost of the jar of peanut butter I had picked up. The cashier was very accommodating, and I was able to pay for the other purchases.

With a word of appreciation, I made a hasty exit. I was unaware of the young man behind me at the checkout counter so when he approached me with a jar of peanut butter in his hand as I was leaving the parking lot, I was taken by surprise. He said, "Good morning. I noticed you forfeited this jar of peanut butter at the checkout counter due to insufficient funds. Please accept this as a gift today and enjoy." I was speechless for a moment and finally was able to thank him for his kindness and wish him a happy day. Finally, in my ninety-two years, I learned to graciously receive! Heretofore, I always felt more blessed to give than to receive (Acts 20:35).

Tips:

If we could each do one kind thing for someone we may not even know every day, think of how the atmosphere of this whole world could change. Encourage your family members to do this and then share the kind things you've done at the dinner table each night.

Give Your Children the Gift of Music

The Idea:

One of the best gifts you can give to a young person is an appreciation and love for music. It doesn't matter what the instrument is, but I think everyone should have the privilege of taking music lessons of some kind.

The Idea in Action:

One of the two nonnegotiables in our home was taking piano lessons. Just like brushing your teeth each day, one of the duties of living in the Glanz household was to take piano lessons from your seventh to your twelfth birthday. Certainly, my children moaned, complained, and did everything in their power to encourage me to let them quit; however, they have all grown up with a true appreciation of music, and many doors were opened to them as a result of their understanding and talent for music.

> When a happy person enters a room, it's as if another candle has been lit.
>
> —Anonymous

Now why would a mother burden herself with such a thankless enforcement? I learned from my own experience with taking piano lessons that there were many benefits besides developing a love for music. First of all, I learned discipline—I had to practice for thirty minutes six days of the week, and the practice came before playtime. Sometimes I would get up at 6:00 A.M. to do my practicing before school so that I was free after school, but in the process I learned responsibility and how to stick to something. I also learned to focus. When you learn to play an instrument, you must be very specific in your focus because every note, rest, and expression mark counts. I learned to memorize, and I also learned the joy that comes from the accomplishment of taking a piece of music, part by part, sometimes one hand at a time, and then putting it all together to play a difficult piece.

All these skills have helped me immensely in life—to study carefully and regularly, to discipline myself toward a higher goal, to memorize quickly, to take tests well because I had learned to focus, and most of all to feel good about myself and my accomplishments. I wanted to provide the same opportunities for my own children. And in the process, they learned to value and respect the gift of music!

Tips:

It is important for you as a parent to determine two or three things that are most important to you to impart to your children and then make them non-negotiables. I would caution you, however, to be absolutely SURE that you are committed to these nonnegotiables for the long term, because it won't be easy to maintain the energy to be firm about their importance, and believe me, most children will try everything they can to wear you down. When Garrett was eleven and in the midst of trying everything to get me to relax my commitment, we heard Arthur Rubenstein, one of the world's greatest pianists, interviewed on television. He shared that when he was eleven, he would have quit playing the piano if his mother would have let him. That made a huge impression on both me and my children. I owe the deepest thanks to *my* mother, who gave me the gift of music.

This is a song David Roth wrote about a beautiful man named Alvin. He created an atmosphere of joy for many hurting people, just as we can create an atmosphere of joy in our home, no matter the circumstances.

More Alvins in the World

There are some who say that laughter is denial
An escape from going deeper into feeling or to pain
But I'd rather take my lifetime ride with those who see the lighter side
And know that there are rainbows after rain

I have a friend who found this out the hard way twenty years ago
His father facing surgery, his mother scared to death
The shuttle bus they took between their hotel and hospital
Was taken every day with bated breath

The driver of this shuttle bus, a gracious man named Alvin,
Must have seen and heard it all with passengers like these
So he'd offer up a smile or two, to help them see their journey through
No medicine could work as well as Alvin's gentle ease

We could use more Alvins in the world
A random act of kindness is more precious than a pearl
On a planet where we stumble while we spin around and swirl
We could use more Alvins in the world

He'd tell a joke or do a bit of magic
He'd help the older women on and ask 'em for a dance
Though the trip was short he made the most of every treasured mile
Because he knew he might not have another chance

We could use more Alvins in the world
A random act of kindness is more precious than a pearl
On a planet where we stumble while we spin around and swirl
We could use more Alvins in the world

"When you see somebody sick like all those people in the hospital
You want to help their families, too" says Alvin with a glow
"Of course you want to cheer 'em up, and someone's got to do it
I was there and so I did, that's all I know"

There are some folks say that laughter is compelling
And Alvin makes the case as well as anybody could
He's a certified constituent of "inverse paranoids"
Who think the world is always out to do them good

We could use more Alvins in the world
A random act of kindness is more precious than a pearl
On a planet where we stumble while we spin around and swirl
We could use more Alvins in the world

CHAPTER FOUR:
_____

A = Appreciation for All

"Become a Thankful Family"

Every charitable act is a stepping stone toward Heaven.

—Henry Ward Beecher

MARK TWAIN SAID many years ago, "I can go two months on one good compliment!" William James, the great American psychologist, said, "The deepest principle in human nature is the craving to be appreciated." And the Bible says, "Encourage each other and build each other up." One of the most basic needs, then, of any human being is to be appreciated.

Diane Geeting, who is a Regional Health Consultant with the U.S. Department of Labor Office of Job Corps in Chicago, Illinois, recently sent me an article titled "The Sound of Two Hands Clapping" by Deborah Shouse.* The article was subtitled, "We all need some form of outward appreciation on a regular basis." In the article Ms. Shouse writes about how she frequently gives applause as an audience member for many different occasions, but because hers is a "normal" life, she misses out on the generous encouragement and enthusiastic support of such tangible appreciation as applause.

Thus, she playfully suggests a "Day of Two Hands Clapping," a day when everyone in her life gives her cheers and standing ovations—from the teachers at her children's school to her coworkers, from the employees at the grocery

_____

*Shouse, Deborah, May 1, 1995, "The Sound of Two Hands Clapping." *Newsweek* magazine.

store where she shops to her own family! She suggests, "There could be applause stations on street corners and in office buildings, and we'd take turns clapping for one another and acknowledging how wonderful we are. One day a month could be designated National Applause Day, and on this day we'd cheer and be cheered. . . . Perhaps we could even learn to clap for ourselves."

She ends the article by telling about an experience she recently had in being roped into a fund-raising walkathon. She said:

After two hours, my new Walk-for-Life t-shirt was wet, my shoes were gnawing into my heels, and my mouth felt like I'd licked 399 envelopes. Along with hundreds of other fund raisers, I doggedly walked the Saturday-morning route, determined not to envy the cool gazes of those gliding by in their air-conditioned cars. I was yearning for water, a fan, and a new bottle of deodorant, when I heard "the sound."

"Yeah, you're great! You've come a long way. Only a few more miles to go. Great job!" The encouragement came from volunteers clustered at the intersection. Suddenly, my legs felt lighter, my mouth was moist. A gentle breeze dried my armpits. Someone has seen my bravery, my determination. Someone has seen me—tired, sweaty, and trying my best. Buoyed by the sounds of appreciation and praise, I knew I could walk a marathon!

Think about what we can do for our family members and others in our world as we freely and abundantly give them praise and appreciation for even the smallest of achievements. This is the GIFT we can choose to give every single day. As we focus on appreciating others, we will undoubtedly become a more thankful people, which in turn will impact the atmosphere in our homes and in our world.

Send an Anonymous Gift of Cheer

The Idea:

It is fun to give surprise gifts that are anonymous and that make the receiver wonder who might have been the one to remember them.

The Idea in Action:

Sylvia Marshall writes about the impact an anonymous gift had on her life:

Close to Home © John McPherson/Dist. by Universal Press Syndicate.

McPHERSON

Having spotted some acquaintances,
Vera activates the instant
grandchildren-photo display
on her purse.

During a period of great personal despair, a subscription to a small monthly prayer book filled with special prayers throughout the calendar month was mailed to me for about a year. I never did find out who sent this to me, but I can tell you I valued that little book. I still have certain pages that I tore out and saved as a keepsake. Some days were harder than others, and the passages in each of the daily pages seemed to hold significance for me alone. It sustained me during those times. I'm so very grateful to that special person who heard my cry and answered my prayers.

Last summer when I went to the front door to get the mail, there was a darling little basket in the door filled with five or six bags of goodies—cookie cutter cookies, brownies, Jordan almonds, and even tea bags. On top was a little poem that read:

> This little basket comes to say,
> You're a special friend in every way.
> Pass it along, but don't get caught.
> Do it in secret as Jesus taught!

I was deeply touched! I enjoyed the treats and then refilled the basket with things I love and left it in another friend's door when I knew she would be away. I thought and thought about who sent it, but I never have found out who my special messenger was.

Tips:

Anyone could do either of these things in their family, neighborhood, or school. You may want to change the faith orientation in the basket poem to one that is comfortable for you, or make up your own poem. I loved filling the basket with things I treasured, like little plastic chocolate-covered spoons, special herbal tea bags, several wrapped Godiva chocolates, a tiny book of quotations, and Pepperidge Farm goldfish!

Make a Thanksgiving Tree

The Idea:

It doesn't just have to be the month of November that we share our gratitude and appreciation for blessings in our lives. One of the ways to keep "an attitude of gratitude" in our homes is to make a Thanksgiving tree.

The Idea in Action:

Many years ago I created a Thanksgiving tree for our home. I took a large manzanita branch, sprayed it gold, and secured it in a base of plaster of Paris. Beside it I kept a basket of small plain cards with holes punched in them, another basket of pieces of colored yarn, and a pen. The tradition in our family is that the month before Thanksgiving, the tree is placed on a table in our living room, and each family member writes down things for which he or she is thankful and hangs them on the tree. We also encourage anyone who visits our home during that month to participate. At the dinner table on Thanksgiving Day we read the cards from the tree as an affirmation of our blessings. Then we save the cards from the year before, and we read those as well. It is a wonderful way to remind us of all the goodness in our lives and reinforces the importance of sharing our appreciation.

Tips:

This could be used year round in a family to focus on the good things happening each day. We found that guests in our home for the month of November would almost always take time to read at least some of the cards on the tree. Many from the children brought smiles to their faces and added a special sunshine to their day. If the tree is kept up all year long, it will be important to remove the cards on a regular basis to make room for others and to encourage continual appreciation.

Write Thank-You Notes

The Idea:

One of the ways to show appreciation and respect is to teach everyone in the family the importance of writing thank-you notes. Even if you have told the person "thank you" verbally, a note affirms the time and effort that person spent in doing something special for you—and it takes only a few minutes of your time.

The Idea in Action:

🎁 When our children were growing up, one of the nonnegotiables in our home was the practice of writing thank-you notes. The children could open their gifts, but they did not become "theirs" until they had written a thank-you note to the giver. When they were very small, they would tell me what to write or write a "pretend" scribbled message or draw a picture. As they got older, I always made sure they had special stationery they liked, so that they could be proud of the notes they wrote. Sometimes, they would write poems or send photographs; but most important, they learned the value early on of what those notes meant to people. And, to this day, my children all write thank-you notes—even without my nagging!

Tips:

Over and over again I read letters in "Dear Abby" and "Ann Landers" about the thoughtlessness of people who don't even respond to wedding gifts. The art of graciousness is slowly being lost in our society because of time pressures and technology that doesn't encourage letter writing. If we want our children to grow up to be grateful people, I believe we must teach them this—and then model it ourselves. One of the best ways is to write short thank-you notes whenever anyone goes out of their way to remember us.

Discover the Healing Power of Praise

The Idea:

Whether you believe good things or bad things about people, most of the time they will prove you to be right! So why not choose to always look for the best in others?

The Idea in Action:

⌂ In his November 1997 *Bulletin*, Dr. James Dobson of "Focus on the Family" writes:

Jaime Escalante, the high school teacher on whom the movie Stand and Deliver *was based, tells this story about a fellow teacher. The teacher had two students named Johnny. One was a happy child, an excellent student, a fine citizen. The other Johnny spent much of his time goofing off and making a nuisance of himself.*

When the PTA held its first meeting of the year, a mother came up to this teacher and asked, "How's my son, Johnny, getting along?"

He assumed she was the mom of the better student and replied, "I can't tell you how much I enjoy him. I'm so glad he's in my class."

The next day the problem child came to the teacher and said, "My mom told me what you said about me last night. I haven't ever had a teacher who wanted me in his class."

That day he completed his assignments and brought in his completed homework the next morning. A few weeks later, the "problem" Johnny had become one of the hardest-working students—and one of the teacher's best friends. This misbehaving child's life was turned around all because he was mistakenly identified as a good student. It's better to make a child stretch to reach your high opinion than stoop to match your disrespect.

Tips:

Really examine your heart. Is there someone in your life whom you don't respect very much or have a low opinion of? How about deciding to change that and letting that person know that you believe in him or her. That is how miracles happen!

Find Creative Ways to Appreciate People

The Idea:

Surprise people, especially those in your family, by finding creative ways to appreciate them.

The Idea in Action:

🎁 Have a special day to celebrate one person in the family. Let that person be "King or Queen for the Day." Have everyone in the family do something to honor that person—write a poem about him, do a skit, tell what they love about him, make a collage of all his favorite things, make one of his favorite foods, or invite him to do something that you know he loves. Often when we celebrate a family member, we give him or her special privileges such as not having to do dishes for a week or getting to eat his or her dessert first or getting to choose all the meals for one week.

🎁 Create a book of _____. Have each person in the family draw a picture or do a collage about the special person, put the pages together in a book, and present him or her with it.

🎁 Instead of complimenting a person directly, let him or her hear you talking to someone else on the phone about them. Write a person's mother to tell her how grateful you are to have her child in your life.

🎁 Barbara McCauley, a delightful person and a wonderful teacher from Salt Lake City, Utah, says, "Whenever you meet a friend, take something to share—a joke, a favorite candy bar of his or hers, a book that you love, a new food, a little trinket that reminded you of him or her, a bookmark, a cassette tape, or something you've cut out of the paper or a magazine that you thought that person would enjoy." It sends a special message that you were thinking about the person even before you got together!

🎁 Susan Stewart from the state of Michigan bought a special "back patter," a large flat rubber hand on a long plastic stick. She said that this year, instead of ringing a bell when they complete their immunization follow-up calls, her coworkers will "pat themselves on the back"! (She says it also works to call it a "pat backer.")

🎁 Janice Kimrey from Mojave, California, wrote about a creative way she found to appreciate someone:

Your advice on creative communication and appreciation at the SHRM conference was exactly what I needed for a personal life situation. I sent a note with a bottle of Dom Perignon champagne to a special gentleman friend. His surprise was obvious, I could tell he felt very special, and it definitely got the desired message across because he's phoned me several times in the past two weeks and has invited me to dinner twice!

"Oh, look at that! First a lawn mower and now a snow shovel! How about a big thank you for your father, Marty?!"

A friend sent me a little gift from The Whistle Stop in Mineola, Texas. It is a small jar filled with tiny folded pieces of paper. The tag attached reads, "This little jar contains reinforcements and reminders of the strength and beauty that are within you. Take one or more a day as needed."

Suzanne and Don Gordon have been married for eleven years. Every week they enjoy their "Friday Night Special." Every Friday evening they exchange cards and drink a toast. Suzanne says, "There is always something you can celebrate!" In all those years, they have given each other the same card only three times!

Carol Baughman from Nationwide Insurance in Columbus, Ohio, tells of a creative way she appreciated family members:

Everyone enjoyed your presentations. I, myself, put into action something I always wanted to do. Well, I did it today . . . it took all day, and I have already received thank-yous. I sent out eleven CARE packages to my family. We never do this among ourselves. I guess, as a part of a large family, it would have been considered as too much extra. Anyway, it seems like your presentation has left a big impression with us—and I had fun, too!

Lynn Ross from Harlan, Iowa, wrote me about something special her mother did for her:

I think my mother was so inspired by the "Johnny" story [see page 89] that she cut out a bunch of "thoughts for the day" for me. I put several under the glass on my desk and then for Christmas she completed the gift by giving me a decorative crock with "Motherly Advice" inscribed on it. Now I have two reasons to smile every day!

🎁 My dear friend Judy Constantino of Middletown, Delaware, recently sent me a "not for any reason" gift, and this was the note she included:

> **Wherever there is a human being, there is an opportunity for kindness.**
>
> **—Seneca**

This is something that I had in my "Judy store." Throughout the year I purchase different gift items and save them in my "store." That way, when I need a special gift, I always have things on hand that I love to give as gifts. Here's the rule of thumb . . . if I don't love it, it doesn't go in the "store."

Then she adds, "The only problem is that oftentimes the items in the Judy store wind up going to Judy!"

🎁 One of my friends told me about a delightful experience of appreciation he gets every time he goes through the tollbooth at Half Day Road on Interstate 94 in Illinois. The tollbooth collectors give "high fives" to each person paying their toll manually! He said this always makes his day, even when he's stuck in traffic.

Tips:

It is such fun to really surprise someone! We all need to be affirmed and appreciated, and it means even more when we know that someone has taken extra time to make that appreciation just for us.

Celebrate Your Pets

The Idea:

Pets become part of the family just like children. Loving them and caring for them provide good training for young people in developing responsible relationships. Find ways as a family to celebrate your pets.

The Idea in Action:

Happy Birthday

📦 Bradley Animal Hospital in Lawrence, Kansas, helps with pet celebrations. When you take your pet to them for the first time, they take a Polaroid picture of you and your special pet. Then on the pet's first birthday they send you the picture with a Happy Birthday card. Do you take a picture of your pet on every birthday?

📦 When our family dog Roscoe died two years ago, it was very traumatic for our children, especially since they were all away from home at the time. He had been our special pet for over twelve years. The following Christmas I gave the children a slate stone with a paw print, Roscoe's name, and the years of his life chiseled on it. We placed it in the backyard in his favorite spot as a memorial to the gift he brought to us as a family.

📦 Jeff Blackman has a dog named Maui. They decided as a family to name their dog after something they all really liked, and he said "Domino's pizza" and "Carnal Knowledge" were just too long!

📦 Jeanette Brancamp, the recreation secretary at the Waukegan Park District in Waukegan, Illinois, tells about her dog's obedience school experience:

On "graduation" night at the recreation center and after all the dogs completed their exercises, my husband set up a cassette player and played a tape of "Pomp and Circumstance." I set two new plastic dog dishes on the registration counter, one filled with dog biscuits for the "graduates," and one filled with sugar cookies in the shape of dog bones for the "graduates' parents." In addition, the dog obedience instructor's wife had printed "diplomas" for each dog.

She said, "This was something we did for the fun of it, not as a part of my job. Sometimes those are the most rewarding things!"

📦 Alice Sehring is a cinematographer who doesn't work in an office, so she keeps photos of her pet bulldog, Georgie, taped to her camera to make her smile and lighten up the set when the actors look into her camera. The photos include Georgie in her Halloween costume as a devil with horns and a cape, Georgie with her basketball, and Georgie smelling a flower. Alice says, "It makes a mother proud!"

📦 Gary Wernlund of Grand Rapids, Michigan, wrote about a tender experience he had at obedience school:

> **Be kind and merciful.
> Let no one ever come
> to you without coming
> away better and
> happier.**
>
> **—Mother Teresa**

During our first session at dog obedience class it became clear that when on opposite ends of a leash, our eleven-year-old daughter was no match for our golden retriever. His exuberance coupled with his weight advantage allowed him to take her for a walk! Having trained a number of large dogs myself, I pulled from my pocket the training aid that we had called the "choke collar." But to my surprise, the trainer quickly instructed us it was a "correction collar." My first thought was that this was the new, politically correct terminology, but I soon realized that it brought different meaning to my tender-hearted daughter. You see . . . she was very hesitant to pull sharply on the leash when she thought it was choking the dog. However, she knew that correction was good for him.

Tips:

Having pets brings both heartache and joy. We worry about them, we laugh at them, and we love them. It is important in a family to hold on to memories and legends, and pets are often a part of these. Do you have pictures and other memories of your pet? (I recently heard about a pet store where you can have your pet's picture taken with Santa!) One family even has a pet scrapbook that the grandchildren now enjoy.

Share Your Appreciation in Words

The Idea:

Sometimes we think we have shared our appreciation of someone; however, I find that often I *intend* to do so, but the tyranny of the urgent keeps me from carrying through the positive intention. When we feel grateful or think appreciative thoughts, it makes us feel good. But if we do not communicate those feelings to the people to whom we're grateful, we have not completed the circle, and they may never know of our good feelings about them.

The Idea in Action:

As I was thinking about this idea one day last summer, I came across a beautiful poem that I decided to use in my Christmas letter this year:

> I have a list of folks I know, all written in a book,
> And every year at Christmas time, I go and take a look.
> And that is when I realize that these names are a part
> Not of the book they're written in, but of my very heart.
>
> For each name stands for someone who has crossed my path sometime
> And in that meeting they've become the "rhythm of the rhyme."
> And while it sounds fantastic for me to make this claim
> I really feel that I am composed of each remembered name.
>
> And while you may not be aware of any special link,
> Just meeting you has shaped my life more than you can think.
> For once you've met somebody, the years cannot erase
> The memory of a pleasant word or of a friendly face.
>
> For you are but a total of the many folks I've met,
> And you happen to be one of those I prefer not to forget.
> And whether I have known you for many years or few,
> In some way you have had a part in shaping things I do.
>
> And every year when Christmas comes, I realize anew
> The nicest gift that life can give is meeting folks like you.
> And may the Spirit of Christmas that forever and ever endures
> Leave its richest blessings in the hearts of you and yours.

📦 Mike Hall of Englewood, Colorado, feels that kids need to get more positive mail and faxes. This is a fax he sent to his daughter Carly:

Dear Carly,

I just wanted to tell you how TERRIFIC you look today. I am so proud to be your father. You are a wonderful daughter, and you make Mom and me the happiest parents in the entire solar system.

Please save a kiss for me—and give your Mom a big smooch too. I love you guys forever and ever.

Let's do something fun after work today—okay?

Love, Dad

This was Carly's reply:

Dear Dad,
I would Love
to go somewhere fun
to night!! I gave mom
a big smooch. I will
do the same to you.
You look TERRIFIC
today too!! how
are you doing at
work today. write
back soon!!!!!!!!!
Love,
carly Hall

I received the following letter from Joe Hoffman of Charlotte, North Carolina, who heard me speak at a conference:

I so much enjoyed your talk this week at the SHRM conference. The opening speaker on Monday also gave each of us a challenge. His challenge was to either write or call an individual who had made a difference in our lives. I would not have taken the time to write or call my special person without hearing your presentation. I wrote a letter to an uncle who had made a difference in my life after his brother, my dad, had been killed in a Kansas tornado. I was thirteen at the time. I had always treated him with respect but had never spoken or written the words to let him know of my appreciation.

Joe also went even a step further in his appreciation. He included with his letter a pair of wonderful navy support stockings for me, adding, "Enclosed is one of the products we manufacture, and as you are on your feet a lot thought you might appreciate. Let me know if they help those tired legs." Thank you, Joe!

When Ray Perez retired from U.S. Customs in Tampa, Florida, he was the recipient of many awards and plaques for his special years of service. At the end of the retirement ceremony, Ray asked for a moment to present an award of his own. He asked his wife, Rosita, to come forward, and he surprised her with a plaque that read "In public recognition of your outstanding support, dedication, friendship, love, and understanding. YOU ARE PRECIOUS TO ME! Thanks for hanging around until I grew up."

Tips:

Have you ever sent your child a love letter or a fax? I have found that I need to have a strategy to remember to do a little something extra to appreciate people. I have chosen Wednesday as my "A" day. No matter where I am in the world, I do not go to bed until I have thanked or appreciated at least one person in a special way—by phoning, sending an e-mail message, writing a note, sending a little gift or card, or telling them in person. Other people keep a large letter "A" on their desks or in their kitchen as a reminder to appreciate others. Find something that works for you—and then DO it!

Surprise Others with Little Treats

The Idea:

One of the ways to delight and surprise others is to either make or share small treats with them. We all know the expression, "The way to a man's heart is through his stomach!" I believe that we can find our way to anyone's heart by giving them a special treat.

The Idea in Action:

📦 One of the priceless gifts my mother gave to us growing up was the gift of sharing. From the time we were very young, she involved us in doing little things for older people who were often alone. One of our favorite things was to go to the Dairy Queen and get several dozen little cups of Dairy Queen ice cream and then deliver them to the residents of the Baptist Memorial Home where many of our older friends lived. Other times we would make cookies or cupcakes and pass them around to the older people. How they loved both the treats AND seeing young people! When I came home with my own children to visit, Mother would often take them to the retirement home to pass out candy or cookies, and of course, they were the center of attention. But most important, they too were learning the importance of giving to others.

📦 Involve your children in recognizing others in your life who have done special things for you by using different kinds of candy. Think about the neighbor who shoveled your walks while you were on vacation, and take him a package of Lifesavers because he "saved your life" by keeping your home safe! Or for a friend who drove the children to a lesson or sports practice when you were

STEVIE, SWEETUMS! YOU FORGOT YOUR LUNCH, HONEY! DON'T FORGET TO BRUSH AFTER YOU EAT!

McPHERSON

In a matter of seconds, Steve's social life was reduced to that of pond scum.

Close to Home © John McPherson/Dist. by Universal Press Syndicate.

tied up, a Nestlē's Crunch bar for "helping out in the crunch!" Or a package of Extra chewing gum for a teacher who helped beyond the call of duty on a child's special project. Or a Nestlē's $100,000 bar to show how much someone's friendship or help is worth to you. Give a Mounds bar with a note that says, "Your gift brought me 'mounds' of joy!" Not only are these treats inexpensive and fun, but they also help get everyone's creative juices going.

🎁 A friend gave the following 3-D "candy gram" made on a huge piece of poster board to another friend for his birthday:.

You are CERTStainly a LIFESAVER and worth $100,000 to us! Sometimes life is a ROCKY ROAD but BAR NONE you are always MOUNDS of JOY, laughs, and SNICKERS! You are a BOUNTY of fun, very CAREFREE, and EXTRA special. SKOR big and count down to PAYDAY. Best wishes, hugs, and KISSES!

🎁 Although this isn't a food treat, it is certainly a treat for the spirit! DiAnne Barron-Binder from Vienna, West Virginia, sent me a little wrapped package with this poem attached:

This is a very special gift
That you can never see.
The reason it's so special is
It's just for you from me.
Whenever you are lonely
Or ever feeling blue,
You only have to hold this gift
And know I think of you.
You never can unwrap it,
Please leave the ribbon tied.
Just hold the box close to your heart,
It's filled with love inside!

The gift was made by wrapping a two-inch-square piece of wood in paper and ribbon and then attaching the little poem to the ribbon. This would be a fun family project to share with others. I have also seen these made with a small magnet attached to keep on the refrigerator.

🎁 Another family in the Midwest has a tradition of making individually wrapped caramels for all their neighbors at holiday time. The mother shared that not only is it a lesson in giving for their children, but it is also a wonderful family sharing time as they sit around the table wrapping each piece of candy separately. Since it doesn't take a lot of thought to do, they end up sharing special conversation with one another that might not otherwise happen. So the process becomes even more important than the end product. In fact, one of their family legends is that one year they discovered that the tip of the paring knife had broken off in one of the caramels, so they had to unwrap and rewrap the entire batch!

🎁 Clara Schuh of Mt. Vernon, Illinois, says that as a birthday treat for one of her friends, she glued Hershey Kisses to a foil-covered board, one for each year, and then a large Hershey Kiss "to grow on"!

Tips:

No matter what the treat is, it is a wonderful feeling for the giver to concentrate on making someone else happy and for the receiver to know that someone has been specially thinking of them.

Every Family Needs a "Red Plate"

The Idea:

For many years the "Red Plate" has been our favorite family tradition. It is just that—a bright red plate with white handpainted lettering along the edge that reads, YOU ARE SPECIAL TODAY. It came with the following explanation:

The Red Plate is the perfect way to acknowledge a family member's special triumphs, to celebrate a birthday or praise a job well done, reward a goal achieved, or simply to say, "YOU ARE SPECIAL TODAY." When the Red Plate is used, any meal becomes a celebration honoring a special person, event, or deed. It is a visible reminder of love and esteem. The Red Plate—make it a tradition in your family, symbolizing the good and happy times. It will speak volumes of love when words just aren't enough.

The Idea in Action:

🎁 The Red Plate is one of the best ways we have found to bring joy, affirmation, and encouragement to different members of our family and friends. Whenever we have a guest for dinner, he or she gets the Red Plate. Whenever there is a special occasion—birthdays, the first night home after being at camp or college, finishing a hard project or getting a good grade on a test, that person gets the Red Plate. (I have even heard of families who bring it with them to a restaurant when they are having a surprise party for someone!)

The Red Plate

However, the most important use for our Red Plate, I think, has been for the hard times, those times when someone has worked and worked to get a part in a play or make a team or win an election, and they have been disappointed. Someone in the family always makes sure that person gets the Red Plate that day as a symbol that they are still special, no matter what has happened.

One of my favorite stories about the Red Plate occurred at a time when our daughter Erin had just gotten home from the hospital and could not return to school for a few more days. She called me at work one of those mornings to tell me she had folded some clothes for me. I said, "Oh, Honey, thank you. That was really nice. Why don't you have the Red Plate for lunch?" She responded, "Oh, Mom, can I?" The Red Plate is always there in the cupboard, but you can see the special significance it has for our family. I now always give it as a shower or wedding gift to special young couples who are starting their own family traditions.

Several years ago I gave the Red Plate to the Robert Freeman family of Lansing, Michigan, and they have found a very special use for it. Since their children are all grown and live all around the country, they sometimes are all together only at Christmas. They started a tradition that each year at Christmas the family votes on who has accomplished or grown the most during the past year, and that person is rewarded by getting to take the Red Plate to their home to use for the next year. Robert related the decision process to me for 1998. He said each of his children had a wonderful year—Jamille is going to teach in Japan for the coming year, Cynthia moved from Iowa to Texas, and Chevelle also moved and got a huge promotion. (Robert says he doesn't say much but just runs the meeting.) The final decision was that all those things were wonderful but sort of "run of the mill" for the girls. The person who really deserved the Red Plate was Dion because he finished his bachelor's degree, the greatest accomplishment of all!

Tips:

The Red Plate can be purchased at many Hallmark and gift stores or ordered from the address in the Resource section of this book. You can also simply make or buy your own version of a Red Plate. It is a fun and visible way to create a new family tradition and to show support, encouragement, and love. Legends grow up around who got the Red Plate and why, and you can even write on the back of the plate with a permanent marker the different times you have used it. Over the years the Red Plate has been the bearer of many deposits in family members' emotional bank accounts!

> **I shall pass through this world but once. Any good, therefore, that I can do or any kindness I can show to any human being, let me do it now . . . for I shall not pass this way again.**
>
> **—Etienne de Grillet**

Find Fun Ways to Be More Thankful People

The Idea:

As families we can help one another be more thankful people by creating an awareness of all the things we can be grateful for.

The Idea in Action:

🎁 One person told me that her family keeps a Gratitude Journal, and at the end of every day they write down five things they are thankful for.

On a piece of paper list the numbers from 1 to 60 (or even more). Then as a family use the letters of the alphabet to list all sorts of things the members of your family are thankful for. List as many of each letter as you'd like:

1. Air	16. Dolls	31.	46.
2. America	17.	32. Jam	47.
3. Artichokes	18.	33.	48. Ocean
4.	19. Electricity	34. Kitchens	49.
5. Beach	20.	35.	50. Pets
6. Books	21. Fall	36. Lakes	51.
7.	22. Family	37. Libraries	52. Quotations
8.	23.	38.	53. Rain
9.	24.	39.	54.
10. Cats	25.	40. Memories	55. School
11. Concerts	26. Games	41. Mothers	56. Shadows
12.	27.	42.	57.
13.	28. Hills	43.	58. Tomorrow
14.	29.	44. Nachos	59.
15. Dogs	30. Ice cream	45. Night	60. Yellow

Barbara McCauley, in her little book *Where Are the Other Nine?*, gives these suggestions for cultivating a grateful heart:

- Wake up in the morning and say out loud: "This is a BEAUTIFUL day for it." (Whatever the weather and whatever "it" happens to be.)
- Think in terms of what you *do have* rather than *don't have*. Make a list of at least fifty things you *do have*, being as specific as possible. You might want to read over this list before going to bed at night and/or first thing in the morning.
- Forget what you have done for others, and remember what they have done for you.

Tips:

These activities are fun to do every few months to see how the lists change—or simply keep adding more lists to have a "Thankful Book."

Give Fun Thank-You Gifts

The Idea:

I have always loved this saying: "Forget all that you give. Remember all that you receive." It is so special to give small thank-you gifts that will bring surprise, delight, and joy to the giver.

The Idea in Action:

Barbara McCauley gives these ideas in her book *Where Are the Other Nine?* for fun thank-you gifts:

- Give a special treat such as a small jar of jelly, a small loaf of bread, or a small loaf of Amish Friendship Cake.
- Make a picture of yourself wearing or using the gift into a postcard. (Postcard backings can be bought, or use a 4 x 6-inch index card. Just remember to have 4 x 6-inch prints made.)
- Send a single flower with a note indicating what that particular flower symbolizes.
- Give a bottle of sparkling cider.
- Send an appropriate quotation, poem, or joke put in a frame.
- Put a wish for the person inside a fortune cookie.
- Make a special tape just for that person or record a special song.
- Write the person's name and write something about the person after each letter, such as:
    - C Classy
    - R Rugged
    - A Attentive
    - I Intelligent
    - G Good-looking
- Send a picture of a bear or small bear figurine or stuffed animal— "Consider yourself hugged!"
- Write your thank-you and cut it into a jigsaw puzzle, or buy a puzzle that is already cut, ready for your message.
- Write out your thank-you in M&M's or alphabet cereal.

- Write the thank-you and then roll it into a scroll and tie it with a ribbon.
- Give a giant kiss made from Rice Krispie treats.
- Give an appropriate bookmark or make your own bookmark and laminate it.

She also gives these wonderful suggestions for a child's thank-you (or for the child in *you!*):

- A picture the child has drawn
- Invisible ink message
- Mirror-image message

Here are some of Barbara's ideas about *whom* to thank:

1. Children—Mothers, thank your children on Mother's Day for the privilege of being their mother.
2. Mothers—Children, give your mother a present on *your* birthday to thank her for giving you life.
3. Hostess—Call or write the day after the event. This will say more. Barbara says, "Joyce Cameron did this for me over twenty years ago, and I still remember that note! I don't remember any of the thank-yous that were said to me as people were walking out the door."
4. People from your past—Whenever something clicks that reminds you of someone from your past that you appreciate, write to that person. She says, "Some of my favorite letters are from students I had many years ago!"
5. Employers!
6. Authors—When we read a book that strikes a chord, let the author know. You can write to an author in care of the publisher. (This is the way Barbara McCauley and I became friends—she wrote to thank me for *CARE Packages for the Workplace!*)
7. People who criticize you—"You may be right. I had never thought of that. Thank you for bringing that to my attention."
8. Teachers—Even those "teachers" who may not know they're teaching us through example.
9. Speakers—A call or note the next day is even better than at the meeting because people often do it then just to be polite.
10. Librarians

11. Manufacturers—If you have used a product you really appreciate, let the manufacturer know.
12. Friends and family—Sometimes we forget to thank those closest to us for the little things because we begin to take them for granted.

Tips:

Barbara says to start today and notice someone you can thank for something:

- a tangible gift
- a listening ear
- a service
- a compliment
- a fun time
- an encouraging word
- an invitation
- just for being who they are

If you look hard enough, you will always be able to find something to be thankful for. Train your eyes and ears and heart to be "thank-oriented." (If you'd like a copy of Barbara's book or you'd like to subscribe to her newsletter "Horizons Unlimited," you can write or call her at 854 Elm Avenue, Salt Lake City, UT 84106, 801-466-1117.)

Nurture Your Spouse

The Idea:

Sometimes we get so busy with the tasks of our lives that we forget our most important relationship.

The Idea in Action:

Christa Paul tells of a way that she shows her loved one that she CAREs:

Being a mother, wife, housekeeper, cook, and full-time employee means that some of my roles aren't always given my all. As much as I hate to admit it, my wife role is one that doesn't get all that it should—after all, he understands, right? Wrong! One of the things that I used to do for my husband was to give him a manicure every other week or so. He's in a profession that takes a lot of wear and tear on his hands, so he enjoyed the pampering, and I enjoyed doing it for him.

After our baby was born and I returned to work, I got pretty stingy with my time. After I would get the baby in bed around 8:00 P.M. or so, I was exhausted but still had dishes, laundry, etc., and wanted some time to myself. Needless to say, the manicures stopped. And when he would ask for one, I would blow up, saying that I didn't even have time for myself—how could he be so selfish!

One evening we talked, and Rich explained to me that I was so busy all the time and

"Mommy's having quiet time now, honey. Go play with the other kids in the family room."

that when we were home, my attention was almost always focused on the baby, and he was feeling neglected. So I've started the manicures again. I try to notice when he needs one and offer to do it, before he even asks. It's not always an easy thing since we are so busy, but I try to keep it up for him. And I understand now that it's a lot more than his hands that I'm taking care of . . . it's his spirit and his heart. He's getting my undivided attention and care—even if just for a short time. And it's then that he knows, in his heart, that I CARE.

Tips:

What special, loving thing might you do to nurture your spouse or significant other?

Hug Your Child with Your Words

The Idea:

The words we use with our children (and others) can either be words of hurt or words of healing. When we use encouraging, loving words with others, it is like giving them a big hug!

The Idea in Action:

🎁 The Indiana Chapter of the National Committee on the Prevention of Child Abuse, with a grant from Target stores, printed out cards with the title "Hug Your Child with Your Words." On the inside was a paragraph titled "Being a Parent Is a Tough Job":

Sometimes you may be so angry with your children you want them to feel as hurt and frustrated as you do. Stop! Take a deep breath. Write down your angry feelings, punch a pillow, yell at the laundry. Then use words that help, not hurt, your children. You will all be glad you did.

In the shape of hearts, these are the words they suggest that help children:

Hug your child with your words

Great job! SUPER!
You are terrific. Thank you!
What do you think?
Let's talk about it.
You are special.
You can do it!
Well
Done.

Good job! YOU CAN!
Nice. I like how you share.
You brighten my day.
NEAT! You're a big
help. I love you.
Wonderful.
Thank
you.

Don't give up! Excellent!
I'm proud of you. You're super!
Way to go! Fantastic.
You're trying hard.
Thanks for being
a big help.
Too
cool!

Words that help children

🎁 Moore and Company Realtor in Englewood, Colorado, give their clients a wonderful rectangular-shaped magnet titled "101 WAYS TO PRAISE A CHILD," and it has a postscript: "Also, works for adults."

Tips:

For one week *really listen* to yourself. How often do you use these words of praise with your family members?

Give Five Compliments a Day

The Idea:

Most of us need a strategy in order to remember to compliment others. Make a plan for yourself such as giving five compliments a day.

101 WAYS TO PRAISE A CHILD

WOW • WAY TO GO • SUPER • YOU'RE SPECIAL • OUTSTANDING • EXCELLENT • GREAT • GOOD • NEAT • WELL DONE • REMARKABLE • I KNEW YOU COULD DO IT • I'M PROUD OF YOU • FANTASTIC • SUPER STAR • NICE WORK • LOOKING GOOD • YOU'RE ON TOP OF IT • BEAUTIFUL • NOW YOU'RE FLYING • YOU'RE CATCHING ON • NOW YOU'VE GOT IT • YOU'RE INCREDIBLE • BRAVO • YOU'RE FANTASTIC • HURRAY FOR YOU • YOU'RE ON TARGET • YOU'RE ON YOUR WAY • HOW NICE • HOW SMART • GOOD JOB • THAT'S INCREDIBLE • HOT DOG • DYNAMITE • YOU'RE BEAUTIFUL • YOU'RE UNIQUE • NOTHING CAN STOP YOU NOW • GOOD FOR YOU • I LIKE YOU • YOU'RE A WINNER • REMARKABLE JOB • BEAUTIFUL WORK • SPECTACULAR• YOU'RE SPECTACULAR • YOU'RE DARLING • YOU'RE PRECIOUS • GREAT DISCOVERY • YOU'VE DISCOVERED THE SECRET • YOU FIGURED IT OUT • FANTASTIC JOB • HIP, HIP HURRAY • BINGO • MAGNIFICENT • MARVELOUS • TERRIFIC • YOU'RE IMPORTANT • PHENOMENAL • YOU'RE SENSATIONAL • SUPER WORK • CREATIVE JOB • SUPER JOB • EXCELLENT JOB • EXCEPTIONAL PERFORMANCE • YOU'RE A REAL TROOPER • YOU ARE RESPONSIBLE • YOU'RE EXCITING • YOU LEARNED IT RIGHT • WHAT AN IMAGINATION • WHAT A GOOD LISTENER • YOU'RE FUN • YOU'RE GROWING UP • YOU TRIED HARD • YOU CARE • BEAUTIFUL SHARING • OUTSTANDING PERFORMANCE • YOU'RE A GOOD FRIEND • I TRUST YOU • YOU'RE IMPORTANT • YOU MEAN A LOT TO ME • YOU MAKE ME HAPPY • YOU BELONG • YOU'VE GOT A FRIEND • YOU MAKE ME LAUGH • YOU BRIGHTEN MY DAY• I RESPECT YOU • YOU MEAN THE WORLD TO ME • THAT'S CORRECT • YOU'RE A JOY • YOU'RE A TREASURE • YOU'RE WONDERFUL • YOU'RE PERFECT • AWESOME • A+ JOB • YOU'RE A-OK • MY BUDDY • YOU MADE MY DAY • THAT'S THE BEST • A BIG HUG • A BIG KISS • I LOVE YOU • YOU'RE THE BEST •
p.s. REMEMBER, A SMILE IS WORTH A 1000 WORDS!

Also. Works For Adults.

Moore
and company
REALTOR

7300 E. Arapahoe Road
Englewood, Colorado 80112
Office: 303/771-3311
1-800-766-9773

MERIKA RUTHERFORD
Sales Vice President

The Idea in Action:

🎁 A person at one of Barbara McCauley's workshops shared an idea she used with her children. *Everyone* was to give five compliments every day, one each to the following people:

1. To their self
2. To their parents
3. To their teacher
4. To their best friend
5. To someone they didn't know or didn't like

Tips:

Could you commit to five compliments a day? It will change your life!

Never Underestimate the Power of Your Smile

The Idea:

A smile can melt the hardest heart and make even a stranger feel special.

The Idea in Action:

Gloria Valentino in her newsletter "Cecilia's Simple Wisdom Messages" writes:

My friend's mother, Mrs. Sullivan, who is in her eighties, heard a story about a man who was considering suicide. He was walking down the street and feeling very, very low. He passed a woman on the street, and she SMILED at him. That smile changed his life! He didn't go through with the suicide plan all because of a SMILE. Mrs. Sullivan was so impressed with this story that she had cards printed with the words, "NEVER UNDERESTIMATE THE POWER OF YOUR SMILE." She's distributed thousands of cards.

I read a story in the August 27, 1996, "Work Week" section of the *Wall Street Journal* that shared the following information: "The Waiters Association tells members they can increase tips by 42 percent by touching diners briefly on the shoulder when placing the tip tray on the table or on the palm when returning change. Smiling more than doubled one waitress's tips!"

In her little book *Friendship Is an Art*, Barbara McCauley suggests this:

Look at each person you meet and say silently to yourself as Og Mandino suggests, "I love you." Then treat that person as the most important person on earth at that moment. Do this with both great people and ordinary people, remembering no one is superior or inferior to you, only unique. We would do well to follow James Michener's example: "I was born to a woman I never knew and raised by another who took in orphans. I do not know my background, my lineage, my biological or cultural heritage. But when I meet someone new, I treat them with respect. For after all, they could be my people."

Tips:

I love the thought, "A smile is a window that shows your heart is at home." A smile is one of the best gifts we can give to anyone—and best of all, it's free! Give lots of them away, starting today.

Send Thanksgiving Cards

The Idea:

Everyone receives so many beautiful cards at Christmas that one of the ways to really get people's attention as well as to send a very special message is to send Thanksgiving cards.

The Idea in Action:

Laurie Trice of Kenosha, Wisconsin, tells about how she got started sending Thanksgiving cards:

The first year after leaving the company where I had worked for fifteen years, I had many wonderful friends to keep in touch with. I decided to send Thanksgiving cards that year, and with each card I wrote how that person was special to me and what reasons I was thankful for their friendship. I included our company caterer, the cleaning staff, everyone who had been a part of my life. At the time my notes were simply an outpouring of my feelings because I missed them. One by one, I realized that these notes were very precious to these people. I came to realize that perhaps we don't get specific enough with our usual holiday cards. I was impressed with how much my friends treasured my feelings when they were put into writing.

This year I decided to send "year end" cards, and I included my new friends at my new job. I decided to tell them specifically how much my new acquain-

> **Sometimes our light goes out but is blown again into flames by an encounter with another human being. Each of us owes the deepest thanks to those who have rekindled this inner light.**
>
> **—Albert Schweitzer**

tance with them meant to me. Again, to my surprise, these cards were received with great enthusiasm, too. Almost everyone thanked me in a very sincere way for the card. I encourage everyone to send Thanksgiving cards and to be very specific in them and tell the person why they are special to you. They will be a blessing to you both!

> **Kindness comes very close to the benevolence of God.**
>
> **—Randolph Ray**

Tips:

I have saved cards like Laurie's for many years, and I read and reread them, especially when I need a boost. It is a wonderful surprise to receive a Thanksgiving card, no matter what time of year it is!

Gift Ideas When the Budget Is Tight

The Idea:

Many times when funds are limited, we get discouraged about gift giving. This is the time to get your creative juices going and get everyone in the family involved in thinking of inexpensive gifts you can make for others.

The Idea in Action:

Karen Sivert of Elburn, Illinois, shares some of the ideas she and her family have used when the budget is tight:

- Take clippings from existing plants to "root" to make a new arrangement for a gift.
- Use hand-me-down clothing to make "new" clothes for children and grandchildren.
- When snowed in on our son Dan's first birthday, his sisters and I made a fabric-and-yarn segmented worm as a gift. It was a creative way to make a gift to give him with his first birthday cake. We had such joy and many giggles as we worked on this special gift.
- Trim spreading juniper shrubs for greens to make wreaths or tie a red bow on them and even add lights for the front of the house.

- Give homemade quick breads or bran muffins. (My sister-in-law Margie Kopec sends over muffins to her neighbor who shovels their snow for them.)

🎁 When our youngest daughter, Erin, was in college, her funds were extremely tight, so she often gave coupons as gifts. For me, she would make several brightly designed flip charts to hang around the room during my speeches. This year for Christmas she gave her dad a coupon for a lunch out and an afternoon doing anything he wanted to with her.

Tips:

There is no limit to the creative ideas you and your family can come up with to make inexpensive gifts. Remember that the gift of one's time is the best gift of all!

Share an Amish Friendship Cake

The Idea:

This is a special tradition in many parts of the country, especially because it keeps growing, so the tradition can go on and on.

The Idea in Action:

🎁 A number of people all over the country have sent me versions of this recipe:

AMISH FRIENDSHIP CAKE

Day 1: Put starter in bowl, stir, cover. You can use a regular sourdough starter.

Days 2, 3, 4: Stir daily and re-cover tightly.

Day 5: Add 1 cup each of sugar, flour, and milk. Stir and cover tightly.

Days 6, 7, 8, 9: Stir daily and keep tightly covered.

Day 10: Add 1 cup each of sugar, flour, and milk. Always hand-mix.

> **Encourage = the act of inspiring others with renewed courage, spirit, or hope. When we encourage others, we spur them on, we stimulate and affirm them. We appreciate what a person does, but we affirm who a person is.**
>
> **—Charles Swindoll, Strengthening Your Grip**

Take out 3 separate cups of starter—two to give away and one to start all over again.

To the remaining starter in the bowl, add:

2/3 cup oil

1/2 teaspoon salt

1 cup sugar

2 teaspoons baking soda

2 teaspoons baking powder

3 eggs

2 cups flour

3 teaspoons cinnamon

1 cup applesauce

2 cups nuts, chopped

3/4 cup raisins

3/4 cup currants

3/4 cup dates

3/4 cup chopped apple

Grease and flour two loaf pans. Bake 50 minutes at 350 degrees.

Tips:

One caution—if you don't use the starter or give it away, it keeps growing and growing. . . . However, this becomes a constant reminder to *share!*

"Pass It On™" Cards

The Idea:

Everyone likes to receive a surprise, especially if it is one that involves appreciation. A fun and easy way to appreciate people is to give out small cards that can be passed on to others.

The Idea in Action:

📦 One of my personal signatures is that whenever I speak to a group, I give each person in the group a small card with a CARE package on the front and the words, "Thank you for CARE-ing." On the back it has my personal motto, "Spread Contagious Enthusiasm™" and the words "Pass it along." I ask them to give this card in the next forty-eight hours to someone who has done some little thing to make a difference in their lives and then to ask them to "pass it along."

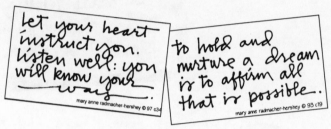

Let your heart instruct you. listen well: you will know your way.
mary anne radmacher-hershey © 97 c34

to hold and nurture a dream is to affirm all that is possible.
mary anne radmacher-hershey © 93 c19

📦 Kathie Hightower of Corvallis, Oregon, uses small cards done in all lower-case script by an artist named Mary Anne Radmacher-Hershey from Cannon Beach, Oregon. These "calling cards" are business-size cards with inspirational sayings like:

> Be strong enough to ask for what you want: be wise enough to have the courage to change.
>
> All you need lies within you.
>
> Find ways to say yes to your best and highest self.
>
> Some days are simply meant for playing.
>
> For tomorrow I offer no answers. For yesterday I hold no apologies. This moment is a gift which I honor by fully living in it.
>
> I will not be governed by the tyranny of immediacy. I make choices.

Kathie sends an appropriate one along with a card or a letter, and she also uses many of Mary Anne's cards and posters to send to friends for inspiration or a lift in difficult times.

Tips:

Preprinted "Pass It On™" cards from Argus Communications in Allen, Texas, come with a variety of sayings on them. These are a few of my favorites:

Some people make the world more special just by being in it.
The difference between ordinary and extraordinary is that little "extra."
Do you mind if I appreciate you?
What you are is God's gift to you; what you become is your gift to God.

The difference
between ordinary
and extraordinary
is that little EXTRA.

Some people make
the world
more
special
just by
being in it.

What you are is God's gift to you;
what you become is your gift to God.

Choose one that feels good to you and that will not offend the person to whom you give it, or even have a variety of cards for different people. These are also easy to create on the computer and can be put in lunches, desk drawers, pockets, in bills and notes, or stuck under office doors as a special surprise.

My wonderful friend David Roth has written a song about appreciation that you will never forget. It's a true story, and I wonder how many of us will be moved to an action of appreciation because of it.

Thank You, Mr. Ryan

The first time I heard that song was a time I well remember
It all goes back some twenty years to Mr. Ryan's classroom
One day he brought his old guitar and sang his favorite songs for us
And the single one that I remember most was "All My Trials"

Something in his simple singing touched my very sixth-grade soul
The harmonies he taught us are the ones that I still know today
The verse about the Tree of Life was wondrous to a twelve-year-old
And many times these twenty years I've wished that I could say

Thank you for the music, Mr. Ryan
The simple gift you gave that day is one I've treasured dearly

I'll always see you sitting up there singing "All My Trials"
You'll never know how much it's meant to me

Went home to see my folks in June, the town that I grew up in
Three of us were sitting in the kitchen having coffee
I mentioned Mr. Ryan, how I wondered what became of him
Mother said she'd heard that he's still working at my school

I grabbed my coat and ran outside, retracing old familiar routes
The shortcut through the playground and the echo of that hallway
And there he was in Room Eleven, wiping off the blackboard
I took a breath and cleared my throat and stepped back into time

Thank you for the music, Mr. Ryan
The simple gift you gave that day is one I've treasured dearly
I'll always see you sitting up there singing "All My Trials"
You'll never know how much it's meant to me

We sat and talked for quite a while, I don't think that he remembered me
But I told him of my work and where I've been and what I've done
And finally he leaned back and said, "It's amazing that you come today
Just last night my mother and I were talking until one

She asked me was I happy, I said, 'Yes, I love my teaching
But I'm sad I never married, that I never fathered children . . .'
'Oh yes,' she said, 'oh yes, my son, you've fathered several hundred.'
And now I look across my cluttered desk, and here you've come

Thank you for the visit, my dear child
The simple gift you gave today is one I'll treasure dearly
I'll always see you sitting up here filling in these twenty years
You'll never know how much it's meant to me

You'll never know how much it's meant to me

CHAPTER FIVE:

R = Respect

"Value People"

I am larger, better than I thought.
I did not know that I held so much goodness.

—Walt Whitman

UNCONDITIONAL LOVE is loving someone "no matter what." It is based on a respect for that person as a unique human being with value in his or her own right. Fostering that respect in your family will ensure a deep feeling of security and belonging that can be an anchor in the midst of the turmoil of this world. Most of us are constantly being judged—by how smart we are, how beautiful we are, how productive we are, how rich we are, even how bad we are. Instead, we must be valued *because* we are! Teaching this to our children and modeling it in our interactions with others will allow them the freedom to be their very best selves.

In his book *If I Were Starting My Family Again*, John Drescher lists the following things he would do if he could start raising his family again, all of which exemplify **RESPECT**:

- I would love my wife more.
- I would laugh more with my children.
- I would be a better listener.

- I would seek to be more honest.
- I would try for more togetherness.
- I would do more encouraging.
- I would pay more attention to little things.
- I would seek to develop feelings of belonging.
- I would seek to share God more intimately.

Think about what you can do *now* in each of these areas to more deeply show your respect for those with whom you live.

Have Family Meetings

The Idea:

Have regular family meetings to discuss schedules, vacations, and how things are working. Allow each family member a time for input, especially when decisions are being made that affect the whole family. Also plan regular times for family fun together.

The Idea in Action:

🎁 One family in our neighborhood has a regular family meeting every Sunday evening. Each person shares what he or she has learned from the last week and a goal for the upcoming week. Then they pop popcorn and play games until bedtime. Other families read a book together one night a week or have family devotions.

🎁 Whenever we had big decisions to be made in our family, we scheduled a family powwow. In 1987 our oldest son was gradu-

"All right! All right! You've made your point, Dad! I'll get rid of my earring, I swear!"

ating from high school and was going to go to an Ivy League college, so I needed to go back to work to help pay the college bills. Our daughters were eleven and thirteen at the time. One of the first jobs I was offered was a job as manager of training with a company in Tampa, Florida. Although it would involve some travel, the good side was that I could choose my own hours as long as my work got done. That meant I would be available to be a room mother, picture lady, and other volunteer activities involving the children when I was home. After our discussion of all the pros and cons, each of the children expressed how they felt about my taking the job. Then each person had a vote: "yes" or "no." (We have three children, so they can outvote us, the parents!) The final decision was a "yes," because in other jobs I would have to be at work all day, every day, and could not be part of their activities at all. It also proved helpful to remind them of the vote when I had to leave town for a few days!

The George Winkler family of Western Springs, Illinois, always had a "Family Fun Night" on Friday night. The children got into their pjs before dinner, they had Pepsi and popcorn, played games, and everyone got to stay up late. Even as teenagers, their children chose to be with the family on that one night a week.

Margaret Rooney of Sycamore, Illinois, shares one of their family traditions:

Our family has a Friday night tradition that my children have come to appreciate. Every Friday night we spread a tablecloth on the floor and have a pizza "picnic" party in front of the TV. We usually top it off with popcorn. Since our family is in transition of moving to a new town and my husband is only home on weekends, this family time is especially important to us. We wait for my husband to get home and then the "party" begins. We really appreciate the time together.

Margaret also shared two other fun ideas to do with the family. On rainy days they like to make play tents using blankets or sheets placed over tables or two saw horses. During a storm it is fun to read stories under the dining-room table. All of these ideas help bring a family closer together both physically and emotionally.

Robert Freeman of Lansing, Michigan, always chairs an annual family meeting over the Christmas holiday. Because their children are all grown and are living all over the country, they find this an important way to keep the family together. At this meeting each person shares his or her achievements and learnings during the past year as well as their plans and goals for the upcoming year and especially things they would like to do as a family. They also each share a projection of what they'd like to be doing in the next five years. Robert says this is a wonderful way to keep the family up to date on each family member, and it keeps them close and involved in each other's lives.

Tips:

If you choose to have family meetings, it is wise to do a Code of Conduct first. Agree on and list all the behaviors you will use with one another in these meetings. Some important ones are things like:

> Do not interrupt another person when he or she is speaking.
> Let each person express his or her feelings, even if no one else agrees with them.
> Do not criticize another's ideas.
> Everyone is equal and has an equal vote.

Also you might let a different family member plan and run the meeting each week when they reach a certain age. These meetings are times that will promote respect and communication, and some of your most valuable family sharing will occur in them.

Share Your Passion and Involve Your Kids

The Idea:

Find ways to help your children understand what you do and let them be involved in small ways so that they feel a sense of your mission and purpose.

The Idea in Action:

Lisa Jimenez, a professional speaker from Pompano Beach, Florida, writes about how she involves her children in her speaking career:

Whenever we dine together as a family, we have an "open mike" time. It's a riot to see each one of our three kids get a turn to tell a story, sing a song, or recite a poem. This Jimenez tradition has brought so much fun to our family dinner table and has helped my kids learn what I do and that "Hey, it ain't always easy!" Ask your kids what they think about a particular speech topic. Put their ideas in your "Things I Learned from My Kids" file. I started doing this just to get them more involved in my work. But the funny thing is I use what they say almost every time! Children are brilliant, simplistic, and honest.

Fred Figge of Marco Island, Florida, shares the passion he has for a hobby with his children and grandchildren. He loves to fish, and when he goes fishing, he always wears a special straw hat. When all his children and grandchildren were visiting last summer, he planned a special outing just for the "guys." He got them all straw hats just like his, and he took them all out fishing. It was a day filled with memories, and the children still love to wear their "Grandpa hats"!

The DMV of Virginia asked the children, grandchildren, nieces, and nephews of their employees to draw pictures of what they thought their family members did at work all day. They then had them framed in plastic frames and posted them all over the DMV, especially in customer areas. Everyone got a chuckle out of the delightful drawings, and the children could come in and see their artwork posted in their relatives' workplace.

When my children were young, I was asked to come back to the high school for a quarter and direct the annual musical, which that year was *The Unsinkable Molly Brown*. After a family conference, I agreed to take the job. However, from the beginning, I decided to involve my children. They came with me to many of the rehearsals, and when it came time for dress rehearsals, the young people in the musical came to me with a request: One of the short scenes took place in a lifeboat leaving the sinking

Titanic. Because there were children on the *Titanic,* they wondered if Gretchen and Erin could have small parts in the play and be with them in the lifeboat. Of course, they were thrilled! Because of his involvement in attending rehearsals, Garrett got to help as a stage hand moving props on and off the stage. Not only was it a wonderful learning experience for them, but they also got to see their mom in a new role.

Even today, my grown children and my husband are very involved in my work. Charlie keeps the books, Erin designs and makes most of the posters I hang around the room, Gretchen makes all of my slides, and Garrett indirectly sells the McGraw-Hill books I've written! They have all heard me speak at various times, so they are much more understanding of the time and energy that goes into my work and the impact it has on my audiences. Rather than being separate from my work, they have a commitment to my mission as well.

Tips:

Think of ways you might involve your family in your profession. Have they visited your worksite? Do they really understand what you do? You might consider creating a videotape of "A Day in the Life of _____." Then ask them for their impressions and suggestions.

Be Creative in the Ways You Discipline

The Idea:

You will teach your children much more if you choose to discipline them in respectful and creative ways.

The Idea in Action:

Melissa Giogvagnoli tells about a friend of hers who had two little girls three years apart. Whenever they were naughty, the mother made them sit on the couch and hold hands and admonished them, "Now, don't you talk!" Of course, they quickly started to whisper and giggle. Today, they not only are best friends, but whenever they write each other, they draw a pair of clasped hands on the envelope!

"It's very simple, Diane. When you leave on a date, you punch out on the time clock. When you get home, you punch in."

Julie Verner-Mackay and her husband, Reay, have a lovely way of disciplining their children:

One thing we insist on in our family is that whenever family members have a "spack" or argument with one another, we get them to hug each other and for the offender to apologize. We have four children, two boys and two girls—Ingrid (eighteen), Chris (fourteen), Katie (five), and Sam (three), so there's plenty of potential for conflict! However, we have found since we implemented this simple "kiss and make up" strategy, relationships have been stronger, and conflict has reduced. We ensure that when the people in conflict hug each other, they do it until we can see the essence of forgiveness and sincerity. It's a pity that this kind of approach couldn't be used in the workplace more often when people come into conflict!

Dan Nygaard of Seattle, Washington, tells of a creative way he and his wife reward rather than discipline. His two-year-old son, Evan, loves stickers, so during his potty training, each time he "does the right thing," he gets a sticker. Dan says that often he is so pleased with himself that we wants to give *everyone* a sticker. Can you picture Dan going to work with a sticker on his hand, and when anyone asks, he replies, "It's a potty sticker. My son went potty!" Isn't it amazing what we celebrate at various stages of our lives? But, Dan says, *"It works!"*

Tips:

Some of the best memories come from the worst experiences handled right.

Teach Your Children Fun Ways to Set Goals

The Idea:

One of the ways we learn to respect others is to learn to respect ourselves. Find interesting, creative, fun ways to help your children set goals and then reach them.

The Idea in Action:

🎁 Mike Hall of Denver, Colorado, shared an idea with me that he and his wife use with his daughter Carly. It is a chart called "Behavior Self!"

Behavior Self!
Reinforcing Behavior to Develop Good Habits!

By G. Snyder & T. Keever. Copyright © 1997 by Performance Management Publications/Aubrey Daniels & Associates, Inc. Reprinted with permision.

The chart has categories of responsibilities such as "Taking Care of Myself," "Being a Family Member," and "School and Play." The authors,

Gail Snyder and Tracy Keever, suggest using the "Keep it Simple" system, and the chart is surrounded with affirming statements like: "I knew you could do it. Wonderful. Excellent. That's much better. You're really doing well! Fantastic! Good! How did you do that?! Wow! Great! What a good job! Super! You've been really helpful. I'm very proud of you!"

Lisa Jimenez writes about having your kids create their own goal poster:

Let them choose something they want and put a picture of it on their goal poster. It could be something monetary or better yet, a special day with you and a special adventure of their own. Then every time you leave for a speech, need time for research or to make phone calls, they can earn a dollar sign or a point on their goal poster for cooperating. When they have accumulated ten or fifteen of these, they get their goal item or adventure. (You could even record that adventure on tape for them to relive when you are not there.) My girlfriend Donna tried this when she was facing a very hectic month. Her daughter Lauren actually booted her out the door on some days saying, "Mom, don't you have some phone calls to make or bookings to go to today?"

Barbara McCauley of Salt Lake City, Utah, tells how she, as the in-service director, used goal setting with the staff at her school in a way that could be adapted for a family or any other group:

I tried one of The Ideas in your book last Friday with our staff at Realms of Inquiry, and it was a great hit! Last month we had each teacher set a goal. At Friday's meeting each teacher reported if he or she had accomplished the goal. (All had!) The teachers then threw a dart at a balloon that had a treat written on a piece of paper inside—a one-dollar gift certificate for McDonald's, a cassette tape, a book, a free hour when the headmaster would teach the class, a one-dollar gift certificate to Baskin Robbins. It was fun! I am thinking that next month we might just have a big cake with "congratulations" written on it.

Tips:

Not only is it good to teach children to set goals, but it is also important to celebrate reaching them—for all of us. As you help your family members set goals, at the same time decide how to celebrate their accomplishment.

Involve the Whole Family
in Doing Things for Others

The Idea:

When a family does things for other people, it teaches the children to respect the needs of others, and it also helps them feel good about themselves.

The Idea in Action:

🎁 Our family did several things that made us all more respectful of other human beings. For several weeks we each drew the name of a family member, and we were to be that person's "secret pal" and do one nice thing for her a day. The children loved doing this, and it really stopped lots of the arguments and bickering in our home. We also learned what "nice" meant to each person in the family!

🎁 After Thanksgiving one year our daughters decided to write to three people they "liked a lot" (adults). In their notes they offered to come over to help them do a job sometime before Christmas. Our older friends loved the attention, and the girls got to do fun things with them like helping bake Christmas cookies, wrapping presents, baby-sitting while the mom did last-minute shopping, and even shoveling snow!

TRY TO HOLD THE NEEDLE STEADY, DANNY. THAT'S GOOD ENOUGH.

ZZZAP!

Take Your Child to Work Day at Fernview Hospital.

Close to Home © John McPherson/Dist. by Universal Press Syndicate.

🎁 Another year we adopted a family from the inner city for Christmas. We tried to pick a family with children about the same ages as ours. Then we gave each of our children thirty dollars (which bought a lot more then than it does today!), and they each got to go to the toy store and pick out things they thought that child would like. They were even more excited than if the toys were for them! Charlie and I bought groceries and several gifts for the adults. On Christmas Eve Charlie picked up the family and brought them to our home. We had our traditional Christmas Eve pizza, went to the family service at church, our new friends opened their presents, and we sang Christmas carols around the piano. It was one of the best Christmases we ever had because we all focused on someone else!

Tips:

A special joy and closeness occurs whenever a family can focus on meeting the needs of someone else. Working together to help someone else inspires cooperation, sharing, and pride.

Find Ways to Spend More Time with Family

The Idea:

Try to find ways you can limit work activities or perhaps even compromise parts of your job that interfere with your family life. Better yet, find special ways to share your rewards with your family!

The Idea in Action:

Joe Heuer, a professional speaker in Milwaukee, Wisconsin, told me that he has been blessed with two-year-old twin girls. Because of his commitment to them, he does not accept speaking engagements that are more than 250 miles from Milwaukee. That way he rarely has to be away overnight.

🎁 To motivate sales managers at its Northeast dealerships, Lexus offered a different kind of travel incentive: trips to Disney World for the whole family. The October 1997 issue of *Selling Power* quotes Marketing Rep Manager John Smiros, "This is the first time we offered family trips. It was a great idea because this way employees get to share the fruits of their rewards with their families." Disney postcards were sent to the homes of all the sales managers so their families could see them. The family members became integral players in the program—when they learned about the vacations, they encouraged the sales managers to sell more cars! And for those who met or exceeded their goals, the whole family got a five-day, four-night, all-expenses-paid trip to Disney World.

Tips:

With some creative thinking, you or your organization may be able to find ways to spend more quality time with your family without sacrificing your career.

Schedule Special Family Time

The Idea:

One of the best ways to ensure quality family time is to make it a definite part of your weekly schedule.

The Idea in Action:

🎁 Amy Clay from Chicago, Illinois, says she and her grown children schedule one night a week to all be together. Since Monday is the only night that they are all home with their busy schedules, it has become their "family night." Whatever they do that night, they do together. Sometimes they rent a movie or watch TV or visit their grandmother, and when people call, they do not answer the telephone. Amy says she has even heard her children's friends say, "It's Monday night. We won't bother you because we know it's your family night." Another family tradition they have is that they all go to her mother's house on Sunday after church.

🎁 One of my daughter's friends, Fran Vegara, always has dinner with her mother and brother on Sunday nights. They live in different parts of the city, and this is a tradition that transcends other activities. Erin loves to be invited to share with them.

🎁 Danny Cox, a member of the National Speakers Association, talks about his family's "Triple F Days." The triple "F" stands for "Forced Family Function!"

Tips:

If you decide to schedule specific family times, make sure that you are fully committed to keeping those times. Only when they are regarded as seriously as other commitments in your life will your children understand the value you are placing on spending time together.

Begin an Intergenerational Sharing Program

The Idea:

My children had only one grandmother when they were growing up, and she lived far away. Because of that, I always felt that our children were missing out on the opportunity to have extended family and to have close relationships with older people. As I met more and more older people in our community, I decided that it would be a wonderful gift for everyone if I could provide ways for my children and others to meet these special older folks and to be able to share their experience and wisdom.

The Idea in Action:

🎁 When our three children were in Field Park School in Western Springs, I volunteered to start an Intergenerational Sharing Program. I spent several months talking with many adults in the community, especially retired people, interviewing them about what hobbies and interests they had that they could share with a group of young people. I found folks who had interesting hobbies like woodworking, baking, gardening, crafts, and music. Other adults were willing to teach cheerleading and languages, to share travel information and interesting things about other cultures, and some even wanted to read to the children. One parent offered to take a group on a tour of O'Hare Airport, where he worked, and another father who owned a landscaping business volunteered to let the children learn about many of his large pieces of equipment.

We created a list of all the activities that different adults had volunteered to lead, and each child in the grade school got a first, second, and third choice. I then worked out the choices so that all children got one of their three choices and many of them got their first choice. Each quarter the children had new choices. Then for three consecutive Thursdays for forty-five minutes immediately after school, the children spent time in small groups, usually just three or four children, with an adult in one of the interest groups, and each child spent time with four different adults during the school year.

Although it was a lot of work, the program was highly successful. Both the adults and the children enjoyed the experiences, and many lasting relationships were formed between an older person and a child.

> **Remember that the value of a man is not measured by what he has, but by what he is.**
>
> **—Pope John Paul II**

The sharing created much goodwill in the community and gave both generations a better understanding and relationship with each other. I also found that there were many retired people in the community who were delighted to be able to share their knowledge and experiences and who had never been asked, and it was a gift for them to feel useful and important as well as for the children who got to make a new friend.

I just read a story in the *Chicago Tribune* about a program at the Golf Middle School in Morton Grove, Illinois. A group of seventh and eighth graders volunteer one afternoon a week to teach basic computing skills to senior citizens, students two generations older. The program gives youngsters an opportunity for community service while introducing computers to the segment of the population least familiar with modems and megabytes.

The computer program was started by Golf School officials, who met with Bud Swanson, the director of senior citizen services for Morton Grove, over the summer and discussed ways of bringing pupils and senior citizens together. The after-school classes in the Morton Grove school's computer lab are funded by a $7,000 grant from the Illinois State Board of Education.

The four-week course has in one semester attracted thirty-four senior citizens. Each adult works one on one with a Golf pupil. They learn how to turn on a computer, operate a mouse, create stories, and print greeting cards. They even log on to the Internet and visit web sites. Even though the instructors have no teaching experience and most of the students haven't been in school for forty years, participants say the program works. Laura Johnson, eighty-five, said, "I had tried taking computer classes before, but they were taught by experts who knew an enormous amount about computers. The kids are easier to work with. They don't try to teach you everything at one time."

The program, along with giving senior citizens valuable computing skills, also gives the middle-school pupils a look at life from the other side of the classroom. Mike Leydervuder, fourteen, said, "I understand now how teachers get frustrated if you don't listen to what they say. I speak a little louder and clearer and slow it down, and I try not to touch the mouse, to let them do it." In setting up the program, Golf teachers asked the seventh and eighth graders to help design the curriculum, create informational packets, calculate the grant's finances, and shop for supplies, including the snacks and soft drinks shared with their older pupils each week.

The class has helped shatter stereotypes between generations, it has given the young people a chance to serve, and the senior citizens not only are learning but also expressed the hope that becoming computer literate would provide a stronger link with young people, especially their grandchildren.

🎁 I read this story in the "Work Week" section of the *Wall Street Journal*, August 27, 1996:

Sesame Place amusement park in Langhorne, Pennsylvania, encourages its student summer employees to bring their parents to work—literally—offering the young people a $25 bonus and donating the equivalents of their parents' daily wages to drug programs. The reason: to encourage intergenerational understanding.

Tips:

If you are thinking about starting an intergenerational sharing program in your school, know that it is much easier to run a program of this magnitude if you have the support as I did of the Parent Teachers Organization. Even though we couldn't run the program during school hours, we had the full support of both the parents and teachers, which was essential because much of the communication about the program went on in the classrooms, and for the program to work well, all children needed to be involved.

Use the Power of Positive Talking

The Idea:

We all need to feel valued and respected. Think about how you are talking to your family members, friends, and neighbors.

The Idea in Action:

Jay Leon, a very special friend from Chicago, writes about his experience with positive talking:

As a teacher for twenty-five years, I've taught every grade from kindergarten through high school. All my years of teaching, however, could not have fully prepared me for the summer of 1995, when I taught G.E.D. (high school equivalency degree) classes at Cook County Jail.

All inmates between the ages of seventeen and twenty-one who are not high school graduates are eligible to go to these classes. The "good" news is that it is voluntary. The inmates must request to live in one of the "school wings" of the jail complex to attend school. The "challenging" news is that some of the school inmates are there simply to relieve the daily routine of jail life.

I consider myself to be a positive thinker. I must admit, however, that on the first day of teaching at the jail, I wasn't feeling very positive. In fact, I was SCARED! As the inmates walked into the classroom, led by a police officer, I thought, "Jay, you'd better come across as authentic and knowing what you're doing, because if you don't, these guys will pick it up in a second."

The first day went smoothly. The inmates and I were "feeling one another out." From the time they walked in until they left, however, many of them used profanity.

This bothered me. I considered my job teaching them to have two parts. The first was to prepare them to pass the G.E.D. test. The second was to prepare them to enter the job market successfully. Using profanity would not help them get jobs. I made up my mind to get them to want to speak correctly.

The second day, the first time an inmate cursed, I knelt next to him and whispered in his ear, "I would appreciate it if you'd speak appropriately in class." His response? "Okay." Without protest. Without defensiveness. Just "okay."

For the rest of that summer session, every time a student used profanity, I made the same request. Surprisingly, the response was always positive. I believe it was due to the following:

- They heard me only use the appropriate language, so they had a consistent model to follow.
- I treated them with respect at all times. For example, I always addressed them as "gentlemen" (as in "Gentlemen, please take your seats").
- I corrected them privately. This preserved their dignity.
- My requests were stated in a positive manner ("Please speak appropriately"), rather than a negative one ("Stop cursing").

From my own experience, I know that if people are told consistently what not to do, they resent it. The difficulty with negative instruction is that when people are told what not to do, they don't learn what to do. It reinforces negative rather than positive behavior.

Before long, the improvement in the inmates' responses was astounding. By the third week of class, when an inmate cursed, all I had to do was walk toward him, and he'd almost jump out of his seat, saying, "Okay, Mr. Leon, okay. I'm sorry, I'm sorry, my fault, my fault," and the cursing would stop. I wouldn't have to say a word. By the fourth week of class, 90 percent of the profanity was eliminated.

A "magical" morning of class occurred at the end of the summer session. Our classroom was needed to test a large influx of inmates for the upcoming fall classes. We were asked to share another teacher's classroom. This was a computer class. Since this was the last day, the other teacher allowed the inmates to work at the computers the entire morning—playing computer games or writing letters to family and friends.

The other teacher's students cursed repeatedly. I felt it would have been inappropriate for me to "whisper" anything to them; it wasn't my classroom. When I asked the teacher about it, he smiled and said that it didn't bother him. I noticed, however, that my students only used appropriate language the entire morning. This was a true "field test."

As we came back to our own classroom at the end of the class, I shook each student's hand and told him what a privilege it had been to work with him. Many thanked me in return; a few of us had tears in our eyes.

We had learned to respect one another.

© Jay Leon, 1997. Reprinted with permission.

"OK, young man, that does it! When we get home you are having a time-out!"

Close to Home © John McPherson/Dist. by Universal Press Syndicate.

Tips:

What a wonderful story of the power of learned respect! Each of us needs to make an effort to model Jay's positive interaction with a very difficult group in our own homes and communities. Thank you, Jay, for the gift you have given us all.

Make People Feel Uniquely Valuable

The Idea:

We all need to feel special. Finding ways to do this with your loved ones and colleagues will be a precious gift of respect and love. Barbara Kerr from Arizona State University in Tempe, Arizona, presented a paper titled "Happy Family Study" at an American Psychological Association meeting in Chicago in August 1997. She studied the family backgrounds of 247 freshman and sophomore college students. While finding it difficult to pinpoint a single family structure as the key to happiness, she discovered that parents who encouraged individuality were more appreciated than mothers and fathers who emphasized achievement.

The Idea in Action:

🎁 Cynthia Jacobsen of Kansas City, Missouri, says that every night she and her son share ten things they really appreciate about one another.

🎁 Suzanne Dorris of Memphis, Tennessee, tells of a family tradition started by her mother:

When my brother and I were children, every summer when school was out, my mother would schedule a day for each of us to spend individually with her. On "our day," we would get to plan anything we chose for us to do! For example, my "day" would usually include the zoo, the children's museum, and lunch at a restaurant of my choice. As I got older, shopping and movies were common choices for me. My brother usually chose the video arcade, baseball game, and other activities that little boys enjoy.

This day outing was usually at the end of the summer, so we would have all summer to think of things to do and look forward to it. My mother was (and still is) a teacher. This family tradition was a way to have quality time with Mom to talk about our plans for the school year and other things regarding the "growing up" process in a fun setting. It made for great memories too!

🎁 Duane Hodgin, Ph.D., assistant superintendent of the Metropolitan School District of Lawrence Township in Indianapolis, Indiana, shared several powerful messages he uses in his work with teachers and students. A notepad he uses is titled "DISCIPLINE WITH DIGNITY," and at the bottom is this quote from Ralph Waldo Emerson: "The secret of education lies in respecting the student."

These are the "Ten Expectations of Lawrence Township Educators":

WE BELIEVE THAT . . .

1. The student is the most important person in education.
2. The student is our partner in education.
3. The student deserves to be treated with dignity and respect.
4. The student is a person who brings us his or her needs. It is our job to fulfill those needs.
5. The student is the purpose of our work.
6. The student is deserving of the most courteous and attentive behavior we can give him or her.
7. The student is deserving of our best teaching efforts.
8. The student is influenced by the behaviors we model.
9. The student is dependent on us, and we are dependent on him or her.
10. Our students are our future.

This is a poem Duane wrote for his teachers:

THE PRIVILEGE AND IMPORTANCE OF TEACHING

Teaching is a **privilege** and a **special art.**
You must have the **skills,** but it comes from the **heart.**
As a **role model, colleague, encourager,** and **friend,**
Your **enthusiasm** and **caring** can never end.

For the **students** you have the **privilege** to **teach,**
Will **cause** you to **examine,** to **stretch,** and to **reach.**
Encourage them to **challenge,** to **question,** even ask "**Why?**"
Expect them to **achieve** and to always "**try.**"

Never forget that the **things** you **say and do**
Leave a **lasting impression;** it's **certainly true.**
So, take **pride** in your **calling,** a **very special profession.**
The **most noble** of all, which is **public education.**

The **demands** are **many** and the **responsibilities**, too.
But, who can **meet** them any **better** than **you**?
As a teacher/educator in **M.S.D.L.T.**,
You're the **"best of the best,"** it's easy to see.

Yes, teaching is a **privilege** and a **special art**.
You must have the **skills**, but it comes from the **heart**!

This poem reminds me of the Human-Business model I mentioned in Chapter Two. I also love Duane's "Educator's Prayer":

> *"I am a teacher; I make a difference" in the lives of my students. That difference may not always be known, but it happens every day. Let me never forget that what I say and what I do, as well as what I don't say and what I don't do, has the capacity to hurt or harass a child or to help and heal a child. Lord, let me always strive to be an encourager, helper, and a healer.*

And this is Duane's message for "Diversity":

Let us not conceive unkind thoughts or acts toward persons who are different from us, as we strive to be more kind and understanding to all students, colleagues, and parents.

Duane also gives out many little cards like these titled **"Care Card"** and **"Success Card."**

Tips:

I am touched by the depth of respect Duane Hodgin expresses for both students and teachers alike. What he has written applies to all of us as parents, as community members, and as friends.

Celebrate "Brothers' (or Sisters') Day"

The Idea:

One mother decided that August needed a holiday because most fun summer activities are over, and there are so many back-to-school things to do. As a result, when her sons were younger, they created "Brothers' Day."

The Idea in Action:

Cheryl Stubbendieck from Lincoln, Nebraska, tells how she and her sons celebrated "Brothers' Day":

This was my response to my son's complaint that there are Mother's Day and Father's Day, but no Kid's Day. They didn't buy that line about every day being children's day, so we created "Brothers' Day."

We planned and budgeted for Brothers' Day just as we would for an adult party, with much involvement from the boys. Each of our sons could invite two friends, who also had to be brothers. They came on a Saturday morning and stayed through the afternoon. There was pizza for lunch, a jelly-roll pan of purple or blue jello to cut as they wished, all the noncaffeine pop they wanted, and a Dairy Queen ice cream cake, among other changing treats.

The boys planned various games, and we did crafts—the year we made sidewalk chalk was especially fun. There was always a paper airplane contest with many winners. Prizes were duplicate toys from Happy Meals, small candies, temporary tattoos. The day culminated in the Great Water Balloon/Super Soaker fight between two teams. It was exhausting for me, but the boys loved it. They also got to choose a "medium" present for the day, which I wrapped even though they knew what it was. Now that they're older, they each have a sleep-over guest on a Friday night and there are fewer organized activities, but they remember the "old days" fondly.

Tips:

What a wonderful idea to show appreciation and respect for one's brother—and also to have lots of fun together! This idea could also be used for "Sisters' Day" or even "Brothers' and Sisters' Day."

Provide Opportunities for Young People to Learn a Better Way of Life

The Idea:

Some children in our world are so disadvantaged that they have not had a chance to learn basic skills to lead a life that is "clean and exact and disciplined." We can all participate in finding creative ways to help them learn.

The Idea in Action:

🎁 Bob Greene in a column in the *Chicago Tribune* writes about a program started at the Salem Baptist Church in one of the grimmest neighborhoods in Chicago, filled with poverty, gangs, prostitutes, and even bullets. This program, started by Rev. Harvey Carey, youth pastor, is called the "Virtuous Young Women" program, and it teaches young women skills to lead a different kind of life. Rev. Carey said:

These are skills no one has ever thought to teach these girls. A lot of the young people who come to our church come on their own—many come from families who have never been to a church in their lives. When they come here, we know they feel the need for spiritual nourishment. But these other things—etiquette and decorating and setting a table—are things they feel a need for, too. Something as simple as "This is how we set a table," "This is how we speak properly and politely." They want to know. When a child has lived a certain way and seen certain things, there is a strong desire to find something different. . . . They are rejecting what is all around them. They hear about a way of life that is clean and exact and disciplined, and they want it. They say, "I've never had a chance to have that," and they want it.

The Spring Workshops are scheduled on Saturday mornings for eighth grade and freshman girls, and they include:

- Sewing
- Operating a sewing machine
- Basic principles of decorating
- Using flowers to decorate
- Table etiquette

For sophomore girls, the workshops include:

- Writing etiquette
- Basic cooking skills
- Speaking etiquette
- "On My Own"—how to develop a standard of living

Rev. Carey said, "In the face of everything, these children want to try for something better. They really do. They want to see what is out there that they have never been able to be a part of."

Tips:

I have been deeply touched by reading about this program, and I am going to volunteer to help in some way. My encouragement and applause go to this church for *doing something concrete* to better the lives of these young women and to help give them some choices they have not had in the past. What might you do in your community to start a similar program?

Give with Respect

The Idea:

When we give to anyone, it is important that we respect their uniqueness and dignity as human beings.

The Idea in Action:

My very special friend Laurie Trice tells of how she gave from her heart with deep respect for one of God's people:

When I first started working in Chicago, I was uncertain what my response should be to the homeless beggars on the street. I knew I couldn't help everyone, and I wasn't sure if putting cash in their cups was really the best thing to do. I was most disturbed that these men stood with their heads down, never making eye contact with the people passing by. I felt they must have lost all self-esteem.

As I began praying and asking the Lord for direction, I was particularly drawn to the man who always passed outside the train station. My first inclina-

tion was to at least say "Hi" when I walked by instead of treating him as a fixture like the concrete column he stood by. I know I caught him off guard, but after several days of greeting him, he began responding comfortably with a "Hi" in return. Within a few weeks he was returning my smile when we exchanged greetings. As time went on, I noticed he held his head up and acknowledged others as they passed by.

At Christmastime, I selected a beautiful card with the real message of Christmas inside. I wrote the following message from John Mason's book, An Enemy Called Average *inside the card and included a cash gift:*

> "Do you know that God made you for a purpose? He has a job for you that no one else can do as well as you. Out of the billions of applicants, only one is qualified, only one has the right combination of what it takes. God has given people the measure of faith to do what He calls them to do. Every person is gifted. Have you found what God created you to do?"

When I gave him the card, I wished him a "Merry Christmas" and asked what his name was. Now, each time I pass him I can say with a smile, "Hi, Cecil!" In all of this God has shown me that I may not be able to help all the homeless, but I CAN make a difference in one person's life. Somehow, I feel that showing Cecil some respect as a person has been more valuable than cash. I will keep praying for him, and I believe someday those prayers will move the mountains in his life, and he'll have a roof over his head.

Tips:

Laurie gave from her heart to a person she respected. What a lesson we can all learn from her story—in just one life, each of us *can* make a difference!

Share What You've Learned from Others

The Idea:

Many times we think about special things we've learned from others; however, we don't take time to put these learnings in writing. What a legacy we can leave both for others and for the person we're writing about when we make these thoughts permanent!

The Idea in Action:

Beth E. Sweitzer-Riley of Indianapolis, Indiana, writes about what she's learned from her mother:

Some of the Lessons I Learned from My Mother, Marie G. Sweitzer

In every day, in every way, the lessons keep appearing in my life . . .

1. *Don't waste electricity.*
   Be thankful.
2. *Don't mix the whites and darks in the laundry.*
   Be selective in your decision making.
3. *Don't let the weeds overtake your garden.*
   A quality end product requires daily care and nurturing.
4. *Measure flour by slowly filling the cup with a spoon before leveling it off.*
   Measure life by slowly building values and character.
5. *Don't impose on others.*
   Learn to be self-sufficient.
6. *"Make Do" with what you have.*
   Enjoy the simple things in life.
7. *When a job needs to be done, step to the front of the line.*
   Don't procrastinate—just do it!
   When the going gets tough, keep going . . .

The most important lesson I've learned is the impact one individual can have on others—an impact so great that the lessons taught are incorporated in both the small things and the big things, without question and without pause. Is there any greater way to say that this life, the life of Marie G. Sweitzer, has made a difference?

Beth E. Sweitzer-Riley
March 30, 1996

Tips:

What a priceless gift Beth has given her mother! Why not write down what you've learned from an important person in your life and then share it with them? You will be demonstrating a respect and a love that will give them sustenance forever.

Share Ways for Senior Citizens to Be Involved

The Idea:

Many senior citizens feel as if they are no longer valuable to society. Help them to find ways they can give of their experience and expertise to make this world a better place—and perhaps have some fun in the process!

The Idea in Action:

📦 Here are some wonderful suggestions for ways seniors can get involved taken from an article in the "Your Money" section of the *Chicago Tribune*, Monday, December 1, 1997:

- **"Passport in Time"** allows you to join activities such as archaeological excavation, caretaking, drafting, laboratory work, collecting oral histories, restoration of historic structures, and much more. Length of projects vary and there is no registration cost or fee. Contact Passport in Time Clearinghouse, P.O. Box 31315, Tucson, AZ 85751; 800-281-9176.

- **Senior Companion Program**—In this program you will be matched up with another person, and you will give individual care to a senior who needs help with transportation or just wants a friend. Volunteers receive a small paycheck and other benefits. Contact National Senior Service Corps, 1201 New York Ave., N.W., Washington, DC 20525; 800-424-8867.

- **Foster Grandparent Program**—This program matches low-income seniors with young people who need various kinds of special help. Volunteers serve as mentors, tutors, and caregivers for children and can also work in schools, hospitals, and recreation centers in their communities. They work twenty hours a week and receive a small paycheck and other benefits. Contact National Senior Service Corps (see above).

- **Retired Senior Volunteer Program** gives retired people a chance to continue to use their professional experience by working with local service organizations doing such things as conducting employment workshops and acting as consultants to nonprofit organizations. Contact National Senior Service Corps (see above).

- **National Forest Volunteers**—Positions vary depending upon your local forest, but can include everything from typing and filing to leading nature hikes. For a list of national forests nearest you, contact U.S. Forest Service, U.S. Dept. of Agriculture, Human Resource Programs, P.O. Box 96090, Washington, DC 20090.

- **National Park Volunteers**—Contact your nearest national park to discover something for you to do, whether it is timing Old Faithful or directing moose traffic. Contact the Office of Public Inquiry, National Park Service, U.S. Dept. of the Interior, 1849 C St., N.W., Washington, DC 20240; 202-208-4747.

- **SCORE, Service Corps of Retired Executives**—Volunteers are retired business professionals who want to share their expertise with the next generation of business owners. SCORE even conducts seminars and workshops covering how to run a business. Contact SCORE, 409 Third St., S.W., Washington, DC. 29924; 800-634-0245.

Tips:

Another excellent resource is the book *Free Stuff for Seniors* by Matthew Lesko and Mary Ann Martello. To learn more, call 800-532-5566. No one should ever have to feel useless or unwanted. Churches and other community groups, too, are always looking for volunteers.

Caring for a Blended Family

The Idea:

When two people with children marry and a blended family is created from that commitment, respect for differences is essential to the success of the family relationship. Here are some ways to demonstrate respect, tolerance, and caring.

The Idea in Action:

Linda Kraig of Western Springs, Illinois, tells how she and her husband, Ray, dealt with their blended family:

In 1988 I met and married the most wonderful man I've ever met. Ray was a single parent also, raising a daughter. When we decided to marry, we made an appointment to see a child psychologist in an effort to educate ourselves about how to best blend our families. The psychologist's advice was simple and to the point: Don't! She strongly felt that, given our children's ages—two fifteen-year-olds, a twelve-year-old, and a six-year-old, statistically, our chances of successfully blending our families were slim to none. We were devastated. We loved each other, we valued the same things . . . most importantly, family. Ray and I wanted to care for our family. We considered the alternatives: We could continue dating until our older children went off to school, but then, what message would that give our children? Were we so fearful of the consequences that we were unwilling to take the chance? Or, we could stop seeing each other altogether.

After seriously considering the psychologist's advice, we made our own decision. As Ray so eloquently put it, we decided to "jump in to see how deep it was!" The important thing was that we trusted each other enough to know that no matter how deep the challenge was, we'd be able to paddle. Looking back (ten years ago now), I think the two most important things we did to successfully blend our families were to practice tolerance and caring. Love just grew naturally from those two seeds.

Tolerance is such an important, overlooked virtue. We learned to accommodate one another by holding family meetings . . . at first once a week. This accomplished three things: It gave [the children] a forum to voice their concerns, it made everyone aware of the others' feelings, and, most importantly, the meetings told the children that we cared. They were important, and we were listening.

Amazingly, we discovered that the concerns were all very similar. Most had to do with trivial things: "They don't fold the towels like we do. He puts the toilet paper on backwards. She plays her music too loud. I can't get a turn at the piano." Ray and I taught tolerance (how important are the towels and toilet paper?) and caring (have the courtesy to turn the music down and take turns at the piano). In order to diffuse eruptions between meetings, we devised the "note" system, instructing everyone to write down their concerns and save them for the meeting. A lot of writing went on in the early days. But everybody paddled.

And then we had to paddle harder! Only two and a half weeks after we were married, I was diagnosed with breast cancer and would have to undergo a mastectomy and chemotherapy. I was devastated—not over the physical loss but because I was supposed to be the Caregiver. To have to burden my new family at this time in their lives was psychologically crushing. I was so afraid my newly formed nest would not be strong enough to withstand the current.

I put a sign on the refrigerator that said EVERYBODY PADDLE, and an amazing thing happened. We bonded. We had to! We really needed each other. The trivial complaints were replaced by genuine acts of caring. We found humor in the crisis, and faith replaced fear. Beth and Kate became sisters, and Patrick fondly cared for his six-year-old brother. In the face of adversity, our family was formed. I am so proud of it!

🎁 Barry Heermann of Dayton, Ohio, tells how his stepfamily created new holiday rituals:

In 1992, when Kipra and I were married, our highest goal was to create a loving and supportive family. At that time my daughter Jennifer was twenty-two, just completing college and starting her career with a diversity consulting firm. Kipra's son Dustin was thirteen years old, and her daughter Tamar was fifteen, both experiencing the challenges of adolescents in two different school settings. Little did we know then that our three kids would find commonalities, get beyond sibling rivalries, and develop authentic, supportive, and giving relationships.

Very early in this process, during the holiday period around mid-November, Kipra and I conceived of a plan to create family rituals and traditions. It was less a plan and more of a commitment to create a space within which the kids could openly communicate about what they wanted to do and how they would like to celebrate the holidays. We invited them to express their ideas over a specially prepared dinner prior to the holiday. These kids love to eat, and a special meal with all their favorite dishes proved an ideal setting for brainstorming possibilities.

In our dialogue with them we didn't use the world family "traditions" or "rituals." Those words and ideas would have seemed foreign and strained, especially for the younger kids. So we used simple language and raised questions about what they might like to do and what they might like to have during these holiday occasions. There was no shortage of ideas!

Some of our holiday traditions begun in that early formative stage in our step family development included the following:

1. We decided on the menu, making agreements about exact food items, including their preparation, for both Thanksgiving and Christmas meals.
2. The kids also agreed that we would hold hands and say a short, spontaneous prayer before all meals, rotating the task amongst each of us. This tradition has continued through this very day.
3. They planned fun things—agreeing to an alternative gift-giving ritual involving a scavenger hunt. The kids were given written instructions that led to clues that led to a present that led to more clues and more presents. The scavenger hunt required that we travel by car to outdoor sites in nearby parks and to homes of friends who participated in this event with us as the location for gifts and/or clues regarding next stops on the hunt.
4. We decided on a process for giving and receiving the gifts that remained under the Christmas tree. Each kid would rotate through the process, while the remainder of the family provided their full, rapt attention, rotating through each family member until all gifts were exchanged and opened.
5. The kids agreed they would also exchange gifts with each other.
6. While Kipra and I decided that joining a religious community would be an important aspect of our new relationship, not just during the holidays but throughout the year, we did not feel "at home" in many of the faith communities we visited in Dayton, and since going to church was a totally foreign idea for all of the kids, we agreed to respect their decision about participating with us in a worship service. Lo and behold, the oldest of the children, Jennifer, called just before Thanksgiving to invite us to join her for church in her home community of Cincinnati. (This was a remarkable invitation as Jennifer had resisted going to church since her childhood, and I concluded that she would permanently avoid structured religion throughout her life.) Over the years two of the three kids have embraced this tradition, and we all feel at home in Jennifer's church.

Tips:

You can see from these two accounts of blending families how important both caring and respect are in making everyone in the group feel important and valued. Think about how you are modeling those attributes in your own family.

Discover Your Child's/Mate's/Parent's Love Language

The Idea:

Love begins at home. A primary human emotional need is the need to feel loved, a need to sense that you belong and are wanted. Child psychologists say that with an adequate supply of affection, the child will likely develop into a responsible adult. Without that love, he or she will be emotionally and socially retarded. Dr. Ross Campbell suggests that there is an "emotional tank" inside your child waiting to be filled with love. When the tank is full, the child will develop normally, but when the tank is empty, the child will misbehave. He feels that much of children's

Bill lets Brenda know that while he appreciates her help, he would prefer that she keep her insightful comments to herself.

misbehavior comes from the cravings of an empty "love tank," a misguided search for the love they do not feel. This need for love, if not met, follows us into adulthood and marriage.

In his book *The Five Love Languages—How to Express Heartfelt Commitment to Your Mate*, Gary Chapman suggests that there are five languages of love, and each of us can seek to "speak the primary love language" of our child, mate, or parent. As we do so, we will be keeping their emotional love tanks full.

The Idea in Action:

📖 As you read about the five languages of love, begin to think of each person in your family and what their special language is:

1. Words of Affirmation—When our children are young, we often give many affirming words to them. Why is it that when they get older, our words of affirmation turn to words of condemnation? To a family member whose primary love language is "words of affirmation," our negative, critical, demeaning words can destroy their self-esteem and leave them feeling unloved and without value. How many middle-aged adults still hear words of condemnation spoken years and years ago—"You're stupid. You'll never make it. You're too fat. You will never be as good a student/athlete/musician as your sister/brother/cousin."

2. Quality Time—Quality time means giving someone undivided attention. When you do this, you are saying that they are important to you, that you enjoy being with them. If "quality time" is the love language of your child and you speak that language, chances are that he or she will allow you to spend time with him or her even through the adolescent years.

3. Receiving Gifts—Sometimes parents and grandparents speak the language of gifts excessively! They think that giving gifts is the best way to show love. However, if the child seldom says thank you, quickly lays the gifts aside, or does not take care of the gifts that are given, chances are their primary love language is not "receiving gifts." If, on the other hand, your child responds with much thanksgiving, shows the gifts to others and tells them how wonderful you are for buying the gift, puts it in a place of prominence, or plays with it often, then perhaps "receiving gifts" is their primary love language. Remember that a gift does not have to cost much money. It's the thought that counts.

4. Acts of Service—Your acts of service to your family members can communicate love in a meaningful way to those whose primary love language is service. If a family member is often expressing appreciation for ordinary acts of service such as cooking special meals, driving them to places, packing lunches, doing errands, helping with homework, that is a clue that they are emotionally important to him or her. Such things are taken for granted by many, but for others, those acts communicate love.

5. Physical Touch—Research shows that babies who are held and touched develop better emotionally than babies who are not. In fact, some babies who are not touched may even die. As we grow, we often stop touching one another except in sexual situations. For those whose primary love language is touch, it is critical to hug and touch them in acceptable ways. If your teenager is regularly coming up behind you and grabbing your arms, lightly pushing you, or sitting near you, those are likely indicators that physical touch is important to him or her.

Tips:

Remember that every family member is different. We must learn to respect and speak each person's love language if we want to keep his or her emotional tank full. Observe your family members. Watch how each one expresses his or her love to others. That is a clue to their love language. Also notice the things they request of you and what they most appreciate. It is very interesting to me how in a relationship we often completely misunderstand the other person's love language because we are blinded by our own and the things that make us feel loved rather than focusing on the *other's* needs. For example, my primary love language is "giving and receiving gifts" and "words of affirmation" while my husband's is "acts of service." How many times we have both felt disappointed and unloved when our expectations were not met—when, in reality, we were simply not speaking one another's love language!

Wonderful friends have added their ideas to this list of ways to express love. Ken Johnston, the founder of Kaset International, says that his language of love is total acceptance of who he is as a person while Ray and Rosita Perez, who were raised in Cuban families, say that to most Cubans, food is the language of love. As their daughter Rachel expressed, "If you're happy, eat something. If you're bored, eat something. If you're sad, eat something. According to the aunts and uncles, if you just eat something, you'll always feel better!"

> **Remove price tags from people! Everyone has worth; the excitement lies in the discovery of their value. Value yourself! The only people who appreciate a doormat are people with dirty shoes.**
>
> —Leo Buscaglia

Get Involved in a Family Literacy Program

The Idea:

One of the best ways to give respect to others is to help them learn to read and write. The whole family can become involved in a literacy program in your community.

The Idea in Action:

In 1993 Yvette Gioannetti and Sister Rachel Sena were asked to work with the large population of immigrant Mayan people in the diocese of Palm Beach, Florida, when a group of the Mayan women asked to be taught to read and write so they could assist their school-age children with their studies. There are estimated to be 15,000 to 20,000 Mayan families in Palm Beach County. Most of them work in the agriculture industry, often holding two or three jobs. While the men have had some formal education (through elementary school), 99 percent of the women are illiterate both in their native language, Q'anjob'al, and in Spanish. They speak no English.

In the Family Literacy Program they teach the mothers basic reading and writing skills in their native tongue and then move them into English as they are ready. They also host an early childhood education program, the Even Start Family Literacy Program, for their preschool children to prepare them to succeed in the public schools. The children learn in the same classroom as their mothers are learning to read and write. The children see their mothers modeling positive study habits while the mothers see their children across the room and are motivated to try just a little bit harder!

Miguel is shy. He clings to his mother, Isabel, when they come to the Family Literacy Center. He won't play with the other children but tugs at Isabel's blouse and whines. The child care worker knows what to do, however. She smiles and makes eye contact. Then, she brings him a stuffed monkey to hug . . . it's Curious George. The next day, she starts reading to two other children but near enough for Miguel to hear the story in Curious George Rides a Bike. *Miguel drifts over to the group. He becomes an active participant for the rest of the year, while keeping an eye out to make sure his mother is still in the room, of course! Isabel relaxes and begins to learn to read and write, too.*

In addition to the literacy training, they offer translation services for the families, transportation to and from the school, medical service support and referrals, home visits, parenting classes, and more, all through local agencies, organizations, and individual volunteers from the community.

These are the people they serve:

Maria's three children are sick, so she takes them to the doctor. The doctor prescribes different medications for each child. But Maria can't read the labels and unintentionally mixes up the medicines. . . .

Juanita bends, stoops, and walks all day in the hot south Florida sun at her job at a wholesale nursery. From time to time, she'll pause to sip some cool water out of a nearby hose. She and her husband are excited about their first child, who will soon be born. But, when that child is born, he has severe physical handicaps. . . . Juanita could not read the sign by the hose that said the water was not potable.

Angela and Armando have saved their money so they can send a precious two hundred dollars to her parents back in Guatemala. She takes the money to a neighborhood store, where the owner gives her what he calls a money order. She mails it. Later, she learns from her mother that the piece of paper was worthless. Angela has been cheated because she could not see that the man had simply handed her a piece of paper with senseless writing. She had no proof that she had ever given him her hard-earned two hundred dollars.

These are just a few of the consequences facing these hard-working families every day because of their illiteracy. The Family Literacy Program helps them overcome such adversities by teaching them to speak, read, and write.

Tips:

I am sure there are similar programs in nearly every community. What a wonderful gift of respect you will be giving these folks by helping them learn to read, and if your family is involved, it will also impress your children with the privilege we have had to learn to read and write. For more information on the Florida program, see the Resource section at the back of the book.

Respect Yourself—Be Self-Fulfilled

The Idea:

Before you can respect others, you must also learn to respect yourself. Part of respecting yourself is "feeding yourself," providing opportunities to grow and stretch and learn. You can do this by pursuing hobbies and interests, developing talents, volunteering to help others, and being involved in causes. Read, travel, take classes, and attend lectures.

The Idea in Action:

"Mikey, turn off Road Runner and try to help Daddy! Tell Daddy what buttons to push to fix a general protection fault error/hard drive failure!"

In her book *Friendship Is an Art,* Barbara McCauley suggests the following ways to fulfill yourself:

- Make a list of things you would like to know more about, and each day for a month, study ten minutes about one of your interests. (One famous person has said that if you study something for fifteen minutes a day, you will be an expert on that subject in five years!)
- Have some of your own personal traditions, such as learning a new vocabulary word each day, buying a new food each time you go to the grocery store, trying a new recipe each week, buying yourself flowers each Monday, or taking a new route to a familiar place once a week.
- Try new things—a new hairdo, a new recipe, a new class, a new food, a new restaurant. Read a book or magazine that you wouldn't normally read. Go to a different kind of movie or visit a new part of the city.
- Have traditions with your friends. Barbara tells of several of hers:

With Linda it was buying season tickets to see the university plays.

With Judy it was celebrating her birthday each year by "grazing" (going to a different restaurant for each part of the meal).

With Joan, Pat, and Kathy, it was getting together once a month for a book club.

With Diane it was having fresh raspberry pie each year for her birthday.

With Kasie and Mindy it was celebrating their half birthday by going to a nice restaurant.

*With Dan it was picking apples from a wild apple tree and making apple pie at
the cabin each fall.*
With Peggy it was giving her something to do with bears each birthday.

And remember—your family members can also be your friends!

🎁 I have made a wonderful friend who works for the Department of Forestry
in the state of Florida. He told me several years ago that when he is having
a difficult time, he sends *himself* flowers—and he sends them to the office
so that everyone asks and wonders who his admirer is! This is one of his
delightful personal traditions.

Tips:

Each New Year I pick something that I want to learn, a place I want to visit,
and a person I want to get to know. These become part of my goals for that
year, and they give me a focus as well as a sense of achievement when I finish
them. You don't have to wait for a new year—you can also do this at an anniversary or a birthday or some other significant time in your life. This is also
a wonderful exercise to do as a family, having each person set his or her goals
for the coming year.

This song of David Roth's, based on a true story, exemplifies the deepest
manifestation of RESPECT:

Dragon to Butterfly

It was early September in Lincoln, Nebraska
Two friends were conversing at dusk on a porch
One was wrapped up in blankets and pillows
The other an old overcoat

Affection was easy to witness between them
The physical closeness, the tender exchange
The one in the coat gently stroking the other
Who struggled but managed to talk just the same

He said, "Do you remember the day we met, Michael?
I heard you were coming and I called many times
I didn't want someone like you to move here
I wasn't used to your kind

But instead of returning my ignorant curses
You just kept answering the phone
And you knocked on my door with a bucket of chicken
The first time you came to my home"

The two men were laughing now, shaking their heads
With a sense of the passage about to take place
"Larry, if someone had said we'd be friends
I'd have called them insane to their face

But you can't always tell what's inside of an apple
And you can't always trust what you see . . ."
And Michael continued to wonder out loud
After Larry had drifted to sleep

How a man can move mountains, a world can be turned
And the greatest distances easily spanned
When the strength that's invested in making a fist
Is transformed into shaking a hand

Michael helped Larry back into the house
And then Michael's wife, Julie, helped Larry to bed
A life-long diabetic confined to a wheelchair
He couldn't do much for himself anymore

So they'd taken him in to unravel the pain
How his father made fun of him, planting the seed
And the root of the anger that grew so completely
Once strangled his heart like a weed

But a man can move mountains, a world can be turned
And the greatest of distances easily spanned
When the strength that's invested in making a fist
Is transformed into shaking a hand

Larry's last breath in his bedroom at Michael's
Came later that night with his friend at his side
"Thank you" was all he could whisper "for changing
A dragon into a butterfly"

For Larry was once a White Knight, a Grand Dragon
With robes and with torches, with scorn and with hate
And Michael the Rabbi who'd just moved to Lincoln
With two open arms and with faith

That a man can move mountains, a world can be turned
And the greatest of distances easily spanned
When the strength that's invested in making a fist
Is transformed into shaking a hand

CHAPTER SIX

R = Reason for Being

"Create a Feeling of Purpose and Belonging"

He who has a why to live for can bear almost any how.

—Nietzsche

I HAVE BEEN DEEPLY touched by Victor Frankl's book *Man's Search for Meaning*, which is based on his experiences in several concentration camps during World War II. As a result of these camp experiences, he has developed a therapeutic doctrine called Logo therapy, which says that the primary motivational force in man is a striving to find meaning in one's life.

What he found in the camps was that even under the most horrible of conditions, each man or woman had a *choice* in their reactions. Even though the external conditions were the same, some people reacted as swine and others as saints. He says:

Everything can be taken from a man but one thing: the last of the human freedoms—to choose one's attitude in any given set of circumstances, to choose one's own way.

He also found that "any attempt to restore a man's inner strength in the camp had first to succeed in showing him some future goal." He even goes on to say, "Suffering ceases to be suffering at the moment it finds a meaning, such as the meaning of a sacrifice." Many of those "saints" found a purpose in *choosing* to accept their suffering and death with dignity.

After he returned to normal life, Frankl began to study in more depth man's need for meaning. A study sponsored by the National Institute of Mental Health and administered by Johns Hopkins University interviewed 7,948 students at forty-eight colleges, asking them what was "very important" to them. Sixteen percent responded, "Making a lot of money." Seventy-eight percent responded that their first goal was "Finding a purpose and meaning to my life."

> **To laugh often and much; to win the respect of intelligent people and the affection of children; to earn the appreciation of honest critics and endure the betrayal of false friends; to appreciate beauty; to find the best in others; to leave the world a bit better, whether by a healthy child, a garden patch, or a redeemed social condition; to know that even one life has breathed easier because you lived. This is to have succeeded.**
>
> **—Ralph Waldo Emerson**

In a more recent eighteen-month-long study, Baxter International Laboratories found that what their employees globally value most is "Being respected as a 'whole' person with a life beyond work." In other words, they want their employer to respect that their lives have a meaning beyond simply working in a job.

Frankl feels that a phenomenon of the twentieth century is what he calls an "existential vacuum," a feeling of total and ultimate meaninglessness in people's lives. He found that 25 percent of his European students were feeling a marked degree of existential vacuum but over 60 percent of American students described their lives as without meaning!

Today that feeling Frankl describes as the "existential vacuum" exists in an even greater degree in people's lives. I see several reasons for this: the increase of technology and the dehumanization of communication; the downsizing and re-engineering of the last several years, which has left many without self-esteem because their feelings of worth and value had become tied to their job; and most seriously, the breakdown of the family and the loss of traditions and values that used to give worth and value and purpose to all human beings. Frankl even in 1984 describes one of the reasons for the phenomenon of the existential vacuum as, "Traditions which buttressed [man's] behavior are now rapidly diminishing."

One of the most important ways we can help people to find new purpose and meaning in their lives is to reinstitute family traditions and values, to give each family member a sense of pride and belonging in a special group, and, as a result, to help each person find his or her unique contribution to making this world a little bit better place. As Frankl says, "What will be the monument of your existence?"

The ideas in this chapter will help you find new meaning and pride in your family group and will help give each family member the foundation and security to be able to find a purpose and meaning in his or her own life. Remember it is not so much the tradition itself that is important but rather the family togetherness and communication and pride that come as a result of the tradition.

"Anytime one of the kids gets an illness we cross it off. When we complete a row, Ed and I are going to Tahiti for three weeks."

Have Family Secrets

The Idea:

It is so wonderful to share a secret with someone. It makes you feel special and builds a sense of intrigue and belonging.

The Idea in Action:

My special friend Rita Emmett of Des Plaines, Illinois, writes about their family secret:

Somehow, some way . . . when my children were small . . . a secret hand-squeeze became part of our family life. I can't describe what the hand-squeeze is because, well, it's a secret. But I can tell you what it means. Every time anyone squeezes someone's hand in this special secret way, it communicates, "I love you."

It was fun to share our "secret" when the children were little, and it was special to receive from an eleven-year-old when our family received bad news, and it was helpful to give when a broken-hearted teen just couldn't talk about something, and it was spiritual to feel that squeeze from a young adult just about to be married, and it was one of the most important communications I'd ever received when my daughter was starting to doze off after blessing this world with the birth of her daughter.

Then, just the other day, I was walking along holding my granddaughter's hand and, with the gentleness of a butterfly, there was that special squeeze. We looked at each other and giggled. Sometimes, secrets can be wonderful!

🎁 Jeff Blackman shared with me that he and his son Chad have a secret handshake that they use before bed each evening. Theirs consists of ten secret steps!

Tips:

What beautiful family traditions. Could you create a special family secret?

Have Fun Family Dinners

The Idea:

When researchers have studied why some people are more successful in life than others, the only variable they could find consistently that differentiated the successful group from the not-so-successful group was that those who were successful had eaten dinner together as a family growing up. And that was *not* with the TV on! I am reading more and more about the importance of family dinners at least several times a week. In fact, the superintendent of our high school shared that the best predictor of a child's high school performance depends on whether the family eats dinner together.

At the American Psychological Association meeting in Chicago in August of 1997, Bowden and Zeisz presented a paper about the behavior of 527 adolescents as it related to family meals. They found well-adjusted teens (twelve to eighteen years) ate meals with an adult member of the family 5.389 days per week, on average. The "nonadjusted" teens—evaluated for substance abuse, depression, academic motivation, and peer relationships—shared similar meals only 3.344 days per week. In 1994 a *Reader's Digest* survey revealed that students who ate at least four meals a week with their families scored higher on academic tests than kids with three family meals or less per week. The same project showed more frequent family meals strongly correlated with self-esteem among girls. A 1996 study by Bruskin-Goldring Research found 42 percent of one thousand Americans surveyed eat dinner with their families every night and 59 percent make it a habit at least five days a week. That leaves 40 percent who do not eat together.

The Idea in Action:

🎁 We almost always had dinner as a family until the children were in the later years of high school and had jobs and activities that interfered with mealtime. Then we insisted that at least three or four nights a week we were all together. We always began each meal by holding hands and someone (we took turns) saying a blessing. Then we often played our own special family games during the meal.

One of our favorites was "Name Three Things." Each person got a turn to ask each other person to "Name Three Things." Then the turn rotated to the next person. Mom and Dad would ask things appropriate to the children's ages that involved some thinking or sometimes even learning: "Name three states that begin with 'A.' Name three kinds of dogs. Name three pitchers in the American League. Name three composers you like. Name three vegetables. Name three words that are onomatopoeias. Name three islands. Name three birds that can't fly."

The kids would often ask each other silly things like: "Name three girls that Garrett likes. Name three foods that are gross. Name three of our friends' dogs. Name three puppets on *Sesame Street*. Name three things that make Mom mad."

Another favorite when they were smaller was "Take a Bite." Each person got a turn to tell everyone else what they should take a bite of. Then if you didn't take a bite of that thing, you lost your turn the next time around. Of course, the parents always said the vegetables, and the kids chose dessert, bread, and milk!

You might also have "theme" dinners where you try different kinds of food and perhaps even dress in costumes. One of our favorites was to have a "grown-up" dinner several times a year where we ate in the formal dining room, used the good dishes and cloth napkins, and had special grown-up food like artichokes and stroganoff. We have decided recently, however, that perhaps we have given our children too good taste. When they choose an Italian restaurant over McDonald's too often, it can be hard on the budget!

The Jeff Blackman family plays some fun games at the dinner table. One of them is "I'm thinking of . . ." Each person takes a turn and adds a new clue until someone finally guesses the right answer:

> I'm thinking of somebody with orange hair.
> I'm thinking of somebody who wears big shoes.
> I'm thinking of somebody who plays the Grand Prize Game.
> (You're right—it's *Bozo!*)

They also play a version of "I spy," again adding a new clue until someone guesses right:

> I see a light.
> I see a light with numbers.
> I see a light with numbers in a circle.
> (I *spy* the clock on the stove!)

Another mother tells of a game that her family plays after dinner called "What's Gone?" (or Kitchen Concentration). She picks at least four but not more than eight kinds of food and puts them in a line on the counter or kitchen table. Each child gets a turn to look at the items and say what each one is. Then, one at a time, a child has to turn around and close his eyes while Mom takes one food away and moves the others all around. When the child opens his eyes, he tries to tell what's gone. After all have had a turn, it's time for dessert (as long as dessert isn't one of the food items that's gone!).

Barbara Swift says her children loved family times of remembering and storytelling about things they had done, especially when they were young.

Over dinner many times she asked them for memories of special times. Sometimes she told a story about a memory of her own to get the conversation started.

🎁 In his book *The Intentional Family*, William J. Doherty suggests three ingredients for success—to promote togetherness and identity as a unit:

Transition phase: There needs to be a distinct movement from everyday matters into "ritual space." It might be dimming lights, lighting candles, playing soft music, setting the table away from a messy kitchen counter, or saying a blessing.

Enactment phase: Eating and talking can be pleasurable if parents aren't using the meal as a disciplinary session. He cautions against going too far with stern talk about nutrition. One suggestion: Each family member tries everything on his or her plate but doesn't have to finish any item (no impolite remarks to the cook). Set an exact time for dinner even if it changes on a daily basis.

Exit phase: Some families don't allow any children to leave until everyone is finished. Others allow family members to drift off at will. There is usually a happy medium. What you want to avoid is ending the meal on a sour note. As for the food, Doherty said even takeout meals on paper plates can provide the makings of a healthful ritual. "You can still set the table, acknowledge you are happy to be together, and participate in good conversation."

Tips:

It is of the utmost importance that you make mealtimes together pleasant. Make a pact that there will be no arguments, criticism, or putdowns allowed. One family even put a sign above their table that said: NEUTRAL ZONE. Some of our happiest and most fun family times have been sitting around the dinner table!

"Sorry, folks, but at the request of other patrons, we're going to have to lower the dome of solitude."

Close to Home © John McPherson/Dist. by Universal Press Syndicate.

Create Precious Memories

The Idea:

Memories of special times shared together in a family can sustain us through many difficult experiences. Making memories for your children will give them the gift of history and belonging, and those memories relived will become the basis for storytelling and joy for many years to come.

The Idea in Action:

Uncle Brian is the most delightful and unpredictable person in our whole family! He is the world's greatest storyteller and the world's most unreliable person when it comes to time. He has lived all over the world; he has been a hippie, a farmer, a college professor, a Buddhist monk, and an executive coach; and he makes friends wherever he goes, from Lord Spenser and Mother Teresa to an upstate New York cowboy/farmer who told my mother he had named a goat after her! He has taught my children to imitate an elephant, smoke a cigar, and play music through their nose.

One of the ways Uncle Brian has created memories for my children is that on every visit he made during their growing-up years, they either made a movie or put on a performance with Uncle Brian as producer and director (and sometimes even an actor in the show). Because we didn't have video cameras at the time, the first thing Brian would do when he arrived was to take the children downtown to buy a roll of Super 8 movie film. Then they would spend the next day in the basement writing the script, rehearsing their parts, and raiding the costume box. Later that day Uncle Brian would begin the filming.

The first movie they made was called *Count Garrettula*, a takeoff on Dracula. Garrett slept in the toy box (coffin), attacked the beautiful princess (Gretchen), then turned into a bat when the hero (Uncle Brian) arrived. A fight ensued, and lo and behold, the hero won! In another segment of magic tricks, Garrett loved that he made his sister Gretchen disappear!

The second movie was *Cowboy Garrett Rides Again*. In this movie Gretchen is Calamity Jane and Erin is Pocahontas, a beautiful Indian princess. The villain is the bad Indian chief (Uncle Brian) who tries to kidnap the beautiful Indian princess. Garrett jilts Gretchen to rescue the

Indian maiden from the bad chief, and the movie ends with Uncle Brian lying on the ground in our front yard covered in ketchup, Gretchen miffed as the jilted lover, and Garrett and Erin riding off into the sunset on a wooden hobbyhorse with a brown paper sack head! While this one was being filmed, Brian ran around our front yard in his shorts with a brown towel hanging over the front and a giant Tinker Toy hatchet, chanting Indian chants and wearing shoe-polish warpaint. I wondered what people going by in our small village must have thought!

The children have watched those movies literally hundreds of times, and every relative, good friend, boyfriend or girlfriend over the years has been introduced to the *Legends of Uncle Brian*. Finally, I did have them put on videotape as a Christmas present so each child could have a copy of his/her own.

Another year, much before the advent of *The Best Christmas Pageant Ever*, Brian came for a Christmas visit. He immediately got all the children in the neighborhood together to put on a "show." They rehearsed all day in our basement, and that night all the parents were invited to the Christmas production in our backyard. They rigged up several scraps of wood and a string of Christmas lights to make a star in the basketball hoop; the garage was the stable; they filled the wagon with potting soil for the manger; and anyone in the neighborhood who had a dog brought it, and they were the "shepherds abiding with their flocks in the fields." Because there weren't enough boys, he chose the "three wise *women*," and for a camel they used the white car with a hump that belonged to one of the moms. The cast was complete with Mary, Joseph, a Cabbage Patch doll Baby Jesus, and the Innkeeper (Uncle Brian, of course). As the Christmas story was read, each child acted out his or her part under Brian's direction. Then he led us all in singing Christmas carols. It was a Christmas no one in the neighborhood will ever forget!

Tips:

It doesn't take money to create precious memories. It simply takes some creative thinking, a little time, and lots of fun. What memories are you creating for your children?

Find Special Ways to Keep
Loved Ones' Memories Alive

The Idea:

Often when a loved one in a family dies, it is difficult for friends and other family members to acknowledge their passing because it makes everyone sad. However, having lost a little son, we know how vitally important it is for healing to talk about the loved one and to keep their memory alive. Otherwise it is as if they never existed at all. Certainly there is sadness because the person is missed; however, finding creative ways to keep their memory alive becomes a celebration of their life.

The Idea in Action:

Nancy Stein from Naperville, Illinois, whose teenage son Jason was killed in a boating accident, shared how she keeps his memory alive in a beautiful way. Every year at the beginning of December, she buys special luminaria bags. Then she sends one to each of her son's friends and family, who are scattered all over the country. She asks them to decorate the bag in a way that helps them remember Jason. Sometimes they attach a photograph with Jason, others write letters of remembrance or poems, and some even make a picture or collage of things they loved to do together. They

Nancy Stein

then send the decorated bags back to her, and on Christmas Eve she puts them around Jason's grave at the cemetery. It becomes a healing for them all—a special celebration of Jason and what his life meant to each of them. Nancy said that she receives close to a hundred bags each year from many people who knew Jason. She invites anyone who wants to come to the cemetery on Christmas Eve night, where they each light a candle as music is played, and they sing "Silent Night." This year the young woman who had received both Jason's lungs sent a luminaria bag to thank Jason for giving her life back to her. Nancy and Jason's ten-year-old brother, Corey, make a copy of each of the bags and put the pictures in a binder as an ongoing memory.

For many years after our little boy died, at Christmas every year our dear friends the Schulzes purchased a children's book and dedicated it in his name to the Western Springs Public Library. The Christmas he would have been twenty-one, Mary wrote that now that he was an adult in heaven, they had decided that rather than donating a children's book, they would make a donation to Habitat for Humanity, a more "grown-up" way to celebrate his short life. Because our child was a baby when he died, none of our family or friends really got to know him, so the Schulzes' gift of keeping his memory alive has meant more than words can possibly express.

When Tom Veazey and his wife of Ashland, Virginia, lost their son Matthew to bone cancer, they began a lovely tradition of sending Christmas gifts to his friends. Because they saw a bright star in the sky the day Matthew died, gold stars and hearts have come to symbolize Matthew's life. One of the gifts was a wand filled with bright-colored stars and hearts. Another was a picture of Matthew in a small heart-shaped frame. They also found small heart-shaped stones at the Nature Store, which they gave to Matthew's friends. These gifts and the ongoing communication have encouraged these young people to come to visit the Veazeys when they are home, which has been healing for them all. Tom says that his wife has even begun an angel collection as a special memory of Matthew.

Bells Across America is a project currently being created to educate America while healing bereaved parents, siblings, and other family members. Their goal is to have church bells rung for three minutes at three P.M. (CST) on a certain day of the holiday season each year. They hope that every family in America who has had a child die can ring the bells at that time in their local church. This will be a very healing experience as parents all across our country come together to speak to all Americans with the sound of bells as they remember their children and the children of all bereaved parents during the holiday period.

Here are some other special ways to honor a loved one's life:

- Each year at Christmas a mother whose young child died picks a needy child the same age as her son would be that year and buys Christmas presents for him. It reminds her that her son is growing up in heaven.
- Another family donates videos at Christmas to the children's transplant ward where their child was treated.
- Bereaved grandparents are becoming involved with volunteer work: he as a tutor and she at their church assisting with young children in honor of their granddaughter.
- Barb Leiber has a tuition scholarship in honor of her son Steven at his school.
- Another family shared that each year at Christmas they write down on a small slip of paper what they're most thankful for and place it in a hollow ornament in honor of their son.
- The Putnam family periodically holds fund-raisers with their deceased son Ken's band-playing friends. They raffle off reproductions of Ken's artwork, and the money raised is sent to the Rainforest Coalition, which was Ken's favorite charity.
- The Paceys founded the Tommy Pacey Foundation in memory of their only child, who died at age three of leukodystrophy. All the money raised is donated to research at Kennedy-Krieger in Baltimore and to the United Leukodystrophy Foundation's research and family support.
- Our three children have made a decision that whoever has the first boy will name him Gavin, after our son and brother who is in heaven.

Tips:

If you or a family friend has lost a loved one, as a family find a special way that you can keep that person's memory alive. It will be a healing experience for you all, and it will help you to focus on the gift of life rather than the loss.

Little Things Can Show Our Love the Most

The Idea:

It is often the little things we do in our families that show our love the most. Ask your children about their memories. Usually their best memories are of things you might not even remember you did. Think of your own memories of growing up. Sometimes we overlook the simple things in order to do what we think are big, important things, when it is the little things we find out later that mattered the most.

The Idea in Action:

John Blumberg shared his thoughts on "It's the simple things we remember":

As our lives unfold day to day, month to month, and year to year, I am sure there are millions of memories built over time. Some are big, and some are small . . . and probably most are forgotten—except for a few very meaningful memories. I am sure the few we truly remember are not the biggest and certainly aren't the most expensive. I would bet most often they are the simplest of all. My most vivid memories of Christmas were never the presents. In fact, I can recall only a couple of gifts that quickly come to memory. But I can vividly remember my brother and me sneaking down the hallway in the middle of the night on Christmas Eve to see if Santa had come! We would practice during the day on Christmas Eve to be sure we had found all the loud creaking wooden boards in the floor, since these "floor alarms" moved around from year to year. I remember the scary thrill of going down the hall hoping not to wake our parents . . . moving almost motionless and covering our inevitable giggles to not make a sound! And I remember the year that, as we were

> **If a man is called to be a street sweeper, he should sweep streets even as Michelangelo painted or Beethoven composed music, or Shakespeare wrote poetry. He should sweep streets so well that all the hosts of heaven and earth will pause to say, here lived a great street sweeper who did his job well.**
>
> **—Martin Luther King, Jr.**

just inches from reaching the coveted closed hallway door that led to the living room of Santa's treasures, my dad burst open that hallway door from the other side. It was only later that we realized he was more surprised than we were!

Janet Swicegood of Galway, Ohio, shared a little thing that meant a lot to her children. She said that when they were young, the budget was tight, so there were many things she didn't buy. The children always complained that they only got generic brands of potato chips and cereal, the tennis shoes that were on sale, and she would NEVER buy Capri Sun drink boxes! One recent Christmas Janet made up a big basket for each of them—filled with Capri Sun, Ruffles potato chips, *real* Cheerios, and all the things she "wouldn't buy" back then! They loved it and realized now that they are grown and have families themselves just *why* she couldn't buy all those things.

Linda Kraig says that even during a time of crisis, her children remember the little, caring things:

In 1985 I was divorced and became the single parent of three children ages twelve, nine, and three. My once safe, secure, family-oriented, home-based existence came crashing down around me and, after a brief period of being paralyzed with fear, I began to rebuild my life, one shattered piece at a time. Until I could find a job, my children and I received food stamps and did not even have a car. And yet, I never for a moment felt desperate. It was one of the times in my life when I had to "Let go and let God." Remarkably, life evolved into a new "normal." I found a great job and a remarkable sitter (through divine intervention, I'm sure).

When I ask my children today what they remember about this emotionally wrenching, financially trying time in our lives, I am always amazed that they do not note the absence of vacations, new toys, or designer clothes (or even good food). They remember that we would all "cozy up" into my bed on Friday night when I got home from work to watch a rented movie (it's amazing how much more a rented movie means to you when you can only afford one per week!) and that we would all four of us sleep in the same bed all night.

They remember the dull-bladed, scuffed-up ice skates from St. Vincent de Paul's Thrift Store and how we turned our backyard into an ice rink. They remember our one-day "vacations" to downtown Chicago and that we always sat on the upper deck of the train. They remember that we needed to depend on each other, and they remember us meeting each challenge together. They remember the caring . . . and they remember that everybody paddled!

Sophia Weibel writes about one of her memories:

> When I was growing up, my father was never home because he was always working late. Sometimes, however, when he would come home, he would come to my room and whisper a few words to me in Greek, "Se agapo polee." These words mean, "I love you very much." I would then whisper back without truly realizing the depth of his love. His absence from home was something I never really understood until I became an adult. Looking back now, I see the deep love he had for me and my family in just those few short words. Today, I can never thank God enough for giving me my father. He is a hardworking, dedicated man, and a man who has taught me by example the meaning of sacrifice, unconditional love, and the blessings of family.

Tips:

How long has it been since you whispered those words to your family members? Even if your situation is one in which it is difficult for you to have much time with your loved ones, the little things you do to show your caring will last throughout their lifetime.

Do Special "Dad" Things

The Idea:

Since the mother in the family is often the primary caregiver and spends the most time with the children, it is important for the dads to do some special things with and for their children. John Drescher in his book *If I Were to Start My Family Again* tells that a group of three hundred seventh and eighth graders kept accurate records on how much time their fathers actually spent with them over a two-week period. Most saw their father only at the dinner table. A number never saw their father for days at a time. The average time father and child were alone together for an entire week was seven and a half minutes! How much time are you spending alone with each of your children?

The Idea in Action:

 Sylvia Marshall of Aurora, Illinois, tells of a special tradition involving the children's dad:

When my children were small, they especially enjoyed Sunday breakfasts, where we would all gather around the kitchen table. The breakfasts were a real treat made special by their dad. He would create special pancakes for each child, spelling out the first letter of each of their names. Those pancake breakfasts are still remembered today, and our oldest child is now twenty-eight years old!

🎁 Another father schedules specific "date" times once a week with each of his daughters. Often he will pick them up at school and take them out for lunch. On their birthdays he ties a helium balloon to their beds before they wake up, and he takes them out of school one day a year for a special adventure just with him.

🎁 One of my friends remembers that his dad always let each of the children paint the house with him. This made them feel very trusted and grown up, and they were together.

Close to Home © John McPherson/Dist. by Universal Press Syndicate.

"For heaven's sake! All he wants to do is play horsey with his dad! Will you stop whimpering and at least try to jump over the coffee table?!"

🎁 A very special father began a daily diary when his first daughter was born. Every day he writes a few lines in it, and he plans to give it to her on a special day in her life. Another father and daughter once a week write in a memory book— he writes on one page and she writes on the other. This has become a treasured time for them.

🎁 One person shared that he remembered how his dad always used to go to the dump once a week to take their garbage, and he always took his little sister along. That routine trip became their weekly "date" time. He said, "That taught me that it doesn't matter where you go with a parent; the important thing is having special time alone."

🎁 Derek Hillyer of San Antonio, Texas, always personally drives his children to school each day even though there is a schoolbus provided. This gives him special and quality time with his teenage sons.

A retired army officer started a tradition with his oldest son on his eighteenth birthday: He promoted him to "adult" status and presented him with an award and pinned him with a medal. The ceremony was complete with a reading of orders and certificates. He hopes to carry on this tradition with his other two sons.

Tips:

Some dads will feel more comfortable sharing time in the backyard with their children while others prefer more verbal sharing. Whatever you enjoy, try to find special ways to have time with your children alone. It is an investment that will be invaluable as they get older.

Have a "Friday Night Campout"

The Idea:

It is a wonderful tradition to do something on a regular basis that children can carry on when they have families of their own.

The Idea in Action:

 A wonderful friend, John Blumberg, writes about his family's special tradition:

As a parent, I wonder what our children will remember in their adult years ahead. There is one tradition that has evolved that I bet will be on their list! It was an idea we borrowed (okay, stole) from two of our best friends in Houston. It all began on a Friday night after a visit to Houston when our kids asked if they could all pull out their sleeping bags and sleep in one room for a "campout." Seeing little harm except for a bit of inconvenience and the concern if they would sleep all night, we agreed. We didn't forecast the tradition that would follow! That Friday night turned into the next Friday night and the next Friday night and so on. Eventually, it simply became known as the "Friday night campout."

The tradition over time began to include much more than a day of the week or just throwing sleeping bags on the floor. Even the exact positioning and layout of the sleeping bags began to take on their own symbolism. Soon, the ritual setup began with putting a blanket on the floor in the center of the room. This came to be what I soon thought of as the "island of security." Ryan, Kelly, and Julie each gathered their own supplies of sleeping bag, pillow, and other unique items. Each of the three sleeping bags began headfirst from the "island of security" and then reached out as spokes in three different directions. Being connected to the island was critical to each of the three kids, but just as important was having their own space which led down its own path.

Soon, the island began to fill with familiar weekly visitors of stuffed animals that each of the children would contribute—making it symbolically an island of shared contribution. There were rules of respect (like quietly getting up the next morning and leaving the room without waking the others) that kept the privilege and the tradition alive. Each respected the rules . . . and the responsibilities of the next morning cleanup because they knew the next campout was less then seven days away!

It always amazed me how each of them looked forward to the next campout, because after all the setup and a quick snuggle, each would almost instantly fall off into their own world of sleep and imagination—although they were never far from their "island of security." I hope our kids look back on a lot of things with gentle kindness, but somehow I think the "Friday night campout" will often come to mind at the top of the list. I guess dreams and memories can sometimes become the same!

Tips:

You can create your own version of the "Friday Night Campout"; it is memories like this that create the bonding in a family that lasts forever and ever.

Create a Collage of Family Values and Traditions

The Idea:

What a wonderful family project to create a collage of what the family values and some of its special traditions. Not only will it help put those values and traditions into concrete form, but it will also demonstrate each family's uniqueness and purpose.

The Idea in Action:

Michelle Fetherolf, a senior in high school in Westerville, Ohio, gave her family a most special gift as she was preparing to leave for college. It was a collage book of several pages. The title page composed of various pictures and words cut from magazines reads:

**Continue FAMILY Values & Traditions
Always Come HOME for the HOLIDAYS**

Page two is titled "FAMILY UNIQUENESS" and begins with the following note, again using words cut from magazines:

*I appreciate my family because we live in HARMONY (most of the time!). We LISTEN to each other and CARE about each other. We know how To Say "I'm Sorry" and AVOID SEEING RED. My parents have taught me so many things. I've learned the importance of **love**, **Friendship**, **KISSES**, and most of all **Education**! I've also learned **How to hear with your heart**.*

Other words on that page include:

Page three is titled, "THINGS I'VE LEARNED." This page includes the words:

Page four is called "FAMILY CHANGES." Words included on this page are:

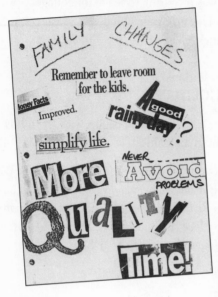

The final page is titled, "WE'VE ALWAYS BEEN . . ." Some of the phrases here are:

Tips:

Michelle gave her family a priceless gift. Did you see some things that reminded you of your family? I hope you'll get a stack of magazines and do this with your family. You might also create an annual "collage of joy" with your favorite photos of the year and do this as a yearly family project. Then keep it out where everyone can see it, adding to the collection as the years go by.

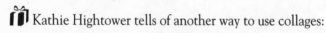 Kathie Hightower tells of another way to use collages:

I love to make collages. I often use these as gifts for others. I've noticed that these tend to be gifts people save forever. When my husband and I attended a military course together (I'm an Army Reservist) for ten months, I made collages for some of our classmates at the end of it. We each had a foreign student in our sections of sixteen. My classmate from the Philippines told me that it is his most treasured gift because of the ongoing memory it provides. (It is also another use for all those duplicate photos I get.)

Find Your Own Personal Way to Make the World Better

The Idea:

Whether you commit to one random act of kindness a day, or your daily work, like mine, has a deep sense of mission that you are making a difference in this world, or you create a giveaway that is uniquely yours, find a personal way to help make this a better world and share it with your friends and family.

The Idea in Action:

I recently received the following beautiful letter from Katherine Wahl of Bellmore, New York:

Dear Barbara,

As an internationally known author and gifted speaker, you have captured the attention and admiration of millions. To have reached your level of success you know the importance of following your dream.

My dream is to make the world a kinder place. Please assist me in my quest by distributing the enclosed cards. I know we can make a difference because I believe all things are possible. I also know that "Caring Is Contagious."

Thank you in advance for helping. I know you must have a busy schedule. If you would like more cards to give out at a lecture, would like to share an experience precipitated by my card, or want to let me know just how my dream has traveled, please contact me. I wish you continued success, good health, wealth, and above all, happiness.

Katherine Wahl

This is Katherine's special card:

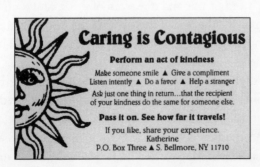

🎁 Gloria Runk from Tampa, Florida, uses the following technique to make a difference in the world. Every day she resolves to:

1. Do something for someone else.
2. Do something for myself.
3. Do something I don't want to do that needs doing.
4. Do a physical exercise.
5. Do a mental exercise.
6. Do something that creates humor.
7. Say an original prayer that always includes counting my blessings.

🎁 Jim Vert from the Michigan Department of Civil Rights in Grand Rapids, Michigan, posted this affirmation on the doors of all his colleagues:

GOOD MORNING, EVERYONE!
Some people make the world more special just by being in it.

🎁 Tom Corcoran of Gloucester, Massachusetts, always carries postcards in his pockets. Then he can send them immediately to people who do something kind for him.

🎁 Maureen Kushner is a teacher who uses humor to bring about a vision of peace to Jewish and Arab children in Israel. She says, "I try to get the children to dream a true vision of peace based on kindness. Through kindness, which was the main attribute of Abraham who is so important to both peoples, we can bring about peace. Humor equalizes the kids in the group and brings out the spark in them."

In Israeli schools, Kushner asks the children to list words they associate with war and violence. Then she asks for words of peace. The next step is a lesson in cartooning. She calls on the children to use their imaginations to draw letters asymmetrically, in varied colors. She asks them to choose one word of war and one word of peace and to draw each, integrating humor. At the end of the exercise the word pictures are gathered together, and the children create a story using the words. The children express their fears and dreams.

In another exercise, "Fix-It Shop," taken from the Hebrew *tikkun olam*, meaning "repairing the world," Kushner explores with the children how the world can be "fixed"—it can be less squeaky, less clogged, and less broken. The children construct a "fix-it shop" complete with tools and first-aid kits, a "love kit" with hugs, kisses, and smiles, and a "joke kit" with humor supplies. The children begin with practical exercises like fixing a toy or repairing a shoe in humorous, innovative ways, and then go on to fixing conflicts between individuals and nations.

Last year at the government religious school in the Jewish Quarter of Jerusalem's Old City, she enlisted children ages five to eleven to create The Happy Tree, a mural of biblical visions of peace. She concludes, "Shlomo Carlebach once said, 'There will never be peace in the world unless people see the holiness and the magic and the warmth and the beauty of all children.' I personally feel more than hope for Israel. With kids like these, Israel can only flourish." Maureen Kushner has found her unique way of making a difference!

Tina Valant Siebelts of Boca Raton, Florida, always includes the following turquoise-embossed cards in all her correspondence, including bill payments:

She's made quite a positive impact!

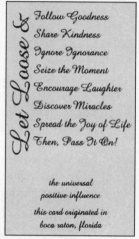

Let Loose &

Follow Goodness
Share Kindness
Ignore Ignorance
Seize the Moment
Encourage Laughter
Discover Miracles
Spread the Joy of Life
Then, Pass It On!

the universal
positive influence

this card originated in
boca raton, florida

Tips:

What might you or your family do as a personal commitment to making this world a better place for us all to live?

Let Family Members Know in Writing How Much They Mean to You

The Idea:

Have you ever written to a special family member to tell him what he has meant in your life? A letter can be read and reread and is a treasure that person will never forget.

The Idea in Action:

Rose Conrad shared with me a touching letter she received from her granddaughter Colleen, who received an assignment in speech class to write about a person who was a significant role model in their life:

Dear Grandma,

You may or may not know that you are a very important person in my life. I just wanted to tell you that and to say thank you for helping me become who you see today.

You are an incredible woman and role model, and I only hope that I can be like you someday. Because of the things you have taught me, I am already like you in some ways.

Something that you helped to teach me is to love all people and to look at the world in an open-minded way, without changing what my beliefs and values are. I can't even begin to explain how much your example of strength helped me to learn how to continue my life after hard times passed by. And one of the most important things you have taught me is how to love God and my family.

Thank you so much for helping me to become me. I love you,

Colleen Rose

Victoria Moran tells of her friend Julie who, for her daughter Katie's thirteenth birthday, created a scrapbook with contributions from every woman who had been important in her daughter's life. She says:

Every page contains a picture of Katie with an older friend from the past or present and a letter or a poem from that woman to the girl just entering her teens. The wealth of support, encouragement, and love in that hand-constructed book will be with Katie through the ups and downs of adolescence and for the rest of her life.

After I had spoken to Nationwide Insurance, I received the following letter from Janice Amato:

Dear Barbara,

I wanted to thank you for the fine seminar you presented to our Nationwide Texas Management Team last week. I left inspired and refilled with hope. I also want you to know that I've shared many of your tips with family and employees—and already I see results.

Most importantly, I completed my assignment about contacting someone who had a great influence on my life and telling them thanks. I completed it last night by preparing the attached letter to my mom for Mother's Day. I cried the entire time and still do this morning.

I want to thank you for prompting me to share these memories with my mom. I hope you have a blessed Mother's Day as well.

This is a part of the beautiful three-page letter Janice wrote to her mother:

Mama,

I wanted to write you a letter for Mother's Day to tell you how much you mean to me. I wasn't sure where to start, so I decided I was going to just write down many of the special things I remember.

I REMEMBER

I remember you rocking me and singing to me every day after lunch . . . I thought you had the greatest voice, and my favorite hymns today are the ones you sang to me. . . .

I remember how you always took care of me when I was sick . . . hot cherry Jell-O always made me feel better. . . .

I remember you always being the homeroom mom at school . . . making the cupcakes, going on field trips, decorating carnival booths. . . .

I remember you always being there to support me in all my endeavors . . . from making mud pies to learning to read to thinking I was a great actress, basketball player, public speaker, and singer. . . . I never thought about failure because you made me feel like the sky was the limit. . . .

I remember you driving countless miles and enduring hours of waiting while all of us took piano, guitar, organ, and voice lessons . . . your love of music, and the message, was passed on to your children . . . I can still hear you singing "by and by when the morning comes, when the saints of God are gathered home" from the kitchen when you were cooking. . . .

I remember the great meals you prepared for us . . . and now that I'm a mom, I am in awe of the special meals you prepared for us daily . . . what a gift I now realize it was to have a mom who was a great cook and added love to every meal . . . your grandkids truly wish I had inherited this trait. . . .

I remember going to church . . . there was never a question about going . . . you set the example . . . I remember you always being a teacher . . . and now I share that joy each week with a whole new generation of kids . . . I remember laying my head in your lap and listening to the preacher while you stroked my hair . . . I knew you loved me just by that touch. . . .

I remember getting a new dress every Easter . . . the excitement of going to Cloth World and picking out material for our new outfits . . . I remember Tom always hating this!

I remember no matter what my gift was to you, it was always the very best in your eyes . . . from mud pies, dandelions and buttercups picked when I was riding my bike, to wood carvings from art class . . . you taught me about being appreciative and thankful. . . .

I remember watching you care for your mom . . . your strong character came from her . . . you honored and loved her and cared for her with such devotion . . . and when she was gone, we knew she lived on through you . . . I hope I will be able to do that for you. . . .

I remember the heartache that all of your kids caused you at some point in time during our lives . . . and how you managed to still love us and let us find our way . . . I hope you are now proud of who we have become . . . you can take a lot of credit for the people we are today. . . .

I remember the hugs and kisses . . . I'm so glad I had a mom who knew how important it was to a child to have these given freely and frequently . . . I love the fact that you still give me these, and I cherish them as much now as I did growing up. . . .

I am so thankful to have so many things to remember . . . and hope that I'll be able to keep adding to my Mom memory book for many years to come . . . you are my friend, my confidant, my prayer partner, and supporter . . . God truly blessed me with a great mother. . . .

". . . A woman who fears the Lord, she shall be praised . . . her children will rise up and call her blessed." Proverbs 31:28, 30

Happy Mother's Day 1997

Tips:

Why not grab a paper and pen and write a note like this to someone you love?

Share Family Tasks

The Idea:

It is important in all families that tasks are shared; however, it becomes harder to pass on the baton of responsibility to adult children. One of the ways is to have sign-up sheets prepared in advance for group get-togethers.

"Oh, that? I thought I told you. "Dateline NBC is going to feature us in a segment titled "Working Couples: Who Does the Brunt of the Housework?""

The Idea in Action:

🎁 One of our family friends has devised a wonderful way to share responsibilities when a number of family members get together at holiday or vacation times. A sign-up sheet is prepared and sent out ahead of time, and each person signs up for the following during the time they are together:

> *Other things may change us, but we start and end with family.*
>
> —Anthony Brandt

One cleanup after mealtime
Cook one dinner
Bring one item to share

The mother says it is really fun to watch some of the guys in the kitchen—*and* difficult sometimes not to jump in and do it all herself. However, she has learned the joy of sharing along with all of the children, and I suspect they all appreciate her much more when they realize what she did for them all those years!

Even when the children were in high school, they were being pre-

"They're done! HA HA! All the school lunches are done for the next 186 days! No more getting up at 6 a.m.! No more messy sandwiches! No more. . . ."

pared to share. Each of them signed up to cook dinner one weekend night a month and to clean up one weekend night.

🎁 Another idea suggested by Victoria Moran in her book *Shelter for the Spirit* is "Fifty-Two Pickup." She says, "Choose any number (fifteen or twenty is more realistic) and pick up that number of items around your house. You can count a dish put away, a newspaper folded, a coat hung up, or a book returned to the shelf." If everyone in the family picks up fifteen things a day, it will cut cleaning time and keep your home neat.

Tips:

It is important to have full support from both parents for this to work—and they must each sign up or participate, too! The wonderful result is that everyone gets to have a good time, and one person doesn't have the full responsibility of cooking and cleaning up.

No Child Is an Island

The Idea:

It is so important for us all to remember that no child can survive alone. We all have a part in raising our children in our homes, our schools, and in our communities.

The Idea in Action:

🎁 Recently I had the wonderful privilege of speaking in Newfoundland, Canada. While I was there, I met Dr. Myrle Vokey, the executive director of the Newfoundland and Labrador School Boards Association. In his office he had the most touching poster of a child, and I asked him about it.

He shared that they had hosted a National School Boards Conference in Newfoundland in 1994, and they had chosen the theme "No Child Is an Island." A local artist, a retired teacher named Robin Cook, drew the poster, and they prepared the following song to use as an accompaniment:

NO CHILD IS AN ISLAND

(anon. music arranged by Eric West
New lyrics by Myrle Vokey and Eric West)

No child is an island,
No child stands alone;
Each child's joy is joy to me.
Each child's grief is my own.
We need love and sharing,
So this wish we send:
All those who are caring,
Will you be my friend?

At the end of the conference the entire group held hands and sang this song.

Tips:

What a powerful message this poster and song share! Please think about the children in your own life, whether they are your offspring, your students, or your neighbors. Do not let them be an island.

Have a "My Family Is Special" Day

The Idea:

We need to help our children have a deep sense of belonging and pride in their family, regardless of what age they are. Perhaps once a month or once every quarter, have a "My Family Is Special" Day.

The Idea in Action:

📦 Here is a suggested plan for the day:

1. Everyone draw a picture of your family. Then share your pictures with the whole family. (These can be saved in a scrapbook as delightful memories.)

2. Decide on some family favorites. (These may change, although my guess is that they will become traditions):
- Our family's favorite dessert:
- Our family's favorite outing:
- Our family's favorite restaurant:
- Our family's favorite book/movie/song:

Add whatever "favorites" here that might be appropriate to your family.

3. Decide on a family slogan or motto. Some examples might be:
We Always Stick Together
God First; Family Second; Then the Rest of the World
You might even create a family cheer!

4. Write a family mission statement—what does your family value, what do you stand for, how is your family going to contribute to the world? If your children are small, begin with their words and rewrite the mission statement as they grow. To work, it MUST be meaningful to every member of the family.

5. Prepare a sheet for each person called "What My Family Likes About Me." Put the person's name at the top.

BARBARA

NAME _____ COMMENTS _____
_____
_____

NAME _____ COMMENTS _____
_____
_____

NAME _____ COMMENTS _____
_____
_____

Then have everyone sit in a circle and have one family member at a time sit in the middle. Have each person in the family tell two things they really like about that person. Encourage them to be creative and not use generic things like, "She's nice." Perhaps the first time you do this or with younger children, have one of the parents go first as a model: "I like that Gretchen is always concerned about the whole family and fairness, and she always remembers things that are important to each one of us." (Then everyone shares what they like about Gretchen.) "I like that Erin is always singing and making us laugh, and she helps us remember what is really important in life." (Then everyone shares what they like about Erin.) "I like that Garrett always helps us learn something new, and he brings many friends to our home." (Then everyone shares what they like about Garrett, and so on.) As you're sharing, designate one person as the secretary and write all the comments down on each person's sheet. At the end of each family member's time in the spotlight, give them their sheet of affirmations to keep and reread whenever they need encouragement.

6. End with a special celebration—perhaps sharing your favorite dessert or going out for ice cream or reading a story together. If you are a praying family, this is a wonderful time to say a prayer for each person and her immediate needs and then for the whole family, thanking God that He made you a family.

Tips:

You may want to add other ideas to this list. Vary your activities depending on the ages of your children. The most important thing is that everyone leaves feeling pride, a sense of belonging, and appreciation for one another. YOUR FAMILY IS SPECIAL!

Create a Family Mission Statement

The Idea:

Bonnie Michaels, the president of Managing Work and Family in Evanston, Illinois, suggests the importance of creating a family mission statement:

Creating Family Mission Statements with all members of the family helps to keep creative communication alive. In our busy world we don't take enough time to talk to each other as family members. Oftentimes, busy parents only have time to delegate responsibilities or are so tired from their busy work schedules that creative communication is lost. The new technical world of computer games and the Internet has also taken away from family interactions. Working together on a Family Mission Statement brings family members to a setting where all are equal and can express their individual desires. Each member can be heard and recognized for his or her beliefs.

This activity also promotes an atmosphere and appreciation for what other members of the family are trying to accomplish—what's important to them. It clarifies each family member's role, which leads to respect for each other's place in the family system. Just like corporate mission statements, the Family Mission Statements help families to work together for common goals that have been previously agreed upon.

> **The question is not whether we will die, but how we will live.**
>
> —Joan Borysenko

Equally important is the understanding it promotes among family members who previously may have been less empathetic or enthusiastic about family rituals. When there is open expression, in a problem-solving environment, for the reasons behind decisions that affect family members, there is often more empathy for that person. It can also trigger enthusiasm, which promotes creative ways to assist that family member instead of sabotaging the idea.

The Idea in Action:

These are some ways Bonnie suggests a family can create a mission statement:

Timing—Choose a time when family members have fewer responsibilities, possibly a Saturday evening or Sunday afternoon.

Advance Planning—Give advance notice that you would like the entire family to meet. Be clear that it is important and not to schedule anything in that time slot.

Promote an Atmosphere of Fun—Hold your first meeting in a place that is comfortable and less formal. Provide some refreshments like popcorn, cookies, or snacks.

FAMILY MISSION DISCUSSION:

Step 1—Discuss with family members the importance of working together for common goals so that there is more harmony and understanding of each other's values and needs.

Step 2—Continue the discussion by asking each member of the family to contribute ideas on the following topics:
1. What does a family mean to you?
2. What do you think the family should do together?
3. What is important to you?

Step 3—After the open discussion, determine what actions the family needs to take in order to promote the mission statement. For example:

1. Planning schedules regularly to ensure family gatherings _____ times a week.
2. Setting up schedules where family members can participate in household chores; setting up systems for children; determining rewards, consequences, etc.
3. Meeting regularly with family members and discussing issues that may arise during the week. Setting up a communication system so that all members can participate and express ideas, feelings, etc., without judgment.
4. Encouraging activities that allow family members to play together and have fun.
5. Determining what spirituality means to children and discussing with spouse ways to encourage it formally and informally.
6. Exploring better ways to develop new family rituals or traditions and still retain some rituals and traditions from the historical ways.
7. Exploring better ways to stay connected with family members while traveling.
8. Role-modeling open affection and acceptance of each family member's differences.

SOME FAMILY MISSION STATEMENT EXAMPLES:

Our family's mission is to work together for harmony, spirituality, and be a bridge from the historical family. We wish to encourage openness, laughter, learning, acceptance, and appreciation of each other's ideas and feelings.

Our mission is to stay afloat financially and to provide quality emotional support for each member.

> **We can help another find out the meaning of life . . . But in the last analysis, each is responsible for "finding himself."**
>
> **—Thomas Merton**

Out family's mission is to listen to each other's ideas and needs and work together to accommodate them. We wish to understand each other better and work toward a cooperative household.

Our family's mission is to provide a nurturing environment where ideas and feelings are accepted and not judged. We wish to incorporate more family activities into our daily lives while still leaving time for individual activities. We wish to understand more about our grandparents and their parents and incorporate some of their traditions into our daily lives.

Tips:

Here are some helpful suggestions Bonnie has for making this process productive and fun:

1. For younger children, you may have to give some examples to get the discussion started.
2. For older children, you may have to deal with skepticism. Be patient and encourage the expression of all ideas.
3. Post the Family Mission Statement in a prominent place when it's finished.
4. Refer to it as goals get accomplished.
5. Have a follow-up family meeting to discuss its progress.
6. Keep a sense of humor. Don't be judgmental. Remember this is for the family and not for work. The process is what is important.
7. Your family mission may change as you and your family members change.
8. The Family Mission Statement may take several meetings to get finalized.

REMEMBER THE GOALS:

- To bring the family together for: **Creative Communication**
- To create an **Atmosphere** of **Appreciation** for all members
- To promote: **Respect** and **Reason for Being, Empathy,** and **Enthusiasm**

Find Ways to Take Care of Our World

The Idea:

St. Francis of Assisi in the early thirteenth century started a Christmas tradition of helping nature by "wishing extra hay and corn for the animals in honor of those present in the nativity." In the 1900s Germans placed corn on their roofs at Christmas, and Scandinavians set out sheaves of grain on poles for the animals. Now one neighborhood family in La Grange, Illinois, has found their special way of helping care for Mother Nature.

The Idea in Action:

Suzie Tatum read about some of these traditions and decided to start one of her own for her neighborhood. Each year at Christmastime the Tatums send out lovely invitations to the children on their block to make handmade edible ornaments to hang on their "nature tree," a fifteen-foot-tall evergreen outside their home. The children bring a variety of cereal strung on ribbon; rice cakes iced with peanut butter and coconut; birdseed and suet ornaments. Tatum suggests other ornaments like dried corn cobs, which need to be collected in the fall, tied with bright red bows on top. Also many items covered with peanut butter work well. She says, "The coconut and peanut butter is good for the birds. It gives them energy and helps their system in the winter." They hang the ornaments the children bring with ribbon or raffia so that the birds can take it off and make a nest later in the spring.

Suzie and her husband, Mike, and daughters Olivia, twenty months, and Sophie, four, prepare the birds for the tree trimming by spreading corn around the base of the tree. They also hang a feeder two weeks prior to the party so that the birds get used to coming to the tree. Suzie describes the tree-trimming party: "It's really fun! The first year we started, it was cold and snowing. It was so pretty! We sang Christmas carols and ate cookies in the snow as we decorated the tree."

After the tree is decorated, the neighbors can watch the ornaments disappear as the birds and squirrels delight in the food. Tatum, who had strung frozen waffles covered with peanut butter, birdseed, and coconut, watched as a bird carried it off in one piece. On Stone Avenue in

LaGrange, Christmas is truly "for the birds"! Suzie hopes her closeknit neighborhood will continue the tradition.

🎁 Karen Sivert tells of how she taught her grandchildren a beautiful lesson about our special world:

One spring afternoon my grandchildren and I planted some sprouting potatoes in the garden. As they dug each hole, they were more excited about the worms they discovered than the potatoes. Months later at harvesting time, with a "treasure hunt" attitude, we headed for the potato patch. As the shovel lifted the potatoes from each plant, squeals of excitement and disbelief were heard. This was a special lesson in God's provisions.

Tips:

It takes only one caring person to start a tradition in a neighborhood. An unknown person anonymously shares his or her appreciation of nature in lovely Lithia Park in Ashland, Oregon. In different spots in the park every week, this nature lover creates an artistic arrangement of flower petals, berries, seeds, leaves, pods, twigs, and other natural items. It is a delightful surprise for anyone using the park, and no one has yet discovered who the gifted artist is. What might you or your family do to help celebrate and preserve our world?

Create a "Dream List"

The Idea:

One Mother's Day I asked, as my gift, for my family to watch the video *Do Right* by Lou Holtz. I figured they couldn't gripe too much if that was what I asked for for Mother's Day! It was a powerful video, and one of the things he mentioned was how he had created a "dream list" of the one hundred things he wanted to do before he died and how much fun it was to have a focus and to check things off his list as he completed them. He also encouraged other people to dream—to write down things that were deep wishes for them, in his case, things like "Having dinner with the president" and "Landing on an aircraft carrier."

The Idea in Action:

 As a result of watching that video, I encouraged each of our children to write things down on their own "dream list." This is the list our daughter Erin, who was eleven years old at the time, wrote down:

1. Be a high-school cheerleading coach
2. Teach preschool or kindergarten for one year
3. Be a lawyer
4. Be a model
5. Have a criminal case and win (lawyer)
6. Run a day-care center for a while
7. Have twins
8. Direct a play or musical
9. Have a lead role in a musical
10. Design some clothes
11. Own my own "party store"
12. Record my own song (singing)
13. Compose a song
14. Be a dancer
15. Be a pediatrician
16. Be in show choir
17. Be in either cheerleading or pom-pon at school
18. Be an actress (movie)
19. Be a deejay for a while
20. Be a ski instructor
21. Make a famous painting or drawing
22. Get asked to homecoming
23. Be in Madrigals
24. Be in the National Honor Society
25. Collect over five hundred pennies
26. Invent my own recipe
27. Be on TV for something
28. Be in a circus
29. Write an advice column
30. Write a book or novel
31. Get tanned in Hawaii
32. Get married and have at least two dogs
33. Be a fashion consultant
34. Be a makeup artist
35. Have a surprise party
36. Be a book illustrator
37. Be five-feet-seven and 110 pounds
38. Dye or highlight my hair
39. Go to a U2 concert
40. Be a photographer
41. Direct a choir for junior high girls
42. Work at a fashion clothes store
43. Get my ears triple-pierced on one side
44. Be a hair designer
45. Design some makeup

Not only did Erin have fun making up this list, but she nearly died laughing when I gave it to her again last year at age twenty! She was amazed both at how "silly" some of the things she wanted were and also at how many of them she has already done.

Tips:

This is a wonderful family activity. It really helps to see what is important to each member of your family and what their real dreams are. Sometimes we need to be encouraged to dream and not always be so tied to reality. Also, the list becomes a focus—if we've never written it down, we will probably never do it, and sometimes (in fact, many times, I believe) our dreams do come true!

Do Special "Grandma" Things

The Idea:

I can hardly wait to be a grandma! For those of you who are blessed with grandchildren, start now to create special traditions with them. They may be even more important to them than their own family traditions because they will be so special.

The Idea in Action:

Karen Sivert tells of some things you can do with your grandchildren:

- Make Christmas ornaments with them to give to teachers and create special gifts to give their parents.
- Take a picture of your grandchildren each month and place the photos in an album to present to their parents for Christmas. (Of course, keep a photo set for your album as well!)
- Keep the grandchildren for an evening or a weekend to give their parents a "date time" and to make some special moments with the grandchildren. (My father used to help Garrett make "forts" out of furniture and blankets when he was little.)
- One grandmother takes all six of her grandchildren for a week's vacation in the summer. They enjoy trips to places like Santa's Village, the zoo, and a picnic in the park.

One special thing my mother, Lucille Bauerle, did for our children starting when Garrett was very little was to send them special decorations for every holiday—a ceramic jack-o'-lantern with a lightbulb inside for Halloween; real eggs hung on ribbon which have hand- painted designs of flowers, nursery rhyme characters, and animals to make an Easter egg tree; a Halloween witch; a Santa plate for cookies; and many others. Each year the children looked forward to getting these special holiday decorations out, and they became part of our family traditions.

In an article titled "Being an Effective Grandmother," Elma S. Bradshaw suggests the greatest gifts to give a grandchild are:

THE GIFT OF CARING—Take an interest in the world of your grandchildren:

- Listen to little ones tend their baby doll or play with a pet. (You can gain insight into how they feel about themselves and their world.)
- Play house with the preschooler and you be the child. (It's surprising what you can learn.)
- Get down on the floor and talk to him or her face to face at eye level. (It helps to see things from that point of view.)
- Make it a habit to attend the events in which the grandchild participates.
- Let your grandchild practice a speech or instrumental number before you prior to the big performance.
- Listen—really listen—with your ears, eyes, and heart to a teen grandchild who has a problem.

THE GIFT OF SELF-WORTH—He or she likes to feel important and to have evidence that what has been done or said is of value:

- Let him see you using the homemade gift he or she created just for you—thank him again for it from time to time.

- Compliment your grandchild in the presence of others.
- Ask him or her to make a centerpiece for the dinner table.
- Provide all the opportunities you can for your grandchild to succeed in varied tasks or activities.
- Write your grandchild a letter on his birthday and list in it all the special qualities he or she has that you admire.

THE GIFT OF HERITAGE—Everyone wants to know who he or she is and who he or she belongs to. Grandparents are children's bridges to the past:

- Write letters or prepare a taped message if they live in a distant city. Tell them what you did as a child when you were their age.
- Write your life story. Give copies to your married children with instructions to share your story with their children.
- Share your old photo album with a grandchild. Tell about the people in the pictures and encourage him or her to start keeping a picture album.
- Write the histories of your own mother and father (their great-grandparents). Then hold a Family Home Evening with your married children at which time you can read the history you have compiled.

THE GIFT OF TEACHING—Most grandmothers have a little more discretionary time than the mother of their grandchildren, so:

- Teach a child to cook his or her favorite food.
- Teach a child to pound nails into a block of wood.
- Teach a child to plant a garden.
- Teach a child a new art or craft.
- Teach a teenage grandchild how to shop wisely in the supermarket. Compare brands, prices, quality, and sizes.
- Teach a child a new song, poem, nursery rhyme, or story.

THE GIFT OF CREATIVITY—Creativity begins with the stimulation of the brain at a very early age in children. Giving even a small baby a variety of interesting things to look at, listen to, touch, feel, and manipulate helps him or her to sort many different images and ideas in his or her mind which he or she can draw on in later life.

- It can be as simple as pointing out, during snack time, that green peas are round and will roll like a ball, while cheese cubes won't.

Or, while on a walk and looking at a house, you might say, "My, isn't this house a tall one? Do you think it is an old house or a new one? What do you think it is made of—bricks or wood or cement?" The wider a child's variety of experience, the greater is his creative potential.

- When our children were infants I placed different, bright-colored fabric shapes all round the bumper pads in our babies' cribs for them to look at. I also took a ribbon and pinned the toe of their sleeper to the crib mobile so that soon they learned that when they kicked, they could make the mobile shake—cause and effect! A plastic pouch with goldfish (real ones) in it is also wonderfully interesting for a baby who has not yet developed enough to move around.

Tips:

A grandmother can make many wonderful memories for her grandchildren. Have fun and enjoy the time you have together.

Give Gifts of Support and Hope

"Adversity is not without comfort and hope."
—Francis Bacon

The Idea:

In difficult times, we can help give others a reason for being and new hope through gifts that create a sense of support and caring.

The Idea in Action:

Chrissy Hancock of Norman, Oklahoma, tells of a way her mother made a wonderful difference during a time of national crisis:

After the bombing of the Alfred P. Murrah Building in Oklahoma City, my mother, Karen White, felt like she wanted to do something to help spread cheer and support for our state and nation. She and my father had visited the bombing site and had just left the parade honoring the rescue workers when she saw a young woman wearing a flag pin made of safety pins and beads. She asked the woman where she had gotten it, and when the woman saw how much my mother liked it, she gave it to her.

After that day, my mother made hundreds of these flag pins and did the same for those who loved

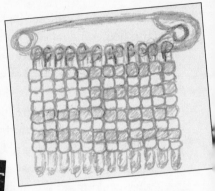

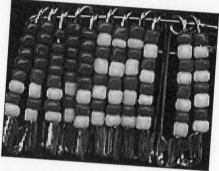

hers. Each time someone showed a genuine interest in her pin, she took it off and gave it to that person. At a time when our city, state, and nation needed it the most, my mother sent her own CARE package to the world!

Carol Ann Cole of Halifax, Nova Scotia, in cooperation with the Canadian Cancer Society, has created the Comfort Heart Initiative in support of cancer research. This is how Carol Ann describes it:

Our Story . . .

In January of 1992, my mother and I were both diagnosed with breast cancer. Within a few weeks we both faced diagnoses, surgery, and decisions regarding treatment. The month became a blur of hospitals and doctors' offices for our entire family. I survived; my mother did not. Radiation treatments gave her eleven months of precious time with her four daughters. On December 20, 1992, two days before my mom's seventy-seventh birthday, cancer took her life.

Our Beginning . . .

Around this time I began putting my personal experience to positive use, lending support and understanding to women with breast cancer. On a visit home to Nova Scotia, I purchased several "Worry Hearts" produced by Oceanart Pewter in Prospect Bay. Both I, and the women with whom I spent time, found it soothing to hold the heart during times of distress. Before long I had given out more than one hundred hearts. I knew there was a source of mutual strength and support from all the "holders of the heart." I also realized the potential existed to accomplish much more.

Our Growth . . .

The Comfort Heart Initiative, dedicated to the memory of my mother, Mary Cole, has grown from that small beginning. Two friends joined my Comfort Heart Team. We approached the owner of Oceanart Pewter with a plan to produce a

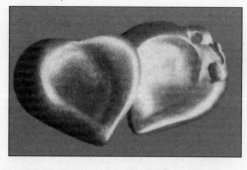

special "Comfort Heart" to raise money for cancer research, and they agreed wholeheartedly. We then approached the Canadian Cancer Society and our idea was met with enthusiasm and support. The Comfort Heart is now available for ten dollars, including shipping and handling and taxes. From every purchase, net proceeds in excess of six dollars go to cancer research.

Our Hopes and Goals . . .

Comfort Hearts are one small way to unite together to win the battle against cancer and to gain strength from each other as we cope with our own personal battles. It is our wish that every Comfort Heart will bring moments of comfort, solace, calm, and hope to each and every friend and supporter. Corporations can give to their community by purchasing hearts for volunteers to offer cancer patients on the corporation's behalf, and the Comfort Heart

is an original and lasting gift that individuals can purchase for those who are dear to them. Our financial goal is to raise one million dollars through the sale of Comfort Hearts. We can do it—with your help. Thank you—from the heart!

See the Resource section at the end of the book to find out how to order a Comfort Heart.

Tips:

What beautiful gifts of love, hope, and caring these both are! Chrissy and her mom have blessed me with my own flag pin, and I have given several Comfort Hearts to friends who are ill. The lovely pewter heart has an indentation in the middle just the size of one's thumb, and I have found it deeply comforting to hold during anxious times. What gifts of comfort and hope have you found to help make some sense from otherwise senseless situations?

This is one of my favorite songs by David Roth. It is based on a true AIDS-related story. I am always deeply touched by the sense of purpose and love that John and Josie express, a noble REASON FOR BEING:

John and Josie

John and Josie's only child, young and handsome, fast and wild
Joined the army at eighteen, left the army at eighteen
Drifted then from job to job, town to town, and love to love
Seven years forever till young Johnny came marching home

But Johnny wasn't looking well, went into the hospital
Days turned into several weeks, Johnny kept on losing weight
Josie said to John, "Sit down . . .", John cried, "Oh God, not my son"
Johnny left at twenty-five, a hole as big as Jupiter

Nothing stronger than the love John and Josie had for Johnny
Threw him his last birthday party, no one from the family came
No one from the family came, turned John and Josie's grief to shame
Shame to anger, anger pain, nothing they needed more of

Two years gone, the telephone is ringing in the dim-lit den
Beneath the wooden crucifix that John had punched the day he learned
That Johnny wouldn't live much longer, now a voice said to his father
"John, we have a baby here and no one seems to want him . . .

The baby doesn't have his parents, two months old and with their virus
Josie grabbed the phone from John, the two of them said, "Yes, yes, yes"
So John and Josie, over sixty, taking in a brand new baby
Named him Paul Antonio, Johnny would have loved him

Nothing stronger than the love that John and Josie had for Johnny
The same love that they have for Paul, they're starting up the wheel again
And of the fear the same thing could happen, losing Paul before his time
    comes
John and Josie look right past it, they're basking in love's mighty presence

John and Josie don't have time, they're basking in love's mighty presence

CHAPTER SEVEN:

E = Empathy

"CARE for the World Both Inside and Outside Your Doors"

There are two ways of spreading light:
to be the candle or the mirror that reflects it.

—Edith Wharton

SPORTY KING, A WONDERFUL FRIEND in Professional Speakers of Illinois, shared with me this lovely thought from Hugh Prather's *The Quiet Answer*. It speaks powerfully about empathy:

JUDGING

Today I will allow all things to be.
I will judge nothing.
I am willing for the weather to be whatever it is.
I am content to have each encounter that is to come. Nor will I resist
    the circumstances in which I am placed.
I will let my friends act however they will.
I will not remain with one word spoken or a single gesture or act.

Instead, I will release my attention from censure to rest on this
gentle moment.

I will allow each member of my family to be what he is, without
defining what he is.

I will attempt to see my children as they are, without interpretations
drawn from my experience and free of motivations I have attributed
to myself.

I will not assign my spouse's role or function or attitude toward me.

I will not cherish a wish for a shift in personality or habits, nor
will I try to push anyone in a direction by moderating my joy or with-
holding my normal responses.

I will let all people be just as they are today, and in this stillness
of thought I will ask what God sees in each one, that He made him
His own beloved child.

Someone once described *empathy* as "your pain in my heart." Although I
think we all have the capacity for empathy as human beings, I also think
empathy must be taught and modeled. In a family there are several levels of
empathy: parents' empathy for their children and the painful experiences of
growing up they must face; family members' empathy for one another and the
different life experiences of each one; empathy for others, especially those less
fortunate, in the world outside of the family; and even children's empathy for
their parents and grandparents and the difficult experience of aging and the
often overwhelming responsibilities of raising a family.

As we each learn to try to experience life from another person or group's
perspective, it broadens our awareness and helps us to find a common "humanness" in our world. In a family there are many activities that can help family
members to better understand one another and their world. I have included
many of these in this chapter as well as many ideas of how to give something
back as a family to this world. One of the responsibilities I think we need to
continually teach each other is a social responsibility, that we all must give
something of ourselves and our blessings to help make this world a better
place. If children are taught to do this as they are growing up, hopefully they
will continue to give back as adults.

Listen with Your Heart

The Idea:

Always listen with both your head (Business level) and your heart (Human level). In fact, the Chinese use this symbol for listening:

Note that on one side is the symbol of the ear, listening with your intellect. However, the other side is made up of several symbols: "you," listening with your full personhood; "the eyes," listening for body language; "undivided attention," listening with your full being; and "the heart," the cornerstone of listening.

The Idea in Action:

A friend shared this story with me:

Boca Raton, Florida, October 6, 1997

Last week I took my children to a restaurant. My six-year-old son asked if he could say grace. As we bowed our heads, he said, "God is good. God is great. Thank you for the food, and I would even thank you more if Mom gets us ice cream for dessert. And liberty and justice for all! Amen."

Along with the laughter from the other customers nearby, I heard a woman remark, "That's what's wrong with this country. Kids today don't even know how to pray. Asking God for ice cream! Why, I never!"

Hearing this, my son burst into tears and asked me, "Did I do it wrong? Is God mad at me?"

As I held him and assured him that he had done a terrific job and God was not mad at him, an elderly gentleman approached the table. He winked at my son and said, "I happen to know that God thought that was a great prayer."

"Really?" my son asked.

"Cross my heart." Then in a theatrical whisper he added (indicating the woman whose remark had started this whole thing), "Too bad she never asks God for ice cream. A little ice cream is good for the soul sometimes."

Naturally, I bought my kids ice cream at the end of the meal. My son stared at his for a moment and then did something I will remember the rest of my life. He picked up his sundae and without a word walked over and placed it in front

Close to Home © John McPherson/Dist. by Universal Press Syndicate.

An unwavering truth of grocery shopping with a toddler: Your child will throw a tantrum, and it will invariably happen when your minister, pediatrician and mother-in-law are walking by.

of the woman. With a big smile he told her, "Here, this is for you. Ice cream is good for the soul sometimes and my soul is good already."

Out of the mouths of babes comes Jesus shining through.

Tips:

This is a wonderful example of one person who listened with her head and another who listened with his heart. Always ask yourself, "Am I listening with my heart?"

This is a poem from St. Michaels Lutheran Church in Hamburg, Pennsylvania:

LISTEN TO THE CHILDREN

Take a moment to listen today
To what your children are trying to say.
Listen today, whatever you do,
Or they won't be there to listen to you.

Listen to their problems, listen to their needs.
Praise their smallest triumphs, praise their smallest deeds.
Tolerate their chatter, amplify their laughter;
Find out what's the matter, find out what they're after.

But tell them that you love them,
Every single night,
And though you scold them, make sure you hold them
And tell them everything's all right.

If we tell our children, all the bad in them we see,
They'll grow up exactly how we hoped they'd never be.

But if we tell our children we're so proud they wear our name,
They'll grow up believing they're winners in the game.

Take a moment to listen today
To what your children are trying to say;
Listen today, whatever you do,
And they will come back to listen to you.

It seems to me that this beautiful poem applies to *any* relationship!

Walk a Mile in the Other Person's Shoes

The Idea:

Not only must we listen with our hearts, but we also need to think about the feelings of others. Sensitivity to another's pain is one of the greatest gifts we can give to family members, neighbors, and others with whom we interact.

The Idea in Action:

🎁 I recently read the following letter in the "Dear Abby" column in the November 29, 1997, edition of the *Chicago Tribune*:

Dear Abby: I am 10 years old and in 5th grade. All my life I have been chosen last. That's my problem.

P.E. is my least favorite class in school, not because I don't like sports—I enjoy them. But it is so humiliating always being chosen last. I dread going to school on days when I know we will have P.E.

Why can't physical education teachers use a different system? P.E. teachers must have never had to experience what I have each day in P.E. I will go into the class again tomorrow to be chosen last.

Why don't they just hang a sign on me that says, "Reject. Last one to pick gets me."

I'm sure there are other kids who feel the same way. There is one in every P.E. class. It really hurts. My mom says not to let it bother me.

Please don't say, "Practice the sport and you'll be great at it and everyone will want you on their team." It doesn't work that way. I'm kind of quiet, and

even if you're not bad at the sport, once you've been chosen last you will be last next week, the week after, and next year too.
   What can I do?

Always Chosen Last, Scottsdale, Arizona

Tips:

Each time I read this poignant letter, my eyes fill with tears and my heart aches—for the ten-year-old child who wrote the letter, for myself in many similar situations growing up, and for all the people in our world who are "chosen last." Why can't we be more sensitive to others' feelings and not so focused on systems? Surely there have been times in each of our lives when we have been chosen last. Remember what that felt like. Wherever you are in your family or career, right now think of ways that you, your family, or your organization unconsciously set up ranking systems that make some people last. For the sake of this child and the hurting child within all of us, vow to do everything you can to find other ways to accomplish the task at hand and still keep everyone's self-esteem intact.

   Whenever I work with any kind of group, I arrange teams in creative, nonthreatening ways such as by birthday months or the colors they have on, their favorite holiday or cartoon character, or the first letter of their middle name. I remember and acknowledge the discomfort and fear that occurs even in a group of adults and especially in groups of fragile young children when they may be chosen last. Never ever let that happen in your presence again!

Do a Project to Help Others

The Idea:

Let your children discover the joy of helping others by volunteering for projects the family can do together.

The Idea in Action:

🎁 Look around your neighborhood to find projects that will help others. Perhaps you can do yard work for an elderly person or bake muffins for a retirement home or homeless shelter. Perhaps you can adopt a grandparent if you do not have one close by. I heard about two maiden ladies in Chicago who decided that their block needed to be cleaned up. One summer day they rounded up all the children on the block from ages five to twelve and asked them if they'd like to help. The city of Chicago donated rakes, brooms, garbage bags, and trash cans. The group spent most of the day picking up debris, beer cans, and other litter and packing it into the garbage bags. At the end of the afternoon, the ladies invited all the children to their front porch for cookies and lemonade. The pride was evident on the expressions on the children's faces when they saw the result of their working together. It takes only a few people to make a big difference!

I recently heard a wonderful idea to encourage young people to help others. A teacher at the College of DuPage in Lombard, Illinois, told the class that they could be exempt from taking the final *if* they found a volunteer task to fulfill. As a result, many college students found meaningful ways to help others. What that teacher was teaching was far more important in life than any subject matter!

Some families make a service project a part of their vacation. When one family took everyone to Hawaii for ten days, the whole family spent two of those days working with Habitat for Humanity, putting a roof on a building that had been damaged by a hurricane. What a wonderful lesson for us all—they spent two days thinking of someone else along with their eight days of fun!

Oliver Truitt of East Camden, New Jersey, is making a difference in his neighborhood, according to a September 1997 article in "Heroes for Today," *The Reader's Digest*. Truitt, seventy-five, decided to take on a challenge after retirement. As he looked out the window of his brick-front house on Mickle Street, he noticed, "Nobody cleaned the street; it was dirty all the time. I don't want anyone driving by to think the people on this block don't care." So, every morning for the past thirteen years, Truitt has been outside with broom in hand, sweeping up trash, bottles, and nails.

He also volunteers his time at nearby Woodrow Wilson High School, where he mows the football field and rakes the long-jump pit. All of this is done voluntarily. The high school principal says, "Whatever needs to be done, he's there. The students have a role model. He shows that when one person has talent to share, it enriches everyone."

In my hometown of Harlan, Iowa, the eighth graders have a very special service project. They advertise on the front page of the local paper that anyone in the community can call them to have their leaves raked in the fall—and this is done for no pay.

Tips:

If you are looking for a project, go to your village offices and ask them for suggestions. As you walk around your neighborhood, keep in mind that this, too, is your home. How might you make it a better place to live?

Teach Your Children to CARE for Others

The Idea:

Encourage your children to do something for others on a regular basis. Even little children can do things for others. John Drescher in his book *If I Were Starting My Family Again* quotes a writer who says, "Work to them is sharing, a sense of belonging, a knowledge that they are individually needed and important to the welfare of the entire family unit."

The Idea in Action:

Norm Swift tells of a neighboring family, the Poynters in Beverly, Illinois, with ten children. One day one of the children knocked on Norm's father's door and asked if he could take his garbage out to the street. Norm's father was delighted and got ready to give the youngster some money. The child responded, "Oh no, I don't want any pay. This is my good deed." His father found out later that each child in the family was required to do one thing for a neighbor once a week without any pay as his or her way of serving others and doing something good for the community. For several years Norm's father received the blessing of having his garbage taken out to the street!

Sylvia Marshall tells of a lesson about giving learned from her mother:

When I was a child, Mother taught us at an early age about the importance of giving and sharing. A day or two before Thanksgiving, Christmas, or at Easter, my sisters and I would gather around the dining-room table, sitting across from each other as we prepared special thanksgiving packages. Each colorful, tissue-filled package was filled with fresh fruit, nuts, candy, popcorn, and other treats that we fastened with colorful ribbon and then distributed to our less fortunate cousins and other needy children selected by my mother. The memory is as fresh today as it was then, even though my mother has been gone for about twenty years now.

It is also important to teach caring within one's own family. One of our family friends told us about a crisis in their family on Christmas Eve night. The youngest child's very special pet bunny was dying. A spontaneous decision was made by the whole family—they *all* went to the vet's office together. What a beautiful way to show support and caring to one they loved!

Tips:

What special ways these families had of teaching their children to care for others and to give something back to the world, no matter how young they were. It is important, however, that we as parents also model this behavior in our lives. How hypocritical it would be to require our children to do something that we did not live in our own actions!

> *Somehow the world is hungry for goodness and recognizes it when it sees it—and has an incredible response to the good. There's something in all of us that hungers after the good and true, and when we glimpse it in people, we applaud them for it. We long to be just a little like them. Through them we let the world's pain into our hearts, and we find compassion.*
>
> —Bishop Desmond Tutu, winner of the 1984 Nobel Peace Prize

Use Your Skills to Help Others

The Idea:

Find something you can do better and enjoy more than someone else, and then show them how much you care by sharing your gifts with them.

The Idea in Action:

🎁 Kathryn Bradford of Naperville, Illinois, shares how she "gives back" to her sister:

> Whenever I go home to Massachusetts, I always stay at my sister's house. She is a professor at Worchester State Teachers College. She has been at the college for thirty-plus years and is a wonderful teacher, mentor, and friend to her students. She spends so much time doing for others that she often finds herself suffocated by the jumble of things and articles she accumulates to share with others.
>
> I go home about twice a year, and I always organize her "junk" room for her—putting like things together and making neat piles for her. If I think something could possibly be thrown out, I make another pile of those things for her to go through for possible discard.
>
> I do this because she never has time and because she would never get through it if she did start on it. She is the type of person who loves to give but hates to receive, and this is one way I can show her I love her that she can accept.
>
> She also saves her tablecloths and linen napkins for me to iron. I hate ironing, but she knows I can handle this simple task and do so willingly. I don't know why, but I find it relaxing and satisfying to see the tablecloths and napkins neatly ironed and stacked for her. Since the ironing is done in the "junk" room, we get a chance to talk while she is going through the items I have marked for discard.

Kathryn has blessed her sister by using her gifts of organizing. I wish I had Kathryn visit my home twice a year!

🎁 The Russett family of Hyannis, Massachusetts, has a unique way of using their skills to benefit others. Because they were well known for their beautiful Christmas trees and helping others improve theirs, they created a "Christmas Tree Inspection" for their friends, neighbors, and communities.

Their flyer says:

Is your tree "legal"??
Experienced tree inspectors available for
festive examination of your holiday tree.
Inspection categories: Shape of tree, Lights, Decorations, etc.
Certificates of Authenticity issued at each inspection.
Inspections will be scheduled at mutually agreeable date/time.
$10 Inspection fee. Proceeds to benefit C.H.A.M.P.S. HOUSE.
The Russett Family Christmas Tree Inspection Company.
References furnished upon request.

Here is a copy of their Tree Inspection Checklist:

Christmas 1996

Tree Inspection Checklist
Home of:_____

Real Tree_____ or a FALSIE _____

Height: Ok for the room _____   Could be taller _____
         Recommend an addition _____   Too short _____

Shape: Good _____   Too skinny _____
         Big and round _____   Just right _____

Fresh: Yes _____   No _____

Decorations: Just right _____   Needs more _____
              Good homemade _____   Place well _____
              Too many _____

Lights: All white _____   Colored _____
         Mixed _____   Well Strung _____

We the undersigned, hereby approve your tree for the holiday season.

_____   _____
Tom Russett , Senior Inspector   Carolyn Russett, Asst. Inspector

_____   _____
Josh Russett, Associate   Tim Russett , Associate
      Inspector   Inspector

Russett Family Christmas Tree Inspection Company

Carolyn wrote to tell me their wonderful, heartwarming story:

This story starts eighteen years ago . . . my husband and I moved to Cape Cod from New York, which moved us quite a ways from both sides of our family. We didn't realize how much we would miss that until we started raising children. It was not easy to see family during the holiday seasons. Most were spent by ourselves and especially at Christmastime, it became a challenge to keep the kids occupied. On many occasions, we would connect with friends who were in the same situation and combine our holiday celebrations. We have a cathedral ceiling in our living room, and my husband has always gotten slightly out of control when it comes to buying a tree . . . we usually end up with at least a ten-footer, and my two boys have followed in his footsteps. We became known among our friends for having one of the most unique trees: not only large but with unique and different ornaments. If family couldn't come up for a weekend to help decorate it, we'd always invite friends over . . . they'd decorate, we'd feed them . . . Such a deal!

> **No man is an island, entire of itself; every man is a piece of the continent, a part of the main; if a clod be washed away by the sea, Europe is the less, as well as if a promontory were, as well as if a manor of thy friends or of thine own were; any man's death diminishes me, because I am involved in mankind; and therefore never send to know for whom the bell tolls; it tolls for thee.**
>
> **—John Donne**

One year, as the boys were older, we were kind of bored on Christmas afternoon, so we decided to go and "inspect" some of our friends' trees. We spent some time devising a "checklist" of items we would inspect—whether there were enough lights, size of the tree, ornaments, etc. So we made our rounds to a few homes, staying just long enough to lighten everyone up, but not too long to intrude on their holiday.

The following year, people asked us if we were going to do it again. We felt we had no choice—but again, we had an awfully good time! The following year as we contemplated yet another round of "inspections," we thought we should make it worth our while. Friends of ours had founded a shelter for homeless teenage boys who could not live at home for a variety of reasons. The shelter was new and greatly in need of money, clothing, etc., so we decided that we would charge five dollars per inspection with the proceeds going to C.H.A.M.P.S. House. We provided a certificate of authenticity for the inspection and made dated ornaments for their homes. We reasoned that even if we only raised a small amount of money, it could go into their petty cash fund to cover small items they rarely had money for. We were a success enough that people were looking for us again the following year.

This past holiday, my boys were seventeen and thirteen. I assumed they were too old to continue the practice . . . boy, was I wrong! When I mentioned that I thought we wouldn't do it this year, they couldn't believe it. My oldest figured this would be his last year since he was going away to school and assumed we would do it one last time. So once again we updated our certificates and prepared for inspections. Before we could sign people up, C.H.A.M.P.S. House suffered a tragic fire and all occupants were displaced. We thought this made our inspections even more important. We raised our fee to ten dollars. A coworker lined up fifteen people in her neighborhood to participate. Many were families that were both Christian and Jewish so we came up with a Hanukkah inspection also. We raised over three hundred dollars with many families writing checks for more than their inspection fee.

We also decided that those displaced persons would need a place for Christmas dinner, so we opened our home to twenty people. We had already done a family Thanksgiving dinner for twenty-five and a tree-trimming party for thirty-five . . . we knew that twenty would be a piece of cake! We asked people in our church if they would "adopt" a C.H.A.M.P.S. resident and purchase a Christmas present. The response was overwhelming—we even had people offering to help with the cooking. Others set up collection boxes in their workplaces and collected toiletries, which was another great need of the shelter.

Even though people do usually rally at the holiday season and do their best to provide extras whenever they can, individuals and businesses and workplaces came together in a unique way for a group that was truly in need this Christmas. And I do believe that my sons had the best time ever with their holiday tree inspections!

Not only are the Russetts helping people have prettier Christmas trees and donating money for a boys' shelter, but they are also having fun and working together as a family, using their special skills to help others have a more special Christmas.

Close to Home © John McPherson/Dist. by Universal Press Syndicate.

"For cryin' out loud, just pick one! He's never going to recognize it!"

The young son of a single mom announced after his father left that he wanted to help earn money, so he decided to sell popsicles to accomplish that goal. The mom made over thirty creative flavors that he sold to the employees of a factory across the street from their home. He placed a cooler in his red wagon and delivered the popsicles at break time to the factory employees. One year he earned enough to buy his own bicycle and a skateboard the next. He and his mom had fun making the popsicles, he helped out with the finances, *and* he learned some valuable selling skills!

Tips:

Sometimes the best gift we can give someone is our time, especially in our family. What are you good at and how could you share that with a family member or a friend?

Give "Angel Gifts"

The Idea:

Think of special ways you can give to others that will surprise them. These gifts are especially meaningful when they are given for no special reason except to show that you care. I call these "angel gifts" because they always seem to come at a time when you need them most.

The Idea in Action:

Two of the most special "angel gifts" I have ever received both came when I desperately needed encouragement and love. When our third child,

Erin, was born, Garrett was seven and Gretchen was two and a half. Just six weeks after her birth, Charlie hurt his back and was completely immobilized, leaving the full responsibility of caring for him, the house, and the children to me.

During the first week he was in bed, I (Super Mom in action!) was boiling water very late one night to make Easter eggs for the children to color the next day since it was Easter weekend and I had not been able to get to it before. At the same time I was talking with a friend whom I'd been too busy to call back earlier in the day. Cradling the phone between my ear and my chin, I carried the pot of eggs and boiling water over to the sink. While pouring the hot water out and trying to carry on a conversation at the same time, I accidentally dumped the boiling water all over my forearm and wrist, causing second- and third-degree burns all up and down my arm. Because it was very late and Charlie was unable to move, I had to drive myself to the emergency room!

Can you imagine what my life was like trying to take care of a baby, an injured husband, and two other young children—with a badly burned arm? Since my mother was unable to come to help, I had a neighbor who came in each day to bathe the baby and another friend who came over to change my bandages twice a day. In the midst of all this, the doctors decided that Charlie needed surgery, so he was taken to the hospital for a laminectomy. Now I was not only trying to care for a house and three young children, but also to be at the hospital to support Charlie, and still breast-feed a seven-and-a-half-week-old baby! On top of everything else, this was a difficult time for us financially because I had chosen to postpone my career and stay home with the children, and Charlie's was our only income.

In those days a good mother used only cotton diapers, which she bleached and washed herself several times a week. It was an extremely time-consuming and unpleasant task! (Young people today probably don't even remember cotton diapers.) Several days after Charlie's surgery, as I returned home from the hospital very late one night, completely exhausted and nearly in tears, on the front porch step sat a huge round plastic hamper, three dozen sparkling white diapers tied in a large plastic bag, and a note which read: "The Edward Burkeen family has given you the gift of diaper service for one month. Please put the soiled diapers in this hamper, and we will pick it up and bring you a new supply of fresh diapers twice a week for the next four weeks. We hope this will help make your life a bit easier." At that moment I truly felt that I did have a guardian angel. Never ever will I forget the compassion and encouragement those dear, practical friends gave me in one of the most difficult times of my life.

My other most memorable "angel gift" came from my younger brother Brian. He was living in Kansas City at the time, serving as executive director of the National Child Abuse Foundation. Remember that I was a stay-at-home mom with three young children, we were on a limited budget, and rarely was there ever time or money for me to do something "just for me."

Brian was coming to Chicago for meetings and called to say that he was going to stay an extra day or two, and he had a surprise planned for his "big sis." He said I was to call a baby-sitter to come for the whole day, I was to dress up in my best outfit, and take the train downtown and meet him for lunch. Then Charlie was to join us after work for a special dinner—all on him!

At lunch Brian announced that "we were going to go shopping to find me a wonderful new dress." I will never forget my absolute delight in going to all the "best" downtown stores and trying on beautiful dresses and then coming out for Brian's approval. Because Charlie doesn't like to shop, I have rarely had the experience of having a man come along shopping and the fun of watching all the sales ladies give you extra attention because they think you'll spend more money. I really felt just like a princess! We finally found a bright red dress (my favorite color) that was simply made for me—and much more expensive than I ever could have afforded. Years later, even though it is nearly worn out, I cannot bear to throw that dress away because of the precious memories of Brian's "angel gift." What amazes me the most is that he was a very young, single man at the time; yet he somehow knew what could touch a young mother's heart and spirit in an unforgettable way. Thank you, Brian, for making me feel so special at a time when I needed it the most!

Amy Hanssen of Batavia, Illinois, tells of two angel gifts she received:

When I was in college and living in an apartment, I didn't have a lot of money or resources to purchase pictures/paintings for the empty walls. One day my good friend, who was also my high school chemistry teacher, came to visit me. She brought me seven framed affirmations (positive encouraging statements) to fill my empty walls. What a difference they made in my life!

When I was finishing college and planning my wedding, I was pretty stressed out. My mom, who realized I was extremely stressed, flew up to Michigan for an engagement party and brought me a stuffed puppy dog (my favorite—a golden retriever). Ever since that day, just seeing my stuffed puppy brings me peace and happiness and good memories. He has traveled with me to four apartments and a house!

When Rachel LaCombe of Gainesville, Florida, was going to have a birthday, her older sister Rita had an idea for an angel gift that involved the whole family. Rachel had not had a day alone for over eighteen months since her son Ryan was born, so the family planned a surprise day of pampering for her. At 8:30 they all met for breakfast to celebrate Rachel. Then while they watched Ryan, Rachel was gifted with a 10:00 massage. At noon her husband picked her up to go out to lunch, and the afternoon culminated in a 3:00 facial. Everyone helped plan and pay for the surprise day, and it is one Rachel will never forget!

Tips:

Think of an "angel gift" you've received from someone. Please tell them again how much that meant to you. Then think of someone in your life who could use some encouragement—and remember, "angel gifts" don't have to cost any money. They simply say, "I care about *you*."

Share Your Blessings with Others

The Idea:

When you are feeling especially blessed, find ways to share those blessings with others.

The Idea in Action:

A very dear person in my life told me about how she is sharing her blessings in the retirement home where she lives:

There are many people living here who have run out of funds, but they are kept here anyway. None of us knows which ones are in need. I had a "brainstorm," so I started a little surprise thing. I put a twenty-dollar bill in an envelope with a little card saying, "Surprise!" or "Merry Christmas" or "Just for Fun" or "From Santa Claus" with a little red heart sticker. These envelopes are put in different people's mailboxes with their names on them. You can't imagine the reactions! People make all sorts of remarks and some say they sure hope it continues and "thank you" if anyone knows who did it. Some put "thank you" notes on bulletin boards, but NO ONE KNOWS (except you now). It is so much fun. So far I've sent almost fifty, and I intend to continue.

Several weeks later this dear giver sent me the following note which was printed in their little publication, the January/February issue:

WHODUNIT?

It's an ongoing mystery on campus. A series of $20 bills appear from time to time, in envelopes addressed for office mail to several different residents. "Just for fun" some anonymous notes have said. My "Merry Christmas" greenback came mid-December.

What fun some sharing, caring person is having! What fun we are having with our conjecture—another resident? a board member? a friendly neighbor? a resident's thoughtful family? a research project? a service group? We wonder . . .

Whoever you are, Mr. or Mrs. Whodunit, Thank You!

Tips:

We are all blessed in so many ways. Find special ways that you can share your blessings, wherever you may be.

Scatter Seeds of Joy Wherever You Go

The Idea:

Find small, thoughtful ways you can bring happiness and joy into the lives of others.

The Idea in Action:

🎁 This letter of November 18, 1996, to "Dear Abby" tells of a wonderful act of kindness:

Dear Abby: Add this to your collection of random acts of kindness:
A boy in our town had three kidney transplants; two failed, the third was suc-
cessful. When he was at his sickest, the local florist decorated his hospital room.
One might have expected flowers, balloons, or a fruit basket, but the florist con-
tacted some of the boy's favorite sports teams, who sent him autographed
pictures and posters. He probably still doesn't know who was responsible. This
happened several years ago, and the young man is doing very well and is a bless-
ing to all who know him.

Proud in Pennsylvania

Marty Hawkins of Independence, Missouri, writes of an act of kindness that we could all emulate:

Several years ago I was working in downtown Kansas City, and I rode the bus
to and from work. On my way every day I saw this older gentleman seated in
his home at the picture window. So one day I sent him a card addressed to the "Man in the Picture Window." After sending several pieces of mail, I stopped by to see him and tell on my-self. He was so happy, and I was glad that I had done it. He was home bound in a wheel chair, and his only pastime was watching the cars go by. My mail gave him something to look forward to. I saw him quite often after that.

> **The gift of "I love you, no matter what" is the best of all gifts . . .**
> **and it is important to remember, "The child who least deserves love is the one who needs it the very most."**
>
> **—Elma S. Bradshaw**

Here are a few other ideas to add joy to this world:

Give a stranger a compliment.
Rake a neighbor's leaves.
Adopt a stray dog or cat.
Surprise a neighbor with a Sunday paper.
Give another driver your parking spot.
Bake a pie or cake and leave it on someone's doorstep.
Leave a note telling a neighbor how much you enjoy his or her yard.
Plant a tree in your neighborhood.

Pick up a piece of trash on the sidewalk.

Buy a cold drink for your row at the baseball game.

Let the person behind you in a line go ahead of you.

Carry birdseed in your car and scatter it for the birds in the winter.

Take a plant to your local nursing home.

Call someone just to say "I love you."

Tips:

Most of the acts of kindness and joy that mean the most are little things. Think about the kind things people have done for you. Try each day to add some special joy to someone's world—you will be happier, too!

Control Worry and Negative Thoughts

The Idea:

According to *Office Professional* magazine, stress management experts say that only 2 percent of the average person's worrying time is spent on things that might be helped or somehow improved by worrying. The other 98 percent is spent in the following ways:

40 percent on things that never happen
35 percent on things that can't be changed
15 percent on things that turn out better than expected
8 percent on useless, petty worries

The Moral: Don't worry unless you can do something about it.

Ask yourself, "What's the worst possible thing that can happen?" It usually is not a catastrophe. The result may not be exactly what you want or expected, but it is not worth all the negative energy to worry about it.

The Idea in Action:

🎁 Sister Anne Bryan Smollin, in her little book *Jiggle Your Heart and Tickle Your Soul*, says:

It is important to address our own perceptions and attitudes. So many of us hold on to negative thoughts without even being aware of what those thoughts are doing to us. They act as shut-off valves in our lives, cutting off all life-giving thoughts. These negative thoughts block the oxygen flow to our brain; before long, we are emotionally comatose.

Since negative thinking clogs the brain, it is obvious that positive thinking unclogs it, allowing creativity and options to flow freely. We begin to find ourselves energized. Our stress level decreases, and our attitudes begin to be positive.

I sometimes believe we work harder at living than we have to. We take 20,000 breaths a day. What are we choosing to breathe in? Negative things? Things that tie a hangman's knot around our throats? Or are we consciously putting our energy into taking in positive air? Life-giving, pure, healthy air? We have learned to put those who smoke in a room by themselves so none of us has to allow that secondary smoke into our lungs. Can't we do the same with thoughts that are killing us—thoughts that are killing our spirits?

Worry can be controlled—the secret is deciding WHEN to worry. Sister Anne suggests that we each have a "Worry Chair." She says:

Pick a chair in your house. Decide that the only time you will worry is when you are sitting in that chair. Then, when you find yourself getting anxious and your mind is beginning to race a hundred miles an hour (we've all been there, haven't we?), tell your body that you are not going to think about that until you are sitting in that chair. When you awake in the middle of the night and you can't fall back asleep, tell your body you are not going to think about whatever is bothering you until you are sitting in that chair. Then roll over and fall back to sleep.

However, you must give yourself time to sit in that chair and worry every day. At first begin with no more than a half hour. Do that for one week. Watch the way your body begins to believe you and gives you the choice of deciding when you will think and worry about what you want. Eventually, you can cut the time down until you will need only about five minutes each day. What a small price to pay for twenty-three hours and fifty-five minutes of worry-free time every day!

Sister Anne says that if we think of something that makes us smile, we feel good and happy. If we think of something that frightens us, our feelings follow. She suggests we try this exercise:

1. Think of something or someone you love. What do you feel?
2. Next, think of something or someone you dislike. Now what do you feel?
3. Finally, think again of something or someone you love or makes you smile.

When we change our thoughts, our emotions quickly follow.

Make a list of things that make you smile, things that make you feel good and cared about and loved—a phone call from someone you haven't heard from in a long time, new snow, a walk on the beach, a note of appreciation, a gift you were not expecting, new underwear, a cold soda on a hot day, the smell of something good in the oven, children's laughter, fresh sheets, a bubble bath, a collection that you love (my dolls!), a good love story, going to the movies, swimming laps in the bright sunshine. Sometimes we may not even really notice when these things happen. Relish them, repeat them in your mind, and think about them instead of the negative thoughts that often overwhelm us. We have a choice!

> *A man's suffering is similar to the behavior of gas. If a certain quantity of gas is pumped into an empty chamber, it will fill the chamber completely and evenly, no matter how big the chamber. Thus suffering completely fills the human soul and conscious mind, no matter whether the suffering is great or little. Therefore the "size" of suffering is completely relative.*
>
> —Victor Frankl,
> *Man's Search for Meaning*

Your List:

_____
_____
_____
_____
_____
_____

Tips:

I often think our mind is like a camera—we see what we focus on. Find yourself a "worry chair" and consciously change your focus to positive things instead of negative.

Remember Older People

The Idea:

Particularly from my growing-up experience with nursing homes and then later with my own children and the visits we made there, I have learned in a poignant way how many lonely, forgotten older people there are whom no one ever visits. How easy it can be for us to brighten their day!

The Idea in Action:

This anonymous letter from a reader in Oklahoma really touched my heart and gave me a wonderful idea:

Dear Abby: I am the director of nursing at a nursing home in Oklahoma City. I recently received a phone call from a woman who asked for the name of a resident who had no family members living. I asked her why, and she explained the following:

Her mother had been in a nursing home for the last few years of her life. The caller had worked in nursing homes and had seen firsthand that many residents had no one to visit or care about them. After her mother died, on Mother's Day, rather than leaving flowers at the grave, she chose to give them to one of those residents in need. She said it had always given her a warm feeling to brighten up someone's life, and she felt her mother would applaud her decision. She never leaves her name; she just signs the card, "Hope you have a great day." The resident never knows who sent the flowers.

I thought this was a wonderful idea and chose someone I thought would appreciate the bouquet. This gesture so warmed me that I'm sharing it with you in the hope that you'll share it with others.

A response to this letter from the executive director of the San Francisco Ministry to Nursing Homes added another possibility:

I can't tell you how much these small gestures mean to lonely elders who have outlived family and friends. The average age of nursing home residents is eighty-five. It affirms their worthiness and restores an important connection to the larger community.

But I would also like to plead that the woman actually meet the resident and give her the flowers in person. She needn't say much—just a quick hello, a brief introduction, a warm handclasp would do. Human touch is healing. It's encouraging. It's life-affirming.

I don't mean to belittle her anonymous act. That's a wonderful step, and if that's all she's able to do, she has done more than most people would. I would just encourage her to take the next step. It would make all the difference in the world to that nursing home resident, who would be forever grateful. She might even make a great new friend—someone, perhaps, like her mother.

🎁 Eric Berry from the Michigan Office of Services to the Aging shared with me something Pamela Hall sent to him. It is the poem "Look Closer at Me," from Disguised: A True Story.

> **One thing I know; the only ones among you who will be truly happy are those who will have sought and found how to serve.**
>
> **—Albert Schweitzer**

I receive mail from many people who hear of my work. One of the most touching letters I have ever read came from Yorkshire, England. It came from a nurse who works in a geriatric ward at Ashludie Hospital nearby. An old lady died in the ward, she explained, and another nurse going through her possessions found a poem she had written. The verses so impressed the staff that copies were duplicated and distributed to every nurse in the hospital. She enclosed a copy of the poem:

LOOK CLOSER AT ME

What do you see, nurses, what do you see?
Are you thinking when you look at me,
A crabby old woman, not very wise
Uncertain of habit, with faraway eyes.
Who dribbles her food and makes no reply,
When you say in a loud voice, "I do wish you'd try";

Who seems not to notice the things that you do,
And forever is losing a stocking or shoe.
Who uninteresting or not, lets you do as you will
With bathing and feeding the long day to fill.

Is that what you're thinking, is that what you see?
Then open your eyes, nurse, you're not looking at me.
I'll tell you who I am as I sit here so still,
As I rise at your bidding, as I eat at your will.

I'm a small child of ten with a father and mother,
Brothers and sisters who love one another.
A young girl of sixteen with wings on her feet,
Dreaming that soon now a lover she'll meet;
A bride soon at twenty, my heart gives a leap,
Remembering the vows that I promised to keep.
At twenty-five now I have young of my own
Who need me to build a secure, happy home.
A woman of thirty my young now grow fast,
Bound to each other with ties that should last.
At forty my young sons have grown and are gone,
But my man's beside me to see I don't mourn.

At fifty once more babies play at my knee,
Again we know children, my loved one and me.
Dark days are upon me, my husband is dead.
I look at the future—I shudder with dread.
For my young are all rearing young of their own,
And I think of the years and love that I've known.

I'm an *old* woman now, and nature is cruel;
'Tis her jest to make *old* people look like a fool.
The body it crumbles, grace and vigor depart,
There is now a stone where I once had a heart.
But inside this old carcass a young girl still dwells,
And now and again my battered heart swells.
I remember the joys, I remember the pain,
And I'm loving and living life over again.

I think of the years all too few, gone too fast;
And accept the stark fact that nothing can last.
So open your eyes, nurses—open and see,
Not a crabby *old* woman, LOOK CLOSER AT ME!

🎁 If you happen to be a retired person, I want to share an idea with you that will help get you perhaps more young visitors than you'd like! My mother has lived by herself in Harlan, Iowa, since my father died twenty-five years ago. Since my brothers and sister and I live far away, Mother has created her own "family" in Harlan. One of the best things she ever did to encourage young people to visit her was to buy a gumball machine. Now she has gained a reputation as the "nice lady who always has cookies and gumballs"! Her doorbell often rings with young visitors who tell her stories, recite poems, and sing her songs. They write her letters and notes, color her pictures, and bring her treats. She has thoroughly enjoyed these children, and we are grateful because we know she's not lonely. You might want to purchase a gumball machine for your home!

🎁 Ella Wilkison, a senior citizen herself who lives in Mesa, Arizona, shares some of the ways she helps her older neighbors and others:

I take a near-blind neighbor to the bank and the store.

I have helped serve meals at senior centers.

I have helped at a golf tournament to raise money for a senior center.

I have given craft articles I've made to raise money for a charity.

I serve in the Legion Auxiliary for hospitalized veterans.

I bowl with problem school seniors once a week.

I sell poppies on Memorial Day for the Legion Auxiliary.

I visit patients in rest homes.

I return family pictures from previous generations to their younger family members.

I pick up friends from the hospital after tests when they can't drive.

No matter what your age, you can find ways to help others!

Tips:

Whenever you are feeling sorry for yourself or as if your life has no meaning, bake some cookies or purchase some flowers, or "borrow" a child for a short time if you do not have one of your own (especially a baby), and make a trip to a local nursing home. You cannot imagine the joy you will bring to otherwise forgotten and hurting people.

A special resource for those of you who want to keep your older family members at home is a new company called Ageless Designs. Their marketing brochure describes their work as "the first organization to dedicate its resources, imagination, and heart to creating smarter, safer living for seniors. By recommending logical, cost-effective architectural modifications, design concepts, and products, homes can accommodate those dealing with multiple age-related conditions. Our basic premise is that as our bodies age, our homes should not become unforgiving obstacles or barriers to safe, comfortable living." See the Resources section for more information.

Begin a "Kindness Campaign"

The Idea:

You can begin a focus on kindness in your home, organization, school, or even in your community. The beautiful little book *Random Acts of Kindness* has opened many people's eyes to the positive impact of small deeds. Encouraging and celebrating these deeds in a formal way is the focus of a "Kindness Campaign."

The Idea in Action:

Rita Blitt, a painter/sculptor from Leawood, Kansas, told me of a very special program that began in Kansas City with her words, "Kindness Is Contagious . . . Catch It!" Several years ago a friend of hers asked Rita to create something "to send around the world to make the world a better place." This was an awesome request, Rita felt, and she wondered if it was possible to create something that might have such a positive effect on the world. Several years later as she was driving and looking at bumper stickers, she said a number of things crossed her mind.

One was a call from a friend whom Rita had helped, wishing that she could repay her. When Rita said no, that wasn't necessary, the friend responded that then she would do something nice for someone else. This excited Rita because it meant that her good deed would go on and on, and suddenly she thought, "KINDNESS IS CONTAGIOUS . . . CATCH

IT!" She immediately called her friend SuEllen Fried and said, "I give you my words. Make magic with them."

Rita envisioned a kindness program for children, and she knew that SuEllen could organize it. Soon after that, SuEllen, also of Kansas City and founder of the STOP Violence Coalition, involved several children's classes in focus groups to talk about bullying and the cruelty of children to one another. To reduce the incidence of teasing, they came up with the idea of placing two jars in the classroom, one labeled "Put-Downs" and the other "Put-Ups." Tokens of some kind would be placed around the jars, and whenever someone received a put-down or a put-up, they would place a token in the jar. As imagined, the visual concept had a dramatic impact on the behavior of the children, and they became much kinder to one another.

Barbara Unell, editor and publisher of *Twins* magazine and a board member of the STOP Violence Coalition, took this idea to the guidance counselor at her children's school, and soon a program was born. Another idea called "Pass It On" was added. In this activity, when a teacher spotted a child performing a kind act, he or she placed a special eraser on the child's desk and then asked that child to become the observer of a kind act and pass the eraser on.

Adults participate in this activity now by wearing a button that says, "Kindness Is Contagious . . . Catch It!" and then pass it on to other people who perform acts of kindness. Legendary stories have evolved as these buttons have spread all over the world!

A partnership developed with a local TV station, KMBC-TV, which sends a letter out to every school district each fall asking the children to nominate the "Kindest Kansas Citians." Over four thousand nominations are returned each year, and three winners are slected and honored at a Kindness dinner. Students write touching stories about coaches, teachers, school custodians, bus drivers, and others who have touched their lives, and the evening is filled with tears of joy.

At the very first Kindness dinner, Rita Blitt was asked to create a small sculpture for each of the "Kindest Kansas Citians" and to present each of the children who read their winning letters a print using her artwork and her words, "Kindness Is Contagious . . . Catch It!" Instead of ordering a few prints to be made, however, Rita decided to order 2,500! She has made it a personal campaign to send them all over the world, whenever and wherever she has heard of a kind person, hoping to plant seeds of kindness. They have been sent to nearly every state as well as to eighteen foreign countries.

The "Kindness Is Contagious . . . Catch It!" activity program guide has now spread to three hundred schools in the greater Kansas City area as well as thirty-four states and Ontario, Canada. Many, many folks have become involved in helping to bring more kindness and love to the lives of the residents of greater Kansas City as well as in other cities throughout North America. In 1996 a joint venture of the STOP Violence Coalition and the United Way held the first "Corporate Kindness Day" in Kansas City the week of February 14, and I was asked to be their keynote speaker. As the circle of good deeds grows, that kindness and love is spread throughout the world.

The program guide on Kindness lists "10 Ways You Can Help Spread an Epidemic of Kindness" that we can all apply in our everyday work lives:

1. Take time to listen.
2. Give praise when earned.
3. Forgive someone who hurt you.
4. Apologize for something you've done wrong.
5. Do a favor for someone in need.
6. Give hugs.
7. Compromise. Don't start a fight.
8. Negotiate. Don't blame.
9. Empathize. Don't gossip.
10. Problem-solve. Don't tease or name-call.

"Ma'am, I've been appointed spokesperson for the other passengers. We're prepared to offer you $637.82 to take a later flight."

Tips:

No matter where you live, you can begin a campaign of Kindness. What a very special way to add more caring and spirit to our world!

In the words of Ivan Misic, the ambassador to the UN from the Republic of Bosnia and Herzogovina, "The highest form of power is not the allocation of external resources, but the harnessing of internal ones. Let us harness the love of all the people of the world. Love, and love alone, can undo hatred."

For information on the Kindness campaign, see the listing for the STOP Violence Coalition in the Resources section of this book.

Find a Charitable Cause You Can Support as a Family

The Idea:

One of the best ways you can teach your children empathy and the spirit of giving is to get them involved in some sort of charitable giving as young children.

The Idea in Action:

When our second child died, we decided as a family that we wanted to do something in memory of Gavin that we could all be a part of. So, nearly twenty years ago, we adopted a little boy in Colombia, South America, through Compassion International. Not only did this involve monthly financial support, but also one of the important responsibilities was keeping in touch with the child and letting him know of our love and support. So each of our children took turns writing short letters to him each month, and we also had fun finding little things like balloons, stickers, postcards, and family pictures that could fit into a #10 envelope. When our first little boy grew up and graduated, we began supporting another, and even today, my husband and I have carried on this tradition.

Someone has purchased this book you are reading, so you have indirectly already made a donation to CARE, the Cooperative for Assistance and Relief Everywhere, the world's largest relief agency and the originators of the first CARE package. I have been so impressed with CARE's work throughout the world that I have pledged a portion of all the royalties from this book to their work. CARE works with 48 million people in sixty-six developing and emerging nations in Africa, Asia, Eastern Europe, and Latin America. Its programs encompass health, nutrition, family planning, emergency relief, girls' education, small business support, agriculture, and environmental protection. As one CARE package recipient said, "It was far more than food for hungry stomachs—it was nourishment for our spirits; someone cared. That aspect meant most. Someone cared." So I deeply value our partnership because that is what I hope my books are helping people to do in our world today. A family donation to CARE is a wonderful way to reach out to others less fortunate in our world. (You can read more about the CARE organization on page 298.)

World Concern, a nonprofit Christian organization based in Seattle, has created a catalog called *Global Gift Guide.* Through it you can, as an individual or as a family, purchase gifts for family members and friends that benefit others less fortunate—a rabbit and two chicks for a Rwandan family for two grandchildren, fish to stock a Bangladesh pond for a brother, prenatal care for women in Bangladesh for a daughter, and you can even give a small business loan to people in Third World countries in someone's name. The Heifer Project International, based in Little Rock, Arkansas, another nonprofit relief organization, also markets gifts such as livestock and seeds through its catalogs. One of the values of this kind of giving as a family is that you are giving something tangible and personal, not just a lump sum of money: "I'm giving *this* goat to Uncle Harry," or "Somewhere in the world there is a water buffalo with my name!"

The catalogs display animals and services available to donate along with prices, descriptions, and photographs. For example, in the HPI catalog a llama runs $150 ($20 for a share), and it explains that llamas provide Bolivian families with transportation, income, and wool used to weave blankets, ponchos, carpet, and rope. Sometimes heartwarming stories are told in the catalog about recipients of previous gifts. This "hands-on" method of giving is a good way to help especially young children with the reality of a contribution to those less fortunate in our world. The family can study the country, the animal, or service, and the child can learn how he or she is helping to make a difference.

The Samaritan's Purse, a nonprofit organization in Boone, North Carolina, has a special project they call "Operation Christmas Child," which would be a wonderful family project to take on. They ask people to fill shoe boxes with things for children from Third World countries for Christmas. The age and sex of the child is attached to the outside of the box and hundreds of thousands of these are distributed throughout the world each year. Think of the fun you can have as a family choosing special, small, creative gifts to fill your boxes!

Amanda the Panda is a nonprofit organization in the state of Iowa for ill and grieving children that has been in existence since 1980. JoAnn Zimmerman, who is Amanda the Panda, the life-sized "bear with a heart," travels the state of Iowa visiting sick children in their homes, hospitals, and schools, visiting over 1,100 children annually. Her mission is a simple one—to bring a smile and a warm and wonderful BEAR HUG to each child she meets and to make them feel special, not different. The group provides the following services for grieving children and families:

- Camp Amanda for children ages six to sixteen who have experienced the death of a parent, sibling, grandparent, or close friend. Through sharing, playing, and being together with peers who have also experienced the death of a family member, children learn that they are not alone and that the feelings they are experiencing are normal during the grief process. These camps take place four weekends a year.
- Individual support for children—Amanda the Panda is available for personal visits to young children when a death has occurred in their family.
- Support groups for grieving children led by a grief therapist or an art therapist.

- Camp Amanda for parents whose spouse, child, or parent has died.
- Fun days for grieving children where the children are encouraged to play, laugh, and have fun again.
- School visits and presentations on the topic of death and dying.
- Consulting services to others wishing to duplicate or begin weekend camps for grieving children in other states or localities.

Like all Amanda activities, the camps are fueled by donations and volunteers who do everything from cooking to counseling. Camp Amanda is the only program of its kind, and all services, including the camps, are completely free to recipients. What a wonderful place for a family to get involved—either in helping with the Iowa camps, in fund-raising, or most important, in helping start such a program in your own area or state. I recently spoke for a fund-raiser for this group, and I was deeply impressed with their work and JoAnn's commitment to grieving children and families. For more information, see the Resources section at the back of this book.

A COMMITMENT TO
ILL AND GRIEVING
CHILDREN

Tips:

There are many wonderful organizations we can support as a family. Find one that touches your hearts in a special way and then get the whole family involved in the project. If you are donating money, let the children earn part of the donation. If you are purchasing presents for a child, choose a child the same age as one of yours so that they can experience the joy of sharing with someone with whom they can identify.

Create a Christmas Cheer Box for Someone

The Idea:

Maybe you are wondering how you can help someone get through the holidays in the midst of severe problems, illness, or grief. Here is the story of how one idea helped and how it continues to multiply every year.

The Idea in Action:

🎁 Carlene Eneroth of Spokane, Washington, lost her husband from a massive heart attack when he was only thirty-one years old. Even though her whole world had come to a screeching halt, Carlene was flabbergasted to discover that life was moving right on even though her grief had kept her out of touch. Most of all, she dreaded her first Christmas without Greg.

On Thanksgiving weekend her parents arrived with a big, open-topped box, covered with bright Christmas wrap and containing many small, gaily wrapped presents inside. Carlene says, "At first I wanted to scream, cry, run, and hide. Didn't they know I didn't want anything in my home that spoke of this awful upcoming holiday season?"

Her mother put the box on the table and explained that since all of them couldn't be together for Christmas, she wanted this box to help her through the hard month ahead. She suggested Carlene unwrap one present each day. Carlene thanked them and then quickly shoved the box over in the corner behind a chair, hoping to forget its very existence.

After a bad day at work on December 1, Carlene remembered those presents and decided to open one. She found a classy new pot holder. The next day she woke up to a "gray" day when, for no reason except her grief, everything was awful. She opened another present—some cute little notepads. Each day she amazed herself by giving herself "permission" to open another little present (knee-high stockings, new ballpoint pens, garden gloves, envelopes of hot chocolate, stationery). Each one subtly reminded her that Christmas was coming whether she liked it or not, and she might as well face it. But most important of all, for a few minutes every single day, she felt loved and remembered.

A couple of years, later when she met a young woman and her three little children who had recently lost their dad to suicide, she remembered her mom's box idea. She said:

I wasn't sure how I could create a "Cheer Box" for a whole family, but I wanted to try. First, I spent some time at the local discount toy store, where I found several little games all the kids could play. Then I included in the box little things for the kitchen along with some special food items and candy/gum treats. As I wrapped each gift, I numbered it to open on a particular day of the month. This helped to ensure that they wouldn't be opening three kitchen items or three toys in a row.

I was a little nervous that the kids wouldn't think it was fun unless they found a game or toy each day, but to my surprise, in January the mother called. She said, "You just wouldn't believe how excited the kids got about the Cheer Box! When we had visitors, the kids even dragged them into the kitchen right away to show off Mom's new kitchen towel. They were as thrilled to open these kind of things as they were about the games!"

After her first experience, Carlene was encouraged to continue, and now she does one or two boxes a year. She begins buying little items she sees on sale all through the year, and when November comes, she is ready to begin planning on who needs a box and what to put in it. One church group decided their Ladies' Circle would try the idea. Each person brought three days' worth of presents.

After the death of Carlene's family doctor last summer, his medical office adopted this idea as something to be done for his wife. A parent on one of the soccer teams in her area suddenly died, and the team parents got together with this idea and made up a fun box for the entire family.

> *It is only by risking our persons from one hour to another that we live at all.*
>
> —William James

Another group knew that one family was missing their mom's cooking of special holiday goodies their first Christmas without her, so they assigned a lady each day of the month to take over hot, fresh goodies that were traditional in their families. An older gentleman in her church had no relatives nearby after his wife of sixty years died. Carlene and his friends wanted to make him a Cheer Box, but she said, "We were not sure what to buy for a man. We decided on a current magazine, hot chocolate envelopes, a new screwdriver, golf balls and tees, and toiletry items—it's the idea that counts, not the gifts themselves."

Reprinted with permission from *Bereavement* magazine, 8133 Telegraph Drive, Colorado Springs, CO 80920.

Tips:

A "Holiday Cheer Box" would be a marvelous family project whether your family is made up of one or two persons or several. Think about someone who is having a struggle near the holiday season and then put your care into constructive action. As Carlene says, "The ideas and possibilities are endless!"

Start a S.O.U.L. Group

The Idea:

Wherever you may be in your life's journey, each of us needs to find a group where we can share our concerns, our joys, and our failures. When my children were young, I found that support in a neighborhood Bible study group. When I was finishing my master's degree, I was a part of a study group that provided encouragement and support. Now I find a great deal of support and sharing with my friends from the National Speaker's Association and the Professional Speakers of Illinois. Are you a part of a support group of some kind that adds meaning and encouragement to your life?

The Idea in Action:

🎁 Tia Vaux, of Coon Rapids, Iowa, shared with me how she and a number of her friends started a group called S.O.U.L.—Stressed-Out Unified Ladies. Here are how several of the group members feel about it:

S.O.U.L. was like opening a gift to myself—a completely unexpected gift! When I heard about the first meeting, something called to me. Somehow, I knew it was going to change my life, or at least my outlook. I was right; we immediately reached out and embraced each other.

We discuss everything under the sun: from our children's latest tantrum to a favorite recipe, to a worthwhile way of helping someone. Out of this, we were drawn together more than any of us could imagine. We were drawn by our similarities as mothers, wives, women—drawn also by our differences, which we respect and love about each other.

We commiserate with each other, share each other's joys and tragedies, we cry together, and mostly we laugh together. We are always there for one another.

What was my gift, you ask? I found my sense of humor restored, some self-confidence, compassion, and love; so much that it filled my heart, my spirit, and yes, my very SOUL! The best thing about my gift is it came all wrapped in friendship.

Diane Andersen

Although I realize that S.O.U.L. stands for Stressed-Out Unified Ladies, for me the letters have also come to mean Support and Overwhelming Unconditional Love. In this group I have discovered not just one friend, but a multitude of friends that I've been able to share my ups and downs with. They are like the sisters I never had. Being with my "S.O.U.L. sisters" is like being enfolded in a warm family embrace. I cherish our times of sharing and thank the Lord for bringing us together.

Laurel Halstead

Ann Kult says:

For me S.O.U.L. has been a spiritual springboard into a deeper commitment to God through regular Bible study and other Christian small-group experiences. Oh, there are days when, as a mother of a pre-schooler, I still feel worn out and overwhelmed. But I keep striving in my walk with Christ. I keep studying God's work, learning how to put Him first and apply His word in my life. Now, when I feel overwhelmed by motherhood and all that goes with it, I am more apt to listen for that still, small voice inside, the voice commanding me, "Be still and know that I am God." (Psalms 46:10)

And Tia Vaux shares her description of S.O.U.L.:

This group has strengthened my family, mind, and SOUL. I no longer feel like I'm the only one going through the stresses in my life. Everyone has similar stresses (and joys) with their home, work, and families. The following quote from Beverly LaHaye sums up S.O.U.L. to me: "In good times and bad, we need friends who will pray for us, listen to us, and lend a comforting hand and an understanding ear when needed." God has brought us together, and I thank God daily for my S.O.U.L. group!

Close to Home © John McPherson/Dist. by Universal Press Syndicate.

"Here's an interesting piece of trivia. Since the baby was born, I've had 957 hours of sleep. You've had 1,429."

These women have met for four years now sharing Bible study, Christian books, and even recipes and baby-sitting services for one another! Patty Petty says:

The bonds from this group have given me the inner strength to laugh, to love, to cry, and yes, to genuinely enjoy life! S.O.U.L. has taught me to treat life with gentle understanding. We share from our hearts the day-to-day challenges, the accomplish-ments, and the sorrows that life brings our way. We laugh, we cry—mostly laugh until we cry! It is in giving that we receive; I have truly found the heart and SOUL of friendship!

Tips:

If you would like information to help you start your own S.O.U.L. group, you may call or write Tia Vaux, 319 Park Street, Coon Rapids, Iowa 50058; 712-684-7793. Another fun idea is a group that has started in the Western Springs Baptist Church called R.O.M.E.O.S. It stands for "Retired Old Men Eating Out"! A group of men in the community get together the first Tuesday of every month for breakfast and good sharing.

Help a Sick Mom

The Idea:

When the mother of a family is seriously ill, sometimes we are not sure how we can be of help, and we say sincerely, "Please call me if you need anything." What most of us don't realize is that when a person is very ill, they are often too tired and too sick to make that call. If we can offer very specific gifts of our time, we will be a wonderful blessing to an ill friend.

The Idea in Action:

📦 A married young woman with three children, a baby, a preschooler, and first grader was battling cancer. In her struggle to beat the disease, people asked many times over the months how they could help. In an issue of *Focus on the Family* magazine before she lost her battle, she shared several ideas:

1. Cook a dinner for my family, *but offer a choice of two entrees. One week we got tuna casserole four nights in a row from well-meaning friends! Bring the food in disposable containers or marked pots. If I can't return your casserole, I will cry at my powerlessness and confusion.*

2. Bake homemade cookies or brownies *and bring them frozen so I can have the delight of sending off fresh goodies in a lunch box the next morning. This will give me the fun of feeling like a mama.*

3. Make your offer specific. *Say, "I want to come over Monday at three o'clock to clean your pantry shelf or do your laundry." Otherwise I won't know what you want to do or when you are free.*

4. Offer to baby-sit—*even if my husband and I stay home. This gives us the freedom of a private adult life in a place my illness can cope with.*

5. Help with holidays, birthdays, and anniversaries. *Ask if there are any special gifts or cards or wrapping paper you could pick up for me. How many times I have wanted to give my husband a special "Thank You" card or put up a holiday decoration but have been unable.*

6. Help my children attend birthday parties *by bringing some prewrapped children's birthday party gifts to our home for future use.*

7. Call before you visit, but drop by for twenty minutes *when you can. Don't assume sickness requires rest at the expense of communication and friendship. (Loneliness is the greatest interrupter of sleep.)*

8. Ask me who you know that I might like to see and bring them by.

9. Take snapshots of my children *over the months. This gives me a feeling that there are permanent records of the temporary happenings I must miss.*

10. Offer to run two meaningless errands *a week for our family—otherwise the small stuff like no hair ribbons, the cleaning, or cologne fall by the wayside.*

11. Allow me to feel sad, *or to prepare for the worst. One of the most difficult problems of serious illness is that everyone wants to encourage the patient. But sometimes, having a good cry with a friend who allows it will let the tension escape.*

12. Even if the joke is terrible, tell it! Read something funny to me or describe a funny story. Speak to the part of me that is more alive than dead, for that is the real me.

13. Touch me.

14. Offer to watch TV with me some afternoon when an old movie is on. Bring a book or a magazine in case I fall asleep.

15. Say the word "Cancer" around me and talk about the real life you are living. This helps me feel less like an untouchable and more like I am still involved with the world of normalcy. One of the hardest things for me as an invalid is the problem of conversation with my husband. If you don't talk to me about the life outside, I am left with only illness and TV to talk about to him, and this is hard.

16. Tell me how great I look considering what I'm going through. I know I look sick, but I still need to feel honestly attractive.

17. Encourage your husband to come over to visit my husband in the evenings. My illness has eliminated many of his pleasures. How happy I am when I hear him laughing with a friend!

18. Pray for me and say you are doing so. The fact that you have faith gives me faith.

19. Talk to me of the future. Next week, next year, ten or twenty years! The power of planning is incredible. If you look ahead, I can too.

20. Remind me of the abundant life that awaits me and is promised, but also recall that there is comfort to be had here and now, in the midst of my illness. The fact that you could care so much in this moment tells me how much God cares for me in all moments.

Tips:

Since every person is different, these ideas may not be helpful for all sick mothers; however, you can use these ideas as guidelines. If your offer is specific and sincere, you can show your caring in your own special way. When I had to be in bed for nine weeks before our middle daughter Gretchen was born, a friend came over and rubbed my feet and put polish on my toenails. To this day, the memory of that special gift fills my heart with love for her.

Have a Baby Shower for the "Big" Brother or Sister

The Idea:

Sometimes a new baby coming into the family can be very difficult for an older child. As a way of helping that child feel important and a part of the event, have a baby shower just for him or her.

The Idea in Action:

Marilyn Webster, a teacher at New Beginnings Christian Montessori School in Bolingbrook, Illinois, shared with me two special baby showers they gave. One was for Briana Griswold and another was for Rachel Kozak:

Briana's baby shower was the first one we ever gave. Mothers are always having babies at our school. Most of our families are young. We cannot give everyone a shower. However, I felt an impression from the Lord that Briana needed a boost. Through the months, she never spoke of her soon-coming sister. Even when we asked her, she seemed hesitant and didn't want to discuss it. That shower was for Briana. It was for her emotionally, and it was for her physically. It was to equip her with something tangible to truly give to her baby sister. It gave her much joy!

In September, one of our three-year-olds experienced her father's sudden death. Her mother was pregnant at the time and already had two young children. She gave birth to a baby boy two weeks early. Children have to face very hard things these days. The Lord impressed me that this baby needed a shower. Not because of the baby items but because of the pictures and the memories and the fact that in his loss at birth, there should be a celebration to recall his specialness. Rachel, too, found much joy in the shower and celebration for her baby brother.

Each child was asked to bring an inexpensive gift to share with Briana and Rachel. The teachers said in their note, "Maybe your child could choose something from the baby aisle at the grocery store, Wal-Mart, or the dollar store." And best of all, these showers were a surprise for the two little girls.

Tips:

This is an idea that helped to heal two small hurting hearts. A shower for the older child could be given in a neighborhood, school, or even in a family to help them feel valued and important.

Begin a Foundation for Educational Excellence in Your Community

The Idea:

Because funding for education has shifted dramatically in most states from the state to local property taxes and those taxes have had to increase, most Boards of Education are reluctant to burden taxpayers with additional funding requests that make the difference between a "very good" program and an "excellent" program. Creating a Foundation for Educational Excellence in your school district or community can help to bridge that gap.

The Idea in Action:

🎁 In 1992 a group of concerned citizens in Western Springs, Illinois, founded a 501(C) 3 not-for-profit corporation called the Western Springs Foundation for Educational Excellence. Their mission is "to acquire and distribute financial and other resources for the benefit of Western Springs School District 101 educational programs and activities which extend and enhance the quality of education and provide students with expanded learning opportunities."

Their primary areas of emphasis are to:

- *Promote student development* by providing funds for such extracurricular activities as computer, music, fine arts, and other camps; after-school seminars and institutes; and summer seminars and institutes.
- *Support unique growth opportunities for all school district employees* by providing funds for staff development, staff in-service opportunities, and resources to encourage and support research; and by providing funds for creative ideas and programs in enrichment areas such as science, math, and technology projects, gifted and talented programs, fine arts enhancement, and classroom mini-grants.

- *Encourage community-school partnerships* by providing a vehicle for individuals, businesses, and organizations to share resources and gifts with the District 101 schools, including business mentorships and partnerships, cash and other contributions, and donation of services.

One of the interesting fund-raisers they are sponsoring is a dinner/dance/auction encouraging all the residents and teachers of Western Springs to contribute to the auction. The teachers are offering creative gifts of special time with children such as music lessons; tutoring; having a birthday party for eight children; making up twenty school lunches; giving a front-row seat at school musicals, graduation, and talent shows; taking several children on a field trip to Chicago; being a deejay at a children's party for three hours; taking a child to their home for a tea party; and taking several children bowling and for pizza. One of the principals has even offered to let a child be the principal for half a day, and she will be a student! Residents are offering gifts of their expertise such as one or more hours of consulting, tickets to various events, products and services from their businesses, tours of their facilities. Even blocks are encouraged to give something as a group such as offering to hold a garage sale for another block. All proceeds go to the Foundation for future educational programs.

> *Friendship is born at that moment when one person says to another, "What! You too? I thought I was the only one."*
>
> —C.S. Lewis

Tips:

What makes this idea really special is that it is involving the whole community in helping to make special educational opportunities available to the children. No matter what your work, you can find something to donate to the auction. (I sent a copy of my last book and consulting time to help someone get their own book published.) Not only is this project making a difference for the children, but it is also bringing the community closer as people get to know one another better. Imagine the delight of a child to have a whole afternoon or evening alone with one of his or her teachers! For more information about the foundation, call 708-246-3700.

Here is another wonderful song by David Roth that truly exemplifies this spirit of *empathy:*

The Dream

There are many professional ball players working in the NBA
Some who make more money in one game than we make in a year
And one by-product of this industry is something called a "sneaker deal"
All you have to do is have a promising career

Then the companies come courting, they see dollar signs in every pair
Of inexpensive highly marked up shoes that they'll be hawking
Then they slap a famous name on footwear cheaply made in China
And they charge a hundred bucks a pair—the athletes do the talking

Unfortunately the targets of these campaigns are not
The rich and wealthy well-to-do's with lots of cash and extra savings
They're the kids of working folks or single parents, some on welfare
Who now have the added pressure of these shoes their kids are craving

Here comes Hakeem Olajuwon, the wondrous Houston center
Who's done everything a player could hope to do in his profession
Except "have a shoe," he's never "had a shoe," can you believe it?
Till the Rockets took the title two seasons in succession

Whereupon a company picked up the ball and dropped a dime and rang him up
They said, "We wanna put your nickname on our sneaker line, Hakeem
We're proud that you're a winner, we can both make lots of money
Every kid'll wanna have 'em, and we'll call the shoe 'the Dream' "

"You want to use my name for what?"
Was all Hakeem purported
"A shoe" they said. "A what?" "A shoe . . ."
"God Bless You," he retorted

But Hakeem, a most religious man, reflected on their offer
And responded with a most resounding "Yes, on one condition . . .
That these 'Dreams' you wish to sell you price at less than thirty-five dollars
If you stick to that you have my permission"

"But who'll wear such cheap shoes?" they reacted in a panic
Knowing full well that the going rate was that and more times three
"I will," said Hakeem to them and that's just what he did
That whole season in the NBA, for all the world to see

That's right, he wore those low-cost brogans right there on his size sixteens
And on each box is printed "make commitments, dare to dream"
Oh, by the way, they sold 1.8 million pairs it seems
Well, 1.8 million and one . . . cuz now I wear the "Dreams"

CHAPTER EIGHT:

E = Enthusiasm

"Create Traditions and Celebrate Those You Love"

Be glad of life because it gives you the chance to love and to work and play and to look at the stars.

—Henry Van Dyke

THE WORD *ENTHUSIASM* has as its root *en theos,* which means "of or from God." Those who are filled with enthusiasm for life and a love for people do seem to radiate a godlike joy. Approaching life as a gift and relishing whatever experiences each day may bring adds a wonder and a delight to living that is expressed in one's enthusiasm for this world. One of my favorite quotations is from Samuel Ullman who says, "Years wrinkle the skin, but to give up enthusiasm wrinkles the soul."

I think enthusiasm can be learned and shared. That is why I've chosen as my personal motto "Spreading Contagious Enthusiasm.™" Enthusiasm IS contagious! We all have experienced being around people who lift us up and make us glad to be alive. They are spreading their enthusiasm for the gift of each day and the wonderful choices we each have to make this world a little bit better. Wouldn't you rather be around an enthusiastic person than one who always sees the negatives and problems in life?

We can help our families to be special places of enthusiasm, joy, and celebration, NO MATTER WHAT OUR CIRCUMSTANCES. There are countless stories about people in desperate, unimaginably horrible situations such as those in the concentration camps in World War II who still found a joy in being alive because life is "of or from God." This chapter contains many wonderful ideas about how to celebrate life and one another—during both holidays and ordinary days. Use these ideas to stimulate your own family celebrations and to "spread contagious enthusiasm!™"

Make Banners

The Idea:

One fun way to celebrate your home is to create a family banner.

The Idea in Action:

Get scraps of felt, beads, ribbon, glue, and all sorts of other materials, and create a banner that symbolizes your family. Do you have a family motto? A special vacation spot? A pet? An inside joke or story? A favorite family sport? Discuss what you want to put on the banner, draw some rough sketches, and then assign each family member a task.

One family decided that their family was made up of many special parts, so they drew a wheel on their banner. Then each person had a segment to create for themselves—what was special about them in the family. The mother added cooking utensils. The father drew a hand to demonstrate all the times he offered a helping hand. One daughter drew a ballet slipper because that was what she loved. Another daughter drew a book because she was the family "historian." The son drew a soccer ball because he loved soccer, and they even had a slot for the family dog. He got a shoe to represent all those he had chewed up!

Another family had so much fun on their family banner that they each created an individual banner as well. When that person had a birthday or achieved a special goal, they flew that person's flag outside the front door.

Tips:

Don't get hung up on the quality of the artwork with this project. Simply allow each member of the family to have a part in the creation. You will treasure this banner for many years afterwards!

Have a Family Guest Book

The Idea:

Have a guest book that everyone who comes to your home signs. Include their name, the date, and any other information you'd like, such as "Comments" or "Purpose of Visit."

The Idea in Action:

Denis and Cynthia Retoske of Costa Mesa, California, have had a family guest book for years. A close friend of theirs who had moved several times after living near them and returned to visit told me how fun it was each time they got together at the Retoskes' home to look back in the book and remember earlier visits. Children's handwriting and comments when they were small were such a delight, and you could trace their growth and development by the entries in the guest book. For the Retoskes it is a wonderful record of friends and good times spent together.

Kathie Hightower of Corvallis, Oregon, tells about the special tradition of friends:

Our German friends, Enno and Babs Probst, have a wonderful tradition. He is in the German military, and they move a lot and entertain. Every time they have guests visit—whether for the evening or overnight—they have them sign their guest book. They never forget. We've known them since we were lieutenants in Germany in 1976. My husband and Enno were in a military German-American partnership program, and we all belonged to a Junior Officers Little NATO group. We've been to their home many times, been to their wedding, and have visited again during our last tour in Germany. It was fun to read through their guest book to read our early entries and to find entries from mutual friends. What a great record of their friendships over time!

Tips:

When your children get their first "home away from home," what a delightful gift a guest book would be to give them.

Create Special Christmas Traditions for the Family

The Idea:

It is wonderful to begin family traditions when children are small; however, it is never too late! They may also be started with grandchildren as you'll see in one family, or even aunts and uncles can begin traditions with their extended families. Family traditions are what give holidays their "roots" and create memories. In fact, being away from home on a holiday is often hardest because of those traditions, so why not plan to take the traditions with you, wherever you may find yourself for the holidays.

The Idea in Action:

Our dear friends, the David Schulz family of Downers Grove, Illinois, shared one of our most special family traditions with us. On the day after Thanksgiving, we put out a small wooden manger that is empty. Beside it is a tray of straw and the following little card:

This is a lovely Christmas custom for children of all ages. The manger needs to be soft with straw to be ready for the Christ Child on Christmas Eve. Each time a good deed or task is done

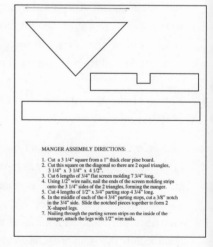

MANGER ASSEMBLY DIRECTIONS:

1. Cut a 3 1/4" square from a 1" thick clear pine board.
2. Cut this square on the diagonal so there are 2 equal triangles, 3 1/4" x 3 1/4" x 4 1/2".
3. Cut 6 lengths of 3/4" flat screen molding 7 3/4" long.
4. Using 1/2" wire nails, nail the ends of the screen molding strips onto the 3 1/4" sides of the 2 triangles, forming the manger.
5. Cut 4 lengths of 1/2" x 3/4" parting stop 4 3/4" long.
6. In the middle of each of the 4 3/4" parting stops, cut a 3/8" notch in the 3/4" side. Slide the notched pieces together to form 2 X-shaped legs.
7. Nailing through the parting screen strips on the inside of the manger, attach the legs with 1/2" wire nails.

without being told, the child has the privilege of putting a straw in the manger. As the manger is being readied, so the child's heart is being readied for the Christ Child's birthday. His thoughts are turning outward, thinking of ways to be helpful and considerate of others.

The idea is to fill the manger with straw by Christmas Day so that Baby Jesus will be comfortable. And Baby Jesus does appear in the manger on Christmas morning. I have to admit that some years good deeds *abound* on the two or three days *just before* Christmas!

Another family uses an object lesson to make the Christmas story come alive. They put the crèche out on the first day of Advent; however, they put the three wise men as far away from the crèche as they can in their home. Then each day the children get to move the wise men a little bit closer to the manger until finally, on Christmas Eve, the wise men reach the stable. What a special way to teach the idea of a long journey to worship the newborn baby!

Barbara Swift of Western Springs, Illinois, shared with me a tradition she has started with her grandchildren. When she puts out the manger scene on the first day of Advent, she wraps the Baby Jesus up in a Christmas package and puts it on the Christmas tree. When the family gathers on Christmas Day to celebrate and unwrap their presents, the youngest grandchild gets to unwrap the very first present, Baby Jesus, and put

"Andy! Start rewrapping 'em now! Mon and Dad just pulled in the driveway!"

him in the manger. Then they talk about the real reason we give gifts to one another on Christmas—because God gave us the gift of Baby Jesus.

Many families always have a birthday cake for Baby Jesus at Christmas dinner. The whole family sings "Happy Birthday, dear Jesus" to remind them of the true meaning behind Christmas.

The George Winkler family of Western Springs, Illinois, had a delightful tradition. On Christmas Eve each person in the family got a new pair of pajamas. Then on Christmas morning, they all wore their new pjs all day long and played games, worked on a puzzle, and read together. That tradition led to an ongoing Winkler family tradition of enjoying many different kinds of games. Even today, when the children and grandchildren come from all over the country for the holidays, they continue to challenge each other to Royal Rummy, Sorry, and Clue!

The Girl Guides, Brownies, and other community groups in Toronto, Ontario, have joined together to make Christmas stockings for the Woman's College Hospital. They have started a special holiday tradition that babies born on Christmas Day will be going home from the hospital bundled in one of these stockings—truly a holiday bundle of joy!

One of our favorite Christmas traditions when I was growing up in Iowa stemmed from a very difficult year for our family. There were four children in the family, and my dad was the Postmaster, so we didn't have a lot of money. Just before Christmas, my mother got pneumonia and had to go into the hospital. Of course, you all know who really makes Christmas happen, so we had to "improvise," and because we were not very old, our ideas were creative but unusual. My brother Brian, who was about seven or eight at the time, decided that he would make Christmas Eve dinner. In those days the only pizza we had was Chef Boyardee that came in a box and you mixed up the ingredients. Brian decided that he should make a little Christmas surprise, so he used food coloring and made one of the pizza doughs red and the other one green. The doctors allowed my mother to come home for just a couple of hours that evening. When she saw our "dinner," I thought we might have to take her back to the hospital again! To this day, it is a family tradition to have the children make pizza on Christmas Eve (although thankfully, we have forgone the food coloring!).

A newlywed couple began one of their own family traditions when they decorated their very first Christmas tree. They alternated choosing ornaments, and as each one put their ornament on the tree, they shared a special memory of the past year.

Joe Hoffman tells of a tradition his daughter has started with her family. They put out the nativity scene the first part of December, but it is empty. The figures are spread out all over their house. On Christmas Eve one of the parents reads the Christmas story from the Bible. As the story is being read, the children bring the various figures to the manger when they are mentioned. Then on Christmas morning the nativity scene is complete.

🎁 Kathie Hightower shares a new Christmas tradition she plans to adopt next year:

For people who live alone or couples without children or with grown children who live far away, Christmas Day isn't filled with gift openings and festivities. My friend Lorraine told me that she and her sweetheart save all their Christmas cards from friends and family and then open them on Christmas Day. Rather than reading them in a rush and forgetting them as many of us do during a hectic holiday season, they read them at leisure and spend the day thinking and talking about their friends.

I am sure this tradition also helps assuage the loneliness because you so powerfully realize you are not alone.

🎁 My friend Rita Blitt, who lives in Leawood, Kansas, shares a special Hanukkah tradition from her family. Because there are so many young family members, if everyone gave each child a gift, there would be too many gifts and too much chaos. So, each year they spin the dreidl, and each child is given a name for a gift exchange for the next year with a price limit of fifteen dollars. Then each child gives and receives one gift. The adults, instead of giving one another gifts, give a monetary donation which is given to a soup kitchen as well as used to buy gifts for several anonymous needy families. As Rita said, it is "so thrilling" to see the real spirit of the season in action.

🎁 Marilyn Webster tells of one of their special holiday traditions:

Each year, we always ask Jesus what He would like for Christmas. If you really want to know, He will tell you!

It was the week before Christmas, and my husband, Chip, and I were in the supermarket shopping. Our buggy was overflowing with holiday food. All of a sudden, we both looked at each other and I said, "I feel that the Lord wants us to give Rose (an employee of Chip's) some food." We finished our shopping, and this time we took a buggy and shopped for Rose. Now Rose had four children, and her husband had deserted her several years prior to that Christmas. As we filled the buggy full of food for Rose, we almost burst with joy because we knew that Jesus had spoken to both of us, and this was what He wanted from us for Christmas.

We loaded our car with food and drove it to her trailer park. As we entered the park, it was almost dark, but two boys were fishing in the ditch near the road with two homemade fishing poles. When Chip walked to the door, he found Rose and her two daughters sitting at the kitchen table praying that God would please help her sons catch some fish in the ditch so they would have something to eat. Chip came out and took all the bags of food to the trailer. Rose was moved with so much joy to think that the Lord would do that for them. Needless to say, my husband and I have never forgotten that night! Through the years the Lord has impressed us to give Him gifts of all varieties. Maybe to pray for someone for a certain period of time or speak words of encouragement or to give money anonymously to someone in need. Our children have been a part of this tradition each year.

> **Whatever you can do or dream you can, begin it now. Boldness has genius, power, and magic in it. Begin it now.**
>
> **—Goethe**

Tips:

Many of the traditions I've mentioned are based on the Christian heritage because that heritage is the origin of the celebration of Christmas, and also that is my family's faith orientation. However, traditions may come from any heritage. One of the delightful things we did as our children were growing up was to ask people from many different beliefs and cultures to share their family traditions with us. Then, even though our family traditions were the most important and familiar ones to us, we all learned to appreciate and enjoy the traditions of others.

Share Christmas with a Needy Child

The Idea:

One of the best ways a family or any individual can share the Christmas spirit is to make or purchase gifts for a child in need, truly focusing on someone else rather than on themselves.

The Idea in Action:

Laurie Trice, who works in downtown Chicago, shares how she made Christmas special in many ways for a young girl:

At Christmastime the Department of Children and Family Services was in the lobby of our building with profiles on all their children along with their Christmas wish list. They were asking employees to select a child and purchase one or more of the gifts on the list. Since my daughter was eighteen, I decided to select a nineteen-year-old girl who was living on her own. I knew how hard it must be for a young girl to make it by herself with perhaps no one to even purchase a gift for her. Her gift wish list was reasonable and very practical.

As I shopped for my daughter, I always picked up a second item for my Christmas child. When it was clothes, I got her a gift certificate so she could make her own selections. Once all the gifts were purchased, I wrapped them in beautiful foil wrappings with the prettiest ribbons. I indicated which gifts were to be opened right away and numbered them in the order they were to be opened.

In the first gift I included a card that had a perfect Christmas message—a beautiful Christmas blessing:

MY CHRISTMAS PRAYER FOR YOU

I pray today will bring you contentment, joy, and peace,
when blessings all are multiplied and daily troubles cease.

I pray the Lord will bless you with a heart full of delight,
And may you always feel that you are precious in His sight.

I pray you feel the hope and wonder of the Christmas star,
And last I pray that you'll feel loved, for after all . . . YOU ARE!
Have a wonderful Christmas.

I wrote a lengthy letter in the card introducing her to our family members by first name and telling her what a blessing it was to include her in our Christmas. I even included a picture of my daughter. I explained that it was important to open the gifts in order because the story would continue.

With each gift I included a card or letter that shared more about our family or why I chose the gift. Along with the Tweety Bird Christmas stocking filled with candies, fun things, and fast food gift certificates, I told her how much my daughter loves Tweety Bird and shared all the Tweety things she has in her room. Since my Christmas child had asked for a night shirt and a warm throw, I got her a darling plaid flannel Tweety nightshirt and included the Tweety slippers that I also bought for my daughter.

I got her a phone card and shared how important it is to call those we love at Christmas and tell them. I got her some stationery and stamps to keep in touch with loved ones and tell them what they mean to her. I also encouraged her to give one of the gifts she had received from me to someone who was less fortunate than her. I explained what joy she would receive in giving—even greater than receiving all these gifts.

The last gift was a New Believer's Bible. I included a card that expressed that the greatest gift ever given was when Jesus came into the world. In that card I put a lengthy letter explaining the Gospel message and how Jesus has impacted my life. I invited her to begin reading the Bible and to find a good church family to belong to. I felt that after taking care of this child's physical needs, it was important to give her the opportunity to understand that Jesus can meet her needs every day, long after Christmas is over.

Tips:

I was deeply touched with the thoughtfulness, care, and love Laurie put into her holiday gifts for a young person she will never even know. What an impact that caring must have had on a young person in need! I encourage you to find someone with whom your family can share their blessings and love next Christmas—or any time of the year.

Give a Holiday Gift of Food
for the Body and the Soul

The Idea:

Often our gifts are for either the body or the soul, but Carol Stanger of Darien, Illinois, created a very special Christmas gift to nurture both.

The Idea in Action:

 Carol says:

At Christmas in 1996 I was not in a very festive mood. My daughter and my only grandchild had left town a couple of months prior, and it looked like I would be spending Christmas for the first time without them. I began thinking about all the people in my life who had been an influence in my Christian "walk" and were always there for me to lend support and encouragement when I was down. These included people from my church family, Christian friends, and also some who didn't include Jesus in their daily lives.

I wanted to do something to say thanks in a special way. Because food is always appreciated, I thought about baking cookies or bread, but that seemed too perishable since the list of people was widespread in area and delivery might not be possible within a certain time frame. Then the thought came to me that all sorts of food was mentioned in the Bible and maybe I could do something with that.

I put my Bible Explorer CD into my computer and began searching for any type of food I could think of and came up with a list of items and Bible verses associated with them. I sorted through and found items that were readily available in the local grocery store which were not too perishable (apples, fish— canned tuna, herbs—herbal mixes for tuna salad—onions, garlic, small jars of honey, nuts in their shells, olives, pomegranates, raisins, wine, bread—small pane loaves which could be picked up at the last minute).

I decided to make up baskets containing these items accompanied by the corresponding Bible verses. I made up a list of the people I wanted to deliver a basket to, and purchased the baskets at a discount store, with colored tissue paper to line the baskets, clear plastic to protect the final package, and big colorful bows to finish them off.

I began purchasing the food items as I found them, leaving the perishable items until close to assembly night. What a night that was, listening to Christmas music and sorting things into the baskets, wrapping and loading them into the trunk of the car as I got them done and planning how I was going to deliver each one in a special way. Two days before Christmas, I made my rounds and left my gifts. I didn't expect any responses, but this is what happened:

- The pastor's family (with three young children) sat and read each Bible verse together as they explored the contents of the basket;
- The young associate pastor and his wife saved it for an evening snack time and said it brought new meaning to each food item;
- One lady refilled the basket and returned it to me on my birthday the next week filled with "comforting" bath items;
- One couple who had not been to church for years said they were reminded of the meaning of the Christmas season;
- One couple appreciated the gifts of food during a hard time financially.

These gifts were in addition to anything which would have normally been exchanged with any of these people, and it gave me great pleasure to share my love of Christ and the messages in the Bible with others.

Carol's card in the basket read:

December 1996
This basket contains significant food items*
which are mentioned in the Bible, some
as far back as The Beginning (Genesis); others given
special meaning as being directly associated
with Jesus as He walked on this Earth.

I wish you Peace, Love, and Joy as we
reflect on the one true gift given to us all:
God's only begotten son, JESUS CHRIST,
and His wonderful Redeeming Grace.

* Each basket is prepared individually and may not contain all items, depending on the space allowed. Each was also filled with a helping of Love.

These were the items Carol included in the baskets, along with their corresponding Bible verses:

God's Food Plan for Us—Genesis 11–12

APPLE—Genesis 2:9; Song of Solomon 2:3
BREAD—Matthew 4:4, 6:11; Mark 14:22

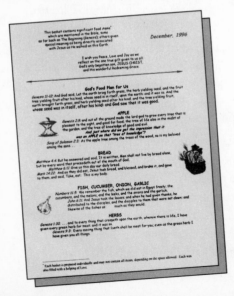

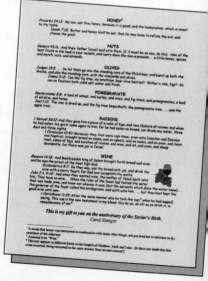

FISH, CUCUMBER, ONION, GARLIC—Numbers 11:5; John 6:11
HERBS—Genesis 1:30; Genesis 9:3
HONEY—Proverbs 24:13; Isaiah 7:15
NUTS—Genesis 43:11
OLIVES—Judges 15:5; James 3:12
POMEGRANATE—Deuteronomy 8:8; Joel 1:12
RAISINS—I Samuel 30:12; I Chronicles 12:40
WINE—Genesis 14:18; Ecclesiastes 9:7; John 2:3, 9–10; I Corinthians
    11:25

Tips:

Every culture and religion has traditions associated with food. What a special
way to share with others your own faith as well as sustenance for their physical bodies!

Give Holiday Gifts That
Focus on the Human Being

The Idea:

Giving a gift anytime is very special; however, when we give gifts
that are different and surprising
and truly focus on the humanness
of a person, the receiver is even
more delighted.

Aunt Ruth had a knack for
getting children gifts that their
parents hated.

The Idea in Action:

My "second mother," Gail
Flynn from Prairie Village,
Kansas, gave me a most wonderful Valentine's gift. The
beautiful cut-out silver box is called the English Silver Friendship Heart,
and on the front of the attached card it reads, "Here is just a sweet reminder whether near or far apart of the very special place you hold dear
in my heart." The inside of the card says:

In renewing an old English tradition, it is told how a special favor is traditionally passed back and forth as the occasion arises and exchanged through the years by friends, sisters, and mothers. It (the heart) contains soothing bath salts to enjoy in a quiet moment. Maybe it will be returned with special chocolates, a piece of jewelry, potpourri, or an antique handkerchief for drying tears. In any case, use your imagination to fill your friendship treasure and pass it back and forth through the years. After all, the real gift inside is the treasure of your friendship.

What a lovely idea and beginning of a special friendship tradition! The manufacturer is Alda's Forever Soap, P.O. Box 45504, Little Rock, AK 72214.

Deb Gauldin, a professional speaker and singer from Winfield, Illinois, and a special new friend, sent me a delightful and different gift this year. It was a darling old-fashioned plastic bathtub (soap dish) filled with a small star candle, a chocolate clock, a "Calm" herbal tea bag, some bubble bath marbles, and a blank list in a scroll titled "Wishes and Dreams," all tied in a cellophane bag with ribbons to match. This is what the card said:

Just a little reminder
from a holiday fairy so rare
She's bringing a special message
One of love and care

In all the hurry and bustle
the season soon will fly by
Where will we go? What will we do?
And then of course, what will we buy?

She dares us to call our attention
to someone most near and dear
Who may lose herself in the chaos
between now and the coming New Year

Midst the trappings of the season
Whatever tradition or view
Her wish is that you will be reverent
and cherish the gift that is

YOU

Promise you will take some time
to sip some tea while you unwind.
To soak in bubbles and make a list
of what you dream and what you wish.

And at the close of every day,
count the blessings on your way.

P.S. Between the turkey
and package stuffin'
Just sit still and don't do nothin'
If you exert any effort at all,
let it be
to watch
the snow
gently
fall.

Tips:

Think of a special gift that you can give to someone you love. It doesn't have to be expensive or big, just filled with love and your own uniqueness. This little treasure was just what I needed this year, and it brought tears to my eyes because of the special way Deb was thinking of me and my needs.

Take Traditional Holiday Photos

The Idea:

One of the ways to create traditions in your family is to always take certain traditional photos each year and then collect these in a special way.

The Idea in Action:

Barbara Swift tells about some traditional holiday photos her family takes:

> On Christmas morning the family always posed for a picture on the stairway as we came downstairs to open presents. I took all the pictures—gift opening, dinner table, sleeping off a big meal, etc., and put them into one album. (It's grown to a set of four since the 1950s.) The albums are our favorite reading material around the holidays, and you can hear frequent, "Oh, remember when I got that truck?" "Look, all the girl cousins had white knit dresses!" "Here's the gingerbread house Aunt Mildred made," "Sandy was just a puppy this year," and much more. My children have really enjoyed introducing their spouses to the family history and their memories through the albums. We frequently have brought them out at other times of the year to show to visiting family or friends to remind them of times they've shared the holidays with us.
>
> Incidentally, as the children married and established their own homes and came over Christmas Day for dinner, we couldn't take the "coming-down-the-stairs-in-the-morning" picture, so now we substitute pictures of each family coming in the door as they arrive laden with children and packages, and the tradition goes on in a slightly altered form.

Tips:

Many families take holiday pictures to use on their Christmas cards every year. We have done that for many years, and in one Christmas letter a former

English-as-a-Second-Language student of mine from China told me that he had all our family pictures for the last twelve years posted on his living-room wall. Because most people live in only one room in China, I realized how special those photos were to him. Another friend's mother gave us a very special gift last year—she had saved our family Christmas letters and photos since 1980 and sent them all back. What delight we had reading and sharing all those wonderful memories!

Make Meaningful Holiday Ornaments

The Idea:

A wonderful family holiday tradition is to create special ornaments as reminders of each year. Some people buy a special ornament for each child every year and label them so that when the child starts his own home, he already has many memorable ornaments to decorate his home. Others make special ornaments each year.

The Idea in Action:

A special holiday ornament you can make with your family every year is an Advent Candy Ribbon. You will need 2½ yards of 42-inch-wide ribbon for the base, two yards of narrow ribbon for the ties, one bell, and twenty-five pieces of candy. On the wide ribbon sew at even intervals narrower ribbon that will be tied in bows. Each bow will hold a piece of candy, and the bell should be sewn at the bottom.

Keep this poem with the Advent Candy Ribbon to read to the children on the first day of Advent each year when you refill the candy ribbon:

December 1st till Christmas
Is the longest time of year.
Seems as though old Santa
Never will appear.
How many days till Christmas?
It's mighty hard to count;
So this little candy ribbon
Will tell you the exact amount.

Untie a candy every night
When the Sandman casts his spell
And Christmas Eve will be here
By the time you reach the bell.

This is a fun family gift to make for friends, especially those with younger children.

📦 The Ed Burger family in Endicott, New York, shared two of their family holiday traditions with me:

Betsey's father used to grow and sell Christmas trees during his years as a YMCA director. Consequently, it is essential that we buy a "live" tree each Christmas. One thing we have done is to make the first cut off the bottom of the tree a straight perpendicular cut only about a half inch wide. Then I drill a hole and burn the year into each side of the wood. After putting ribbon through the hole, we have a very nice ornament. The kids look forward to this each year.

📦 *Another idea that is strictly on the "QT" was originated by my daughter, Erin. Although both Erin and Eric still believe in Santa, they are no longer at an age where they feel comfortable visiting him at a mall. On Erin's last visit to see Santa two years ago in 1995, she found a penny next to Santa's chair and handed it to him. He told her that was very nice of her to give it to him and that he might just leave one for her under the tree that year. Since then, I have similarly made ornaments from a penny for each of my children for their stockings. I always find a current-year penny and drill a hole in it and place a ribbon through the hole. This is another tradition they always look forward to each year, and of course, they always ask Santa for this in their letter to him on Christmas Eve.*

Tips:

It is easy to see from Ed's story how easily a holiday tradition can get started. It is these traditions and the memories they invoke that give a family roots and a sense of belonging.

Special Holiday Recipes Become Traditions

The Idea:

Many families have special recipes that they make only at holiday times, so these recipes become a part of the family's traditions, and they are often carried on from generation to generation as the family grows.

The Idea in Action:

🎁 One of the holiday recipes that is a tradition in the Glanz family is making rosettes. Grandma Glanz brought her special irons when she came over to this country from Germany, and these irons have become a treasure of the Glanz family. Because it takes several people to hold the irons in the hot oil, it is a wonderful family project for the holiday season. Over the years the grandchildren have begun borrowing the irons so that they, too, can make rosettes for their friends.

🎁 Niki Gombis, who grew up in Athens, Greece, shared several of their special holiday recipes with me. It is especially interesting to me that in Greece people don't have ovens in their homes, so all desserts are made on the stove. Also she shared that rarely do the Greek people have desserts with a meal except on holidays, Name Days, or if you are serving a guest. Here are the directions for one of their favorite holiday desserts:

Bring 6 cups milk to a slow boil.

Add peel of one lemon (cut in a single piece around the lemon), cinnamon sticks, 10 whole cloves, and 10 whole allspice. Let this mixture simmer for 30 minutes.

Melt 2 sticks of butter in a Dutch oven. Then brown a 15-ounce package of coarse semolina in the butter until it changes color to a dark blond. (It is optional to add slivered almonds and 1/2 cup golden raisins to the semolina, and Niki recommends doing so.)

Turn off the fire. Add 2 1/2 cups sugar and 1/2 cup honey to the milk. Stir to dissolve it completely.

Then pour the milk mixture into the semolina. (Niki cautions you to wear mitts as you do this as the mixture will bubble up and rise as you're pouring.)

Stir over low heat for 2 to 3 minutes to let it thicken to the texture of runny mashed potatoes.

Then put the mixture into one 10-cup or two 5-cup molds. Push down as you add it in layers to avoid air bubbles. Let sit for ten minutes.

After you remove the mixture from the mold, decorate it with almonds and sprinkle it with cinnamon and/or nutmeg. Serve it at room temperature.

Niki says it is not only delicious, but it is also nutritional for the members of the family!

Niki also shared another favorite Greek holiday recipe, which they eat only at Christmas and New Year's:

NIKI'S KOURBIEDES

Cream together 1 pound (4 sticks) butter and 5 tablespoons powdered sugar. Add 2 egg yolks and beat the mixture until smooth.

Then beat in 1 jigger (1/3 cup) brandy or whiskey.

In a separate bowl, mix 1 teaspoon baking powder into 4 1/2 cups sifted cake flour. Stir this mixture into the dough.

Stir in 1 cup finely chopped walnuts or almonds at the end.

Refrigerate the dough for an hour or more. Then roll the dough into small balls or pear shapes. Stick one whole clove in the top of each.

Bake at 350 degrees for about 20 minutes. They should not be brown. As soon as they come out of the oven, sift powdered sugar over the cookies or roll them in red or green sugar. Makes 5 dozen cookies.

Niki says her children especially like putting the cloves into the cookies. And in her words, "They'll melt in your mouth—the best cookies you've ever eaten!"

My daughter-in-law, Ashley Glanz, shared a special Dobert family tradition. Each year on Christmas Eve they make two Christmas casseroles, one for their family and another to give away. Since they must be made the night before, on Christmas morning all you have to do is put it in the oven and enjoy the rest of your day.

DOBERT CHRISTMAS CASSEROLE

1 pound pork sausage links
6 to 8 slices bread, cubed
1 cup grated sharp Cheddar cheese

4 eggs
¹/2 teaspoon dry mustard
2 cups milk

The day before serving, fry the sausage, drain well, and cut into thirds. Alternate layers of bread cubes, sausage, and cheese in a buttered 2¹/2-quart casserole dish. In a separate bowl, beat the eggs, add mustard and milk, and pour over the ingredients in the casserole dish. Cover with foil and refrigerate overnight. Bake at 325 degrees for 45 minutes. For vegetarians, substitute mushrooms or green pepper for the meat.

Tips:

Judy Motzenbecker of Kaneville, Illinois, always makes cinnamon squares from the leftover pumpkin pie crust, and they roast the pumpkin seeds from the children's jack-o'-lanterns at Halloween. Do you have special recipes that you make only on holidays in your family? That is one of the things that family members most look forward to and also what makes it hard when you are not able to be with your own family on special days. Sometimes it is very difficult to be away from home for a holiday, so why not share one of your family traditions with the family you are visiting?

Start Special Grandparent Holiday Traditions

The Idea:

If you are fortunate enough to have your grandchildren nearby, it creates wonderful memories to begin special holiday traditions with them.

The Idea in Action:

🎁 Julie Wiksten of Dallas, Texas, shares an idea her parents have begun with her children:

My mother and father are grandparents to four boys ranging in age from six to eleven. Starting last year, one weekend in December, they are all invited to spend the night with GranJan and GranDe (Jan and De Wiksten). The boys are told to bring some spending money and some new unwrapped toys.

During the evening of their sleepover, they get to go "shopping" for family Christmas gifts. But the store is indeed a special one! All year long, GranJan has gathered small gifts to stock "the store inventory." Each boy decides what family members he needs to buy a gift for and has the opportunity to select just the right thing. They pay the "cashier," GranDe, whatever they feel is appropriate for the gift, usually a dollar or two.

Once all the gifts are selected and purchased, the rest of the evening is spent wrapping and tagging them. Each tag is custom-made by the boys, and they are often more special than the gift itself!

The next morning, the entire group piles in the car and visits a nearby charity. The new, unwrapped toys are donated as well as all of the money they have used to "purchase" the gifts from GranJan and GranDe. This year, the cash donation was over seventy dollars.

On Christmas Eve, the boys distribute their gifts to family members and watch in delight as each card is read and the specially selected gift is opened. This tradition is now two years old and already the boys ask eagerly how long it will continue. This is their special time with GranJan and GranDe that gives them the opportunity to experience the true meaning of Christmas on many different levels.

> *Years wrinkle the skin, but to give up enthusiasm wrinkles the soul.*
>
> —Samuel Ullman

 I so fondly remember a tradition that my grandparents started for me and my two brothers and sister. Each Easter they chose one of us, and since we lived in a very small town in Iowa, they took that child on a special trip to Omaha, Nebraska—the next closest city—and they bought him or her a new Easter outfit—including everything from new underwear and shoes to accessories. I will never forget my special outfit when I was about nine years old. It was a little suit (very grown-up for a nine-year-old!) with a red jacket and a black and white short checked skirt. Then they bought me a red felt hat with a hole in the top and a feather (they were in style in those days), black patent shoes, a little patent purse, white gloves, and all new underwear. I felt like a princess—I had never had a completely new outfit before! However, it wasn't the outfit that meant the most—it was the special time alone with them. They had me model lots of different outfits before we chose "the one," we went to all the nicest stores and got lots of attention from the salespeople, we went to fancy restaurants for both lunch and dinner, and then I talked to them all by myself all the way home. My grandfather lived only five years after that, so it is one of my most treasured memories.

🎁 My parents started a tradition that we have begun to carry on with our children. The Christmas I was pregnant with our first child my parents gave us a Super 8 movie camera so that we could record memories (video cameras did not exist in those days). That camera took pictures of us bringing each of our children home from the hospital, their first steps, their first day of school, and birthdays, vacations, and Christmases in between, including pictures of two grandparents they never really got to know. Just this Christmas when our son and his wife were expecting their first child, we passed the tradition on—we bought them a video camera to record their family memories.

Tips:

These memories are priceless to children, especially since grandparents may not be alive for later years of their lives. If you're blessed to be a grandparent, think of a holiday tradition you could start with your grandchildren. You will be giving them a gift that will live on forever in their hearts.

Celebrate Other Holidays

The Idea:

Choose several special holidays and create family traditions around them.

The Idea in Action:

🎁 Barbara Swift and I both remember a family tradition of celebrating May Day on May 1. Barbara said they made little baskets from construction paper and filled them with flowers and then hung them on neighbors' and friends' doors. In my hometown of Harlan, Iowa, we either made or bought the little baskets and then filled them with all kinds of candy. You always gave the largest baskets to your best friends, of course! Part of the tradition was that you were to leave the basket at a friend's door, knock on the door, and then run away. If they caught you, they got to kiss you. So it was always with eagerness and anxiety that you approached the home of someone of the opposite sex that you "liked"! One of my fondest memories is about a boy who had a crush on me in about the fourth or fifth grade. He was so nervous that I might catch him when he brought my May basket that he knocked so hard on our storm door he broke the glass! (You can imagine how much fun my little brothers had with that one. . . .)

Wanting simply to face the inevitable, many parents have begun to organize chicken pox parties.

My dear friend Rita Emmett tells how her family celebrated St. Patrick's Day:

My parents, who were both born of people "from the old country," leaned over backwards to be as American as possible. As a result, they tossed out all the wonderful old traditions. So, when my children were small, I decided to create some traditions of my own.

The evening before St. Patrick's Day, I would casually make a bowl of red gelatin dessert and put it in the refrigerator. Then after the children were in bed, I'd run over to a neighbor's house, give her the dessert, race back, and make green "Jell-O Jigglers." We called them Knox Blocks. (For those not familiar with them, it's a special way to make a gelatin dessert that you can pick up and hold in your hand—but if you drop it, the thing bounces all over the house!)

Early the next morning, I'd wake up the children by hollering that I caught a leprechaun. As soon as the first child came running around the corner, I'd look at him or her and—of course, everybody knows that the only way a leprechaun can escape is if you look away—that little elf would immediately disappear! So, even though I caught one every St. Patrick's Day morning, my children never saw him because it's a mother's natural instinct to look at her child when he or she comes running and hooting and hollering into a room.

Then we'd all go through the house together to find out what the little mischief-making leprechaun did to us this year. Sometimes he'd turn our milk green. It looked terrible on oatmeal, pretty cool on Rice Krispies, and tasted just like regular milk! Some years he'd set our places at the breakfast table with pots and pans and put the dishes on the stove. The pranks were always silly, always harmless, but EVERY SINGLE YEAR he changed red regular Jell-O into green bouncy stuff!

Maybe this tradition doesn't exist in Ireland, but now my children are married and have children of their own—and you'll never guess what happened at their houses last St. Patrick's Day!

🎁 Peggy Weidner from St. Charles, Illinois, tells of an Easter tradition that her family began:

> **Life is either a daring adventure or nothing.**
>
> **—Helen Keller**

Our Easter tradition was out of necessity as our youngest son has many food allergies. The traditional Easter basket contents would have been poison to him, so we decided to change the tradition. In our children's Easter baskets we changed the focus from chocolate bunnies to rebirth and things that give life—such as packets of flower, vegetable, and gourd seeds. One year birdhouse gourds were the family's gifts to all the relatives. We dried, decorated, and actually made functional birdhouses from the Easter gift of life! Another year the Easter basket gift was an aquarium with all the trimmings including books on fish and how to set it up, again a focus on life. The budget dictates whether it is a packet of seeds to plant or a more costly item; however, it can be done at any cost level very successfully. As a family, on Easter we share the fruits of life.

🎁 In a large family it is often hard to have meaningful communication. One of our dear family friends has the following tradition at their Thanksgiving dinner. The table is set with an unlit candle at each person's place. The first person begins by lighting his or her candle and sharing something about the past year: perhaps what things they are thankful for, what was the hardest obstacle they had to overcome during the past year, or how God touched their life in some special way. Then that person lights the candle of the person next to him or her, and they share something about their year, and the light keeps getting passed on. The mother told me what a touching experience this is for all of them and how even their guests enter in the sharing.

In another family each year the father writes a special blessing for each person in the family, focusing on things they have achieved or learned in the past year and affirming them for that. He reads the blessing to each one of them individually at their Thanksgiving dinner as he holds him or her on his knee. Even when the children have grown up, he still holds them, and they still love it!

Another wonderful family tradition that was shared with me is that on New Year's Day each family member writes a letter to the other members of the family, appreciating them and sharing special things about them that they really like. Then these letters are rolled up, tied with a ribbon, and put in everyone's Christmas stocking.

Laurie Trice shares how their neighborhood celebrated the Fourth of July:

One of our neighbors, Florence Perry Heide, is an author of children's books, and she always did a very creative thing each Fourth of July. Many of the neighborhood children were very young, and parents didn't always want to take them to the big city parade. So Florence organized her own children's parade! She would have her children or grandchildren announce parade details by writing them in crayon on paper plates and hanging the plates with yarn from trees all around the neighborhood. All the children decorated their bicycles, Big Wheels, and wagons with Fourth of July decorations.

The parade started in front of Florence's house on the sidewalk. Her older children would carry a boom box, drums, and whatever other instruments they could muster up. Children and moms and dads all followed as they led the parade around the block. At the end of the parade, Florence served everyone ice cream in her front yard. Florence has moved away now, but someone in the neighborhood is keeping the tradition of the parade alive. Last year you couldn't tell the beginning of the parade from the end—it went all the way around the block!

Many years ago I started an Easter tradition with our family that today many families have adopted. I bought several dozen plastic Easter eggs of all different colors. Then I used a sharp instrument and melted holes in the top and bottom pointed ends of each egg. Through the holes I threaded floral wire so that I made a loop to be able to hang the egg. Then at the beginning of the Easter month, each child got to invite a friend, and we created an Easter egg tree in front of our house by hanging the eggs all over the branches. Twenty years ago this brought lots of traffic in front of our house for a few weeks!

🎁 Debby Heltzer of Cedar Rapids, Iowa, has a special Valentine's Day tradition. She hand-makes beautiful valentines and then sends them to single friends who may not receive any valentines from others. What a loving gift she is giving!

Tips:

Choose one or two holidays that are meaningful to you and make up your own traditions. You will, like Rita, be amazed that often these traditions move down through the generations.

Do Group Cooking

The Idea:

These are fun party ideas for a family, class party, a neighborhood get-together, or a community event.

The Idea in Action:

🎁 Make "Friendship Soup." The hostess starts the soup, using chicken broth or beef or vegetable stock. Then each guest brings a vegetable to add to the soup. They may bring them chopped and peeled, or they may do that when they arrive. While the soup cooks, the group can play games or other activities. When it is ready, they all share a "community" meal.

This is a great idea for families with tight budgets, college students, or even small children learning about various vegetables. And the soup is good! Ashley, my daughter-in-law, even tells of one incident when her family was hosting the party, and the locusts were out. Several of the neighborhood boys "added" a handful of the locusts to the soup, and it was still eaten! (I'm not sure I recommend this. . . .)

🎁 A family with nine children have started a special tradition as they have become adults. Once a year they fly in from all over the country and meet at a sister's home in Washington, D.C., for a special meal. She is a gourmet cook, and she plans the menu and assigns each one of them a task in preparing the meal. Not only is it a wonderful sharing time with everyone pitching in to make the day successful but it is also fun to watch the men in the kitchen! They often hear things from the sports jocks like, "What in the heck does 'marinade' mean?"

John and Mary Graff of Sanibel, Florida, have a wonderful tradition with their grandchildren. At holiday time they make this special punch just for the children:

> Two 10- to 12-ounce packages frozen sliced strawberries, thawed
> 2 tablespoons lemon or lime juice
> 1 bottle (25.4 ounces/750ml) Catawba or Welch's sparkling grape juice, chilled
> 1 bottle (28 ounces) lemon-lime soda, chilled
>
> In a bowl press the strawberries through a sieve or put them in a food processor or blender. Stir lemon or lime juice into the pulp. Cover and chill.
> Put the strawberry pulp in a large bowl. Carefully pour grape juice and soda into the chilled pulp, stirring with an up-and-down motion.

They freeze a gelatin mold with whole strawberries in it and float that with sliced lemons on the top. They serve it in Mary's mother's antique milk glass punch bowl with punch cups, in a very "grown-up" way, and the children love it. What they love the best, however, is that after the first bowl is gone, they get to go in the kitchen and make the recipe for the next bowl!

The Jerry Pavloff family of Ligonier, Pennsylvania, have family International Cooking nights. Jerry says:

On these nights, all four of us cook the meal, which usually has a theme to it. For example, we had a guest from India once who cooked an Indian meal for us. She also gave us a cookbook as a hospitality appreciation gift. When we are "hungry" for Indian food, we take out the cookbook and as a family decide the menu. We divide up the responsibilities, i.e., the slicing, dicing, seasoning, frying, and everybody works. We've done this following visits of guests from Israel and Italy. Although we haven't had guests from China, included in the cuisines for these nights are stir-fry and other oriental recipes.

Aaron is now nine, and Evan is seven. We've been doing this for two years, and the boys love it. These events inspire some of the best cooperation that we enjoy with our family. And, you never have to coax them to eat on these occasions. They "clean their plates," and sometimes we even run out of food before they are finished!

Tips:

Isn't the kitchen the primary meeting/sharing spot in most of our homes? Whenever you create sharing times such as these around food, you bring people together in a most basic and significant way. We are truly "breaking bread together."

Do Silly Things Together

The Idea:

At least once a week do something silly as a family. It will relieve stress, make everybody laugh, and create a feeling of humanness and belonging.

The Idea in Action:

🎁 Trish Walker Webb tells about one of their silly family traditions. Every Sunday afternoon as they were changing their clothes from church and getting ready for Sunday supper, the whole family listened to Casey Kasem's *American Top Forty* on the radio. As the show counted down from the number 40 tune to the number 1 hit of the week, the entire family danced along with the music. She said, "We couldn't believe my mom and dad and how much fun they had dancing right along with us!" How long has it been since your family danced together? The kids might be surprised at what their folks can do!

🎁 Whenever a family we know gets a package, they all fight over who gets to pop the bubble wrap. In fact, sometimes they seem more interested in that than the package, one of them told me! When is the last time you popped bubble wrap in weird and creative ways?

🎁 Take an oval-shaped gelatin mold, fill it with pink gelatin, and keep stirring it a little bit as it hardens to make "brains." Then serve these to your family as a salad for dinner!

🎁 Matt Weinstein of Playfair, Inc., suggests these silly fight diffusers for a family or marital spat:

- *Hide props around the house. When tempers flare, don a fake nose and mustache.*
- *Call for "write mode." Jot down the reasons why you're angry, along with a favorite joke. Give the list to your family member or partner.*

If things get too serious, do what Weinstein did during his first marital bout. "I broke an egg over my head," he quips.

These silly things help to put small disagreements into perspective, and if you end up laughing, it breaks the tension and makes it easier to talk more rationally about one another's needs.

🎁 Even traditions can be silly! Our daughter-in-law Ashley tells about a Christmas present her brother Mark gets every year. Many years ago her father started giving her brother some kind of gross food gift for Christmas. One year Mark received a bag of pickled pig's lips in his stocking. It was so disgusting that he threw it away. Ashley's Dad secretly retrieved it, froze it, and each year from then on, Mark gets it again. Father Earl has come up with some pretty good "disguises," according to Ashley!

Tips:

Your children may complain at first, but they really love for you to be silly. How long has it been since you blew bubbles together and chased them all over the yard? Painted with water? Had a pillow fight? Ate dinner with your hands? Dressed up in silly clothes? Your children will never forget those times.

Find Fun Recipes That the Whole Family Can Enjoy

The Idea:

When my children were little, one of their favorite things to do was to be with me in the kitchen while I cooked. Often I let them "help" (Gretchen even liked to lick the bowl of Crisco when I was making pie crusts!); however, sometimes I needed to distract them with their own fun while I concentrated on making dinner. At other times we did these recipes together.

The Idea in Action:

The children loved to play with Play Doh, but it seemed to get lost easily or harden up or the dog ate it! Bev Buer, a creative friend with children about the same ages, gave me a recipe for *homemade play dough* so that it was always available:

> 1 cup flour
> 1/2 cup salt
> 1 cup water
> 1 tablespoon cooking oil
> 2 teaspoons cream of tartar

If the children wanted to save one of their creations permanently, we baked the dough on low for a short time, and that caused the dough to harden.

Because the little ones always want to put things in their mouths, another favorite recipe was for Peanut Butter Play Dough, and the delightful thing about this recipe is that the children can play with it and then *eat* it!

PEANUT BUTTER PLAY DOUGH

> *Peanut butter (smooth)—start out with a couple of tablespoons*
> *Honey—about a teaspoon (can be more or less or none)*
> *Nonfat dried milk powder—enough so the peanut butter is not sticky*
> *Mix with a spoon and then roll into a ball.*

📦 Another fun activity is to make *pretzel animals*. You need:

> 1 *package dry yeast*
> 1 1/2 *cups warm water*
> 1 *tablespoon sugar*
> 1 *tablespoon salt*
> 4 *cups flour*
> 1 *egg, beaten*

In a big bowl mix together yeast, water, sugar, and salt. Stir in flour.
Knead on table until dough is smooth. Shape dough into animal shapes.
Brush with beaten egg. Sprinkle with additional salt. Bake at 425 degrees for 15
minutes or until browned.

📦 *Mr. Peanut Butter Head* is a version of Mr. Potato Head. Cut a slice of bread into an oval and cover with peanut butter. Then provide the children with various edible foods to create the face—bread crusts, carrot slices, raisins, nuts, seeds, shredded cheese, olives, and so on. The children can make their lunch and eat it too!

📦 *Painted Cookies*—Slice your favorite refrigerator cookie recipe and place on a baking sheet. Make "paint" from evaporated milk and food coloring. Paste food coloring sets are a good investment for the best colors. Use inexpensive watercolor paintbrushes to "paint" the cookies. You may also do this on cut-out shaped cookies.

📦 A *Valentine Cake* is a heart-shaped cake for a special holiday family treat—or simply to say "I love you"! Mix a two-layer cake recipe and then bake in one 8-inch or 9-inch square and one 8-inch or 9-inch round pan. Cut the round layer in half and frost as shown in the diagram:

Younger children can decorate with red hots, red licorice, sprinkles, gum drops, thumb prints, or animal crackers. Older children may draw or cut out paper decorations and tape them on toothpicks.

Tips:

Especially with the peanut butter play dough, make sure the children wash their hands first! These recipes provide wonderful ways for the whole family to express their creativity together. We often made things from the play dough, and then the other family members had to guess what they were. Another fun food my mother made we called "ribbon sandwiches." She cut off the crusts of bread and alternately spread peanut butter and jelly on the sandwich four to six slices high. Then she cut each one into four slices so that the peanut butter and jelly made them look like ribbons.

Celebrate Good Neighbor Day

The Idea:

September 4 is Good Neighbor Day, a program started in Jackson, Mississippi, in 1994 by florists. Local mayors are asked to proclaim the day "Good Neighbor Day" in their respective communities. The Good Neighbor Day theme is the florist industry's response to cynicism and mistrust in the world. It is a time to turn to optimism.

The Idea in Action:

On Wednesday, September 4, 1996, all nine Phillip's Flowers & Gifts shops in the western suburbs of Chicago, Illinois, began a new tradition as a part of Good Neighbor Day. They gave away ten thousand flowers! Each store visitor received one dozen roses while supplies lasted, according to J. R. Phillip, chairman of the family-owned business, which was founded in 1923. Those who received the twelve-rose bouquet were asked to keep one flower and give one to each of eleven neighbors as an expression of friendship. Phillip was quoted in the *Suburban Life* newspaper as saying, "A little thoughtfulness goes a long way in making life pleasant for both the giver and the receiver. That is what the event is all about."

Tips:

Not only can you mention this special program to your own local florists, but you can also think of things you might do in your community on September 4 to celebrate "Good Neighbor Day."

Discover Special Ways to Celebrate the Seasons

The Idea:

One of the wonderful ways we can honor the changing seasons with our families is to find creative, delightful ways to celebrate the beauty and uniqueness of each special time of the year.

The Idea in Action:

Some families plan special day trips during different seasons of the year. When we were growing up in Harlan, Iowa, one of our family traditions was a fall trip to Mondamin, Iowa, a state park known for its wild beauty. We each got to pick a friend, my mother prepared a scrumptious picnic lunch, and we all packed into our Ford station wagon for the trip (with four children *and* their friends, it was a pretty tight squeeze!). Each of us had our special places in that park. My brothers and their friends played cowboys and Indians, hiding in the trees and roaming the hills looking for arrowheads. I loved a kind of tepee made from logs where my friend and I could sit in secret and tell stories and talk about boys! My little sister loved going with Dad to look for animals, and my mother always picked bittersweet to make arrangements when she got back home. It was a wonderful day, and even though we had to go back to school, we always looked forward to fall because of this fun family day.

If you live in a northern climate, there are many fun ways to celebrate winter. I recently saw a snowman in our neighborhood that was colored! Evidently the children had used food coloring, and each layer of the snowman was a different color—green on the bottom, pink in the middle, and blue on top. A friend told me that at the Creative Day Preschool in Elmhurst, Illinois, they made a huge Barney snowman, and he was even purple! Snow sculptures are a delightful way to help your children celebrate winter.

November is a good time to have a nature scavenger hunt. Here is a list of ten things your child and some friends or your family may enjoy looking for. Substitute any other items you'd like:

1. An acorn or other nut
2. A brown leaf
3. A smooth stone
4. Something fuzzy
5. A rough twig
6. A pine cone
7. Something white
8. A few pine needles
9. A dried weed
10. Three round berries

Tips:

You might celebrate the first daffodil of spring by buying a bunch for your kitchen table, or summer's first strawberries by making shortcake or dipping the berries in chocolate or powdered sugar. Celebrate the return to school in the fall by making a big deal out of shopping for school supplies. I still love buying a box of sixty-four crayons each fall! Welcome the first snowfall by making paper snowflakes and sharing hot chocolate. Some families attend fall or spring festivals as a tradition. You can pick apples together in the fall or strawberries or blueberries in the spring and summer. Look through a guide from the Chamber of Commerce for your part of the state to find what kinds of festivals exist in your area. Then begin your own family seasonal traditions.

Plan Theme Birthday Parties

The Idea:

One of the wonderful, creative gifts you can give your children is to plan birthday parties with a theme. The more creative you are, the better. Your children (and their friends) will never forget your efforts.

The Idea in Action:

When our children were young, our budget was tight; however, I decided that one of the things I could do that was special for them was to create unique, theme birthday parties, different from the ones everyone else had.

I didn't spend much money, but I used lots of imagination and their interests at the time. Here are some of the favorite birthday parties we had:

• **A Barbie Party.** When Gretchen was really into Barbies, we planned this party. Each little girl was asked to bring her favorite Barbie doll in her best outfit. Then we had a Barbie fashion show with each little girl telling about her doll's outfit. The cake was a rounded cake I baked in a metal mixing bowl, and when it was placed upside down and a Barbie doll stuck up to her waist in it, it looked like a Barbie in a large hoop skirt. I decorated it and the top of the doll with pink frosting for the dress and then added flowers for trim. We played several Barbie games, and each little girl received a handmade Barbie outfit for her doll as a favor.

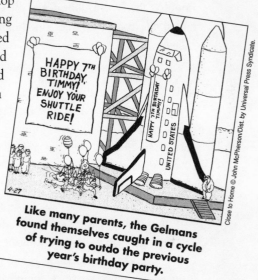

Like many parents, the Gelmans found themselves caught in a cycle of trying to outdo the previous year's birthday party.

• **A Mother Goose Party.** This party was for Erin's fifth birthday, when she was in kindergarten. Each child was asked to come dressed as his or her favorite nursery rhyme. Then we had a parade and everyone guessed what rhyme each child represented. Shortly into the party, the doorbell rang, and we had the arrival of a special guest—Mother Goose herself! (This was a high school baby-sitter who was in theater and volunteered for the part.) The children were delighted. Mother Goose then played several theme games with them and read them nursery rhymes. The cake was a re-creation of "The Old Woman Who Lived in a Shoe." Using several different loaf pans, I created a large shoe, decorated it with frosting and red licorice for shoelaces and then populated it with wooden Fisher-Price people. Favors were tapes of Mother Goose rhymes.

• **A Monster Party.** Each child was asked to come dressed as a monster of some kind. Garrett was Count Dracula. We decorated the basement with all kinds of spiderwebs, bats hanging from the ceiling, and various masks stuffed and put on poles. The cake was a sheet cake with spider-webs made from red and black string licorice covered with black plastic bugs and spiders. We played monster games, danced the "Monster Mash," and watched the movie *Abbott and Costello Meet the Mummy*. The favors were various monster things such as fake blood, a rubber finger, ghoulish masks, and other body parts.

- **A Pirate Party.** The boys were asked to dress in pirate gear while Garrett was Captain Hook. The cake was a treasure chest filled with gold coin candy and gumdrops strung as necklaces. Favors were gifts from Disney World's "Pirates of the Caribbean," and all the paper goods had skulls and crossbones on them. We watched the movie *Treasure Island*.

- **A Shopping Mall Party.** This was Erin's party when she was twelve and really into shopping. We gathered all the girls into three vans and drove to an indoor mall, where we played three games. One was a hunt for the five adults who had come along. Each adult stationed themselves in a part of one of the stores (it is a large mall!) while the girls stayed in one spot in the center. They then had thirty minutes in teams to try to find all the adults and get each of their signatures. Next we gave them each two dollars. They had thirty minutes to see how much they could buy with it and then come back and show the group. The "winner" was the one who got the most for her money. Last we had a scavenger hunt in teams. We gave the girls a list, and they had to ask clerks in the stores for certain items. Then we came back to our house and had cake and ice cream. The cake was in the shape of a shopping bag, and their favor was the book *Secrets of the Shopping Mall* and a bag of chocolate gold coin money "wrapped" in—a shopping bag!

- **A Magic Party.** Garrett practiced his magic tricks for this party! The cake was a top hat with a white chocolate rabbit coming out of the top of the hat. (I had a little trouble with this one and had to have several soup cans to hold the brim of the hat up!) Each of the guests received his or her own magic trick and then had to perform it for the whole group.

- **A Japanese Party.** When Gretchen was ten, she was really interested in anything Japanese. We had a Japanese girl who was staying with us for a short time, and she helped plan the party and taught them several

Japanese games and how to say a few words in Japanese. We had tea, rice rolls wrapped in nori, and Japanese cookies and candy, and we ate sitting on the floor with chopsticks. We decorated with Japanese lanterns, Gretchen wore a kimono, and the children received Japanese fans for favors.

- **A "Boring" Party.** When our son Garrett was going to be sixteen, he and his friends always found everything "boring," so I decided to have an unusual surprise birthday party for him. The invitations to his friends read, "IF YOU WANT TO BE BORED, COME TO GARRETT'S SURPRISE PARTY. PLEASE DRESS IN YOUR MOST BORING CLOTHES. WE GUARANTEE THAT YOU WILL HAVE AN EXTREMELY <u>BORING</u> NIGHT!" As the fifty-plus guests from his school and youth group arrived, I gave them each a box of crayons and paper and asked them to draw a picture for Garrett while we waited for him to come home from work. After the "surprise," I served them their "boring" dinner—American cheese sandwiches on white bread with no mustard or mayonnaise, unsalted potato chips, and milk. The "boring" dessert was plain white cake with plain white frosting and plain vanilla ice cream.

  They then went to the family room for their "boring" entertainment. I rented two silly, boring movies—*The Attack of the Killer Tomatoes* and a documentary called *Those Hairy Apes*. Afterward in each room I had set up children's games such as Twister, Monopoly, Chinese checkers, Clue, Candyland, and Chutes and Ladders. As a final "boring" activity, I got out all Garrett's childhood photo albums, scrapbooks, and baby book for them to look at, and we showed home movies of "Garrett growing up." Many of the kids stayed until two A.M., and they talked about the "Boring" Party for years!

🎁 In her book *Shelter for the Spirit* Victoria Moran tells of one of their best celebrations—an impromptu **birthday party for Mozart**:

Rachael was eight and quite taken with the thought of someone her age composing, so on the draggy winter afternoon—January 27, to be exact—that the newspaper told us was his birthday, we played Mozart tapes and baked a sheet cake. There was some half-used cake decorating gel left over from the birthday of someone still living, so we used it to regale Wolfgang's cake in quarter notes and sharps and flats. Then we rented the film Amadeus. A week later I over-

heard Rachael asking one of her friends what he had done for Mozart's birthday. Holidays are in the home of the beholder. We now do Mozart's birthday every year.

🎁 When Ryan LaCombe of Gainesville, Florida, was two, his aunt Rita planned "Ryan's Rainbow Parade" to celebrate his birthday. He picked his favorite color of the rainbow, which was red, and dressed in it. Then each of his cousins dressed in one of the other rainbow colors. Aunt Rita made them each a flag of their rainbow color to carry as they rode their Big Wheels and trikes and bikes in the parade. She also created huge cardboard number 2s, which she hung from the branches of the trees in the park to guide the parade to where the party would be held. Ryan's cake was a drum with chopsticks for drumsticks to go with the parade theme. What a special idea for a young child's celebration!

Tips:

It is important that the theme of the party be something appropriate for your child's age and his or her interests. I would ask my children what kind of party they wanted, and then our creative juices would start flowing. Several times when I was really swamped, we took the children special places for their parties—to an ice skating rink, to McDonald's, and to Second City Theatre. But the best parties of all were the theme parties. Both my children and their friends (and their friend's mothers) still remember some of those parties!

Start Birthday Traditions in Your Family

The Idea:

One of the best kinds of traditions to start in your family is something that revolves around birthdays. Because most of us celebrate birthdays anyway, beginning a tradition tied to them is easier than starting a whole new tradition.

The Idea in Action:

🎁 Tracey Wolski tells of a family birthday tradition started by her mother, Maureen Frost, of Villa Park, Illinois. Birthdays are very important in the

Frost family. Whenever anyone has a birthday, at the beginning of the present opening, the birthday person gets a "Bombardment Gift" from each member of the family. Tracey told about some of the "Bombardment Gifts" that had been received:

- Her husband loves a certain kind of hair gel, so on his last birthday everyone gave him a bottle of it. Now that he has ten bottles, his hair will look wonderful forever!
- On Tracey's birthday she received all different kinds of spoons. The last time her mother had visited her home for a party she was nearly out of serving spoons.
- Her son, in Tracey's words, is a "super sucker fanatic," so on his birthday everyone got him some kind of a sucker. He has enough to have a sucker every day for weeks (and Tracey has to pay the dental bills!).
- Her twenty-six-year-old brother told them he wanted toys for his birthday, so his bombardment gift was a matchbox car from everyone.
- They got her sister rolls of film because she always takes thousands of pictures.
- Tracey's mom got all kinds of knee-high nylons, which she needed, and Tracey said that several other members of the family had also gotten socks.

Usually Maureen, the mom, decides what the bombardment gift will be; however, when it is her birthday, Tracey gets to choose the gift. She says it is one of their most treasured family traditions and makes birthdays even more fun.

Barbara Swift of Western Springs, Illinois, tells of a favorite birthday tradition in their family:

On birthdays all four children piled into our bed in the morning and opened birthday gifts that were piled in the chair in our bedroom. The pile of gifts was always covered with the same old bathrobe. I still have the bathrobe. I can't part with it even though I never wear it. Mothers have happy memories, too!

Rosemary Meyer is the mother of five children, and it was very difficult for her to plan a birthday party with all five of them needing her, so her mother, Anna Delfs, began a birthday tradition that lasted throughout her children's growing-up years. Whenever one of them had a birthday,

The Lubermans prepare for Willie's third birthday party.

the grandma came over very early i the morning and took all the chi dren to her house. She brought the party clothes and then planned special day for them while Rose mary got everything ready for th party.

First, she took the birthda person out to get a new outfit an then they did a special craft pro ect. She gave the children a kinds of old magazines and cor struction paper. Each of them cut pictures out of the maga zines they liked and paste them on the bright-colore paper. Then they punche holes in the construction paper and tie it with yarn to make special scrapbooks. Later Grandma woul get them all ready in their party clothes, and when they came home everything for the party would be ready. So *everyone* had a good day—th children had a special day with their grandmother, and Rosemary had a day alone to plan the party!

Karen Sivert shared how her mother always baked a personalized, beaut fully decorated birthday cake for each of her six children each year wit "Happy Birthday" and their name on it. Karen says, "We felt so special. don't remember what the gifts were—but I sure remember the cakes!"

Tips:

Have your children think of something special and fun that you might do i your family for birthdays. Perhaps the birthday person wears a special crow that is passed around, or maybe they get to stay up as late as they want on the special day, or perhaps they get to choose all the meals for their whole birth day week.

Have a "Come-as-You-Are" Party

The Idea:

A delightful way to get a group of friends together is to have a "come-as-you-are" party. The idea is that they must come to the party exactly as they are—no showering, shaving, doing hair, or dressing up.

The Idea in Action:

As I was growing up, one of the most fun things my mother did with me was to plan "come-as-you-are" parties. Usually they were planned only a day or two ahead of time, and we always did them on a Saturday morning or a holiday. My mother would drive, and we would go early in the morning to all my friends' houses, where I would wake them up and sometimes drag them out of bed to the party. As we picked up more and more people (we had a station wagon, and there weren't seat-belt laws in those days), the whole group would go in to get the new invitee, so it became lots of fun to "surprise" our friends. Sometimes I even had another mother in on the surprise so we had two cars picking up. It was amazing to see the different outfits the girls wore to bed!

When we arrived at my house with everyone in their pjs, we always had the party on the sun deck out in back. We had a large picnic table, and my mother would always have it set with juice, milk, and fresh fruit, and then she would make homemade doughnuts. Of course, we laughed a lot and took a lot of pictures, but the best was the doughnuts. To this day when we have reunions, my friends remember those parties and those homemade doughnuts!

Tips:

This idea can work with boys as well as girls or even with adults, although it is probably safer to pick them up later in the morning or on a Sunday afternoon or evening rather than rousting them out of bed! As my friends got older and the boys discovered we had these parties, we had to have them inside the house. . . .

Give Gifts from Your Heart and Personal Passion

The Idea:

True giving comes from a pure heart and the desire to please another. It may also come from the intense desire to share something you love with another.

The Idea in Action:

Sophia Weibel of Naperville, Illinois, writes about one of her most memorable gifts:

> It is much easier to give than to receive for me. I feel that I need to work harder to become a better Christian and therefore, I do not feel worthy of the many gifts and blessings that I receive. There is one time, however, in which receiving was such a wonder, I can never forget it. . . .
>
> I have a sister who is four years younger than me. As we were growing up, my sister always wanted to do what I did and follow me around. I know now how much she loved me, but back then I had a very different response. It was around my birthday, and I was about to turn nine. My older brother gave me something "cool" he made in school, and my parents got me a toy that I wanted. My sister suddenly disappeared from the kitchen and ran upstairs in a frenzy as she was determined to get me a gift I'd really enjoy.
>
> She came back down a few minutes later with two square presents wrapped in Sunday comics. She handed them to me with the biggest smile on her face, and she said she knew I'd like them. When I opened them up, I found they were my favorite books, which she took from my bookshelf. It made me smile, and I hugged her so tight. . . . I loved the books, though they were mine already, but I loved the thought even more, and from then on, I understood the love my sister had for me. To this day, I'll never forget her thoughtfulness . . . although I must admit, she still follows me around (smile).

Some of the best gifts my children ever received were born of the love and passion others had for their work. Uncle Bruce, who lives in Grand Junction, Colorado, has a double doctorate in Biology and Zoology and teaches survival skills at Mesa State College. He has given both us and our children some of our most memorable and educational gifts, all associated with his passion. When Garrett was in fourth grade, his Christmas gift from Uncle Bruce was a fully preserved small shark, complete with a dissecting kit and instructions. Not only did Garrett learn a great deal about animal biology, but he was also the hit of the grade school as he got to visit every classroom and present a "show and tell" like no other!

Another year his present was a stuffed white rat from Uncle Bruce's lab lying on its stomach with its little feet out in front of it. It's head was "caught" in a wooden rat trap, and the other end of the trap had a small, hollowed-out place which contained a square glass ashtray. The card attached said, "Smoking is gross, so here is a gross ashtray!" Needless to say, Garrett got the message! (And he had the most unusually decorated room of any of his friends. . . .)

My mother, who was a former art teacher, has given them many wonderful art projects to create, and Uncle Brian, who is a world traveler, brought them gifts such as an Afghan warrior's sword and a centuries-old pot from the canals of Thailand. Uncle Brian is also a dog lover, so another year he surprised us all with "Roscoe G. Simpson," a cockapoo puppy who was a dearly loved member of the family. Because I love books and reading, each Christmas and birthday, even as adults, I give the children special books.

Kathie Hightower suggests a wonderful gift idea that she got from a military spouse and that has been adopted by many others:

When my husband was being promoted to lieutenant colonel, I wanted to give him a special gift. I bought a photo album with a three-ring binding. I sent individual pages to all his friends and family with a letter asking that they fill the page with memories of Greg. That could include photos, funny memories, poignant memories, or whatever. Then I put the pages together. It's a gift that he looks at over and over as the years go by. It would be a great way to do a gift for a special anniversary or a special birthday. It doesn't cost much—just time. And it means more than most other gifts ever could.

Maria Marino of Ontario, Canada, tells of a story in the newsletter of the Avenue Road Art School: "Student Arei Rosenberg created a four-foot 'Guardian Bunny' in a Papier Mache class for her first grandchild, Sophie. The Bunny's vest is adorned with ancestral photos dating back to Sophie's great, great, great grandparents." What a gift of the heart!

Tips:

The best gifts are those truly given from the heart, like the one Sophia's little sister gave. Help your children realize that gifts don't have to cost money. Then think about what your passions, loves, and interests are. Are you sharing those gifts with your loved ones?

Find Romantic Things to Do
for Those You Love

The Idea:

We all need to keep the romance and caring alive in our relationships. My friend Scott Finley of Dallas, Texas, is one of the most romantic men I have ever known. I asked Scott for some of his secrets.

The Idea in Action:

Scott says, "First of all, romance doesn't always mean a red rose, a bottle of wine, and satin sheets. Under my definition, it also includes these ideas which cost you little or nothing and are easy to do":

- *Backing her car out of the garage and turning it around in the driveway to face the street on cold mornings.*
- *Noticing that her car is out of gas, taking it, and filling it up for her.*
- *Making the bed.*
- *Doing the laundry (Men take note: Look at the "how to care for" tags in her clothing!).*
- *Doing the dishes (including unloading the dishwasher).*
- *Dropping off and picking up dry cleaning.*
- *Doing the grocery shopping.*
- *Vacuuming and dusting.*
- *Rubbing her shoulders.*
- *Brushing her hair.*
- *Leaving a little message in her jewelry box: "Hello to the most beautiful woman in the world!"*

- Bringing her a cup of coffee or hot chocolate or tea in the morning while she's doing her makeup and hair for work.
- Taking care of the cat boxes (It's a nasty job, but someone's got to do it, and you're fooling yourself if you think the Persian is going to get in there with a little shovel!).

Now, if you want to spend a little money:

- Stop and get a box of Godiva chocolates and a card for her on your way home.
- Rent a movie you know she wants to see.
- Take her on a Saturday shopping excursion and buy her lunch. (Please note: It's HER dollar at Nieman Marcus, but she'll enjoy just spending time with you!)
- Surprise her with a limo ride and a really fancy evening.
- Make her birthday an annual "big event" and try to top what you did last year.
- Memorize her sizes and pick up something nice at Victoria's Secret.
- When you go to the store, pick up her favorite brand of beverage.

Here's how I proposed to Jana (on her birthday, December 17, 1994):

I had my marriage proposal typed into the program at Ballet Dallas' *Nutcracker*. It was in just one program, printed at the bottom of the donor page, and I picked up that special program when I picked up our tickets at the will-call ticket counter. I later switched out her "normal" program with my fixed one. A limo had picked us up at home, taken us to eat, then to the theater, and then picked us up from the theater to look at Christmas lights.

When we got back to the house, I had already had my next door neighbor come over and set out flowers, champagne, cheese, turn on the Christmas lights, and have music playing on the stereo. How it ended: She never looked through the program to see the proposal until we were back home, and it wasn't until I asked her (for the third time) to check out the list of donors to see if anyone we knew was on it that her eyes finally traveled the length of the whole page!

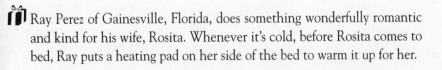 Ray Perez of Gainesville, Florida, does something wonderfully romantic and kind for his wife, Rosita. Whenever it's cold, before Rosita comes to bed, Ray puts a heating pad on her side of the bed to warm it up for her.

Tips:

What I realized after reading Scott's suggestions is that Charlie is more romantic than I thought he was! I also remembered an ad I had seen recently posted in Lansing, Michigan, for Precious Party Planners, Inc.:

Precious Party Planners, Inc.
presents "Romance in a Basket"
for
SWEETEST DAY
(date)
Instead of waiting away your Sweetest Day in a long line,
Why not order a picnic basket for two.
Dine in your car overlooking the sunset, or that magical place where you met.
Dinner comes to you all prepared (in the Lansing area)
Baskets will include:
Two candles/with matches
Two wine glasses (plastic)
Sparkling Cider
LOVE CHOCOLATES
Main course and your choice of two sides
And dessert
(Call to place your order with at least one week's notice)
TREAT YOURSELF TO SOMETHING SPECIAL AND DIFFERENT!

Isn't this a wonderfully romantic idea? For those of you who live in the Lansing area, call them. For those of you who don't, why not create your own basket and surprise your significant other or your family?

I was deeply blessed to first meet David Roth at the International Humor and Creativity Conference in April 1995 where we were both presenting. After experiencing his deeply sensitive words and music, I shared with him "The Johnny Story" from my book CARE *Packages for the Workplace—Dozens of Little Things You Can Do to Regenerate Spirit at Work*, hoping that he would create something that would be able to touch many lives on a different level from my writing and speaking. This is the song he has written to *celebrate* Johnny and to *celebrate* how one enthusiastic, joyful, committed person can make a difference in this world:

A Little Something More

I run a local grocery store, a friendly place to shop
One day a boy came to my market looking for a job
He said his name was Johnny, I could see that he was different
I also saw a sparkle in his eye and so I hired him.

I started him collecting carts and sweeping up the floor
In no time flat young Johnny was a bagger in my store
He took such pride and worked so hard it rubbed off on my crew
And just because he only did the best that he could do.

Johnny is a bagger in our local grocery store
Packing people's food away as they go out the automatic door
Just a job ten thousand other people do
But Johnny found a way to make it new.

Johnny came to work one Monday grinning ear to ear
He told me that his dad was teaching him to use the home
    computer
Typing this and printing that, whatever he had done
The look on Johnny's face that day was brighter than the Indiana
    summer sun.

A couple weeks went by and I began to notice something
It started in the parking lot after people had done their shopping
They were digging through their groceries and coming out with
    smiles
I made a mental note and came inside to check the aisles.

The store was pretty busy, must be five o'clock, I guessed
And here the line in Johnny's lane was twice as long as all the rest
"No waiting on 1 through 4," I said, they didn't seem to care
"We want to be on Johnny's line," they said, and stayed right there.

That's when I discovered Johnny's magic secret brainstorm
A little note he put in every shopper's bag before they went home
And every note had what he called his "thought" for that same day
And Johnny signed the back of each good thought he gave away.

Johnny is a bagger in our local grocery store
Packing people's food away as they go out the automatic door
Just a job ten thousand other people do
But Johnny found a way to make it new.

I can't begin to tell you how the mood in our store shifted
Whoever heard of coming home from shopping so uplifted
We see new people every day we've never seen before
And some folks say they come in now each time they pass our
     store.

Of course Johnny's got the longest lines of any shop in town
He's also got some syndrome that the doctors label "Down"
If you ask me how one person makes a difference anymore
Come on by, see Johnny at our store.

Johnny is a bagger in our local grocery store
Packing people's food away as they go out the automatic door
And he's making things a little better than they were before
The most important person in our store
Johnny always gives a little something more!

I run a local grocery store, a friendly place to shop
One day a boy came to my market looking for a job . . .

Afterword

THINK ABOUT YOUR FAMILY. How would you answer the question, "What is a family?" Edith Schaeffer in her book *What Is a Family?* suggests several answers, each one forming a chapter in the book:

A Changing Life Mobile
The Birthplace of Creativity
A Formation Center for Human Relationships
A Shelter in a Time of Storm
A Perpetual Relay of Truth
A Door That Has Hinges and a Lock
A Museum of Memories

When Jeff Herring, a columnist for the *Tallahassee Democrat* and a licensed marriage and family therapist, reviewed my first book *CARE Packages for the Workplace—Dozens of Little Things You Can Do to Regenerate Spirit at Work*, he asked the following questions:

- What would happen in our families if we applied the same **CARE** acronym at home? What would it be like to find **creative and fun ways to communicate** with those with whom we live?

- What would it be like for the teenager who has been giving you trouble to find a note from you under the pillow that simply says, "I love you and I'm glad you're here **(appreciation)**."

- What would it be like to come home to an **atmosphere** where you can be yourself, feel loved, and grow to your full potential?

Close to Home © John McPherson/Dist. by Universal Press Syndicate.

- What if your **"reason for being"** was your relationships? How would life be different?

- What would happen in our families if we brought as much **enthusiasm** home with us as we had at the football game? Could home become an exciting place to be?

Ask yourselves these questions—over and over again. I hope this book has given you lots of ideas to regenerate spirit in your family, but it is ultimately your CHOICE. You have to be the one to answer these questions in your own life, and then act in a way that demonstrates your commitment. Remember the elements of a spirited family:

C = Creative Communication
A = Atmosphere and Appreciation for All
R = Respect and Reason for Being
E = Empathy and Enthusiasm

As each family member learns to CARE, your family life will be richer in every way!

Resources

Ageless Design, Inc.
(resources for helping prepare your home for age-related concerns)
12633 159th Court North
Jupiter, FL 33478
561-745-0210
Fax: 561-744-9572
ageless.design@ibm.net

JoAnn Zimmerman, president and founder
Amanda the Panda
1000 73rd Street, Suite 12
Des Moines, IA 50311-1321
515-223-HUGS (4847)
Fax: 515-223-4782

Bereaved Parents of the USA
(a support group for parents who have lost a child)
National Headquarters
Theresa and John Goodrich
P.O. Box 703
Hinsdale, IL 60522-0703
630-325-2816

CARE
(Cooperative for Assistance and Relief Everywhere, Inc.)
151 Ellis Street
Atlanta, GA 30303
800-422-7385

info@care.org
web site: www.care.org

The Comfort Heart Initiative
(providing comfort for cancer victims)
Box 27013
Halifax, Nova Scotia B3H 4M8
Canada
(Make checks or money order for $10.00 per heart payable to
    The Canadian Cancer Society)

Compassion™ International
Colorado Springs, CO 80997-0009
800-336-7676

Family Literacy Program
641 S.E. 15th Avenue #200
Boynton Beach, FL 33435
561-533-8130 or 561-738-2614
emdfl@worldnet.att.net

Focus on the Family
Colorado Springs, CO 80995
800-232-6459

Focus on the Family Canada
Box 9800
Vancouver, BC V6B 4G3
Canada
(The monthly magazine *Focus on the Family* is free.
    Write if you would like a copy.)

Barbara McCauley
Horizons Unlimited
854 Elm Avenue
Salt Lake City, UT 84106
801-466-1117

The "Red Plate"
Waechtersbach USA
4201 N.E. 34th Street

Kansas City, MO 64117
816-455-3800
Fax: 816-459-7705

David Roth
Maythelight Music
18952 40th Place NE
Seattle, WA 98155-2810
Phone/Fax: 206-364-7128
RothDM@aol.com
web site: http://songs.com/dr

Samaritan's Purse
"Operation Christmas Child"
P.O. Box 3000
Boone, NC 28607
704-262-1980

The Scrap Exchange
(Check the yellow pages to see if there is one in your area.)
Northgate Mall
1058 West Club Blvd.
Durham, NC 27701
919-286-2559

STOP Violence Coalition
(Kindness Campaign)
5811 W. 63rd Street, Suite 112
Overland Park, KS 66202
913-831-9221
Fax: 913-831-9312

WHERE DID THE FIRST CARE PACKAGE® COME FROM?

In the process of researching this book, I learned about the wonderful history of the CARE package, which originated with CARE, the international relief and development agency. I'd like to share this story with you.

On a sunny afternoon, in May 1946, a small crowd formed on the docks of Le Havre, a French city still in ruins from the war. A local resistance hero, Marcel Fernez, stepped through the gathering of friends and neighbors to sign for a food parcel sent to him by an American he had never met. As he hoisted the parcel up onto his shoulder, Fernez became the recipient of the very first CARE Package®. This plain brown package of food was the creation of a new American charity—CARE—founded to help survivors of World War II. In the years that followed, Americans sent some 100 million CARE Packages to people in need all over the world; and CARE continues to help the world's poor today.

CARE® (which stands for "Cooperative for Assistance and Relief Everywhere") still provides people with the ability to touch lives and make a difference. Several of CARE's current donors are people who have become self-sufficient through CARE programs and want to give others the same opportunity. This spirit has helped make CARE the world's largest relief and development agency in existence today, and it literally thrives on the unconditional caring felt by Americans that transcends politics, race, nationality, and all other barriers separating people.

CARE continues its mission of working with the world's needy and giving them the tools to achieve economic and social well-being. CARE now works with 48 million people in sixty-six developing and emerging nations in Africa, Asia, Eastern Europe, and Latin America. Its programs encompass health, nutrition, family planning, emergency relief, girls' education, small business support, agriculture, and environmental protection. And fifty years after the first CARE Package arrived in France, CARE has returned to Europe to assist the people of Bosnia recovering from war and ethnic strife.

Over its fifty-year history, CARE has brought its message of hope to more than 1 billion people in 125 countries. For more information about CARE, please see the organization's site on the World Wide Web at www.care.org. Or contact: 151 Ellis Street, Atlanta, GA 30303; 800-422-7385; or info@care.org.

CARE and CARE Package are registered service marks of the
Cooperative for Assistance and Relief Everywhere, Inc.

Biography

BARBARA GLANZ is the mother of three children on earth and one in heaven, a grandmother-to-be, and a wife of thirty-one years. She grew up in Harlan, Iowa, went to college at the University of Kansas, has lived in Western Springs, Illinois, for twenty-nine years, and is seriously contemplating a move to Sarasota, Florida, with her husband, Charlie, in the near future. She is a pianist, a reader, a lap swimmer, and a lover of people, food, travel, dolls, and a good bargain!

In her professional life she is the author of three best-selling business books: *The Creative Communicator*, *Building Customer Loyalty*, and *CARE Packages for the Workplace—Dozens of Little Things You Can Do to Regenerate Spirit at Work*. Known as "the business speaker who speaks to your heart as well as to your head," her exciting, motivational, action-oriented keynotes and workshops focus on three areas: **Improving Internal Communication**, **Building Customer Loyalty**, and **Regenerating the Spirit in Your Workplace and in Your Home**.

Barbara has spoken on three continents and in forty-six states to conferences, associations, and organizations such as IBM, the State of Michigan, AT&T, Mobil Research & Development Corporation, Hilton Hotels, First Chicago Bank, Rockwell International, the Gap, Nationwide Insurance, the EPA, the International Customer Service Association, Abbott Labs, Blue Cross Blue Shield, Southwest Airlines, USAA, the Conference Board of Canada, the Hellenic Management Association, the U.S. Department of Energy, the IRS, the Shedd Aquarium, Delta Air Lines, Boeing, and A&E Television. She was recently selected as one of eighteen speakers worldwide to participate in two internationally marketed live satellite business TV series called Masters on Motivation and *The Evolving Workplace*.

Barbara earned a B.S. in English and an M.S. in Adult Continuing Education and is the former director of quality in training for Kaset International, a Times Mirror training company. She is a member of ASTD, the Board of Professional Speakers of Illinois, the National Association of Female Executives, the National Speaker's Association, Gamma Phi Beta, the Advisory Board of Loyola University's Center for Ethics, and is featured in *Who's Who of American Women, Who's Who in Entertainment,* and *Who's Who in the Midwest.* She recently earned her CSP, Certified Speaking Professional designation, from the National Speaker's Association. Fewer than 298 people internationally have earned this honor.

More than just an exciting speaker, consultant, and author, Barbara has three additional "claims to fame": her great-grandfather laid the cornerstone where the four states come together (Page, Arizona, is named after him); she played the piano on the TV show *Talent Sprouts;* and she directed David Hasselhof of *Knight Rider* and *Baywatch* fame in his first high-school play! Barbara lives and breathes her personal motto, **"Spreading Contagious Enthusiasm."**™

Bresnahan Portrait Studio

More CARE Packages
for the Home

IF YOU HAVE unusual family traditions or heartwarming stories of things you or family members or friends have done to make your homes more caring places to live, please share them with me for a second edition of *CARE Packages for the Home.*

Often we are so close to our own actions and traditions that we don't consider them "special"; however, when we share them with others, we realize that we are making a difference right where we live, and we do have something important to share.

Also, I would love to hear from you about how this book has impacted your life and family.

Barbara Glanz
More CARE Packages
4047 Howard Avenue
Western Springs, IL 60558
708-246-8594
Fax: 708-246-5123
bglanz@barbaraglanz.com
web site: http://www.barbaraglanz.com

If you are interested in having me do a speech or a workshop for a group to which you belong or an organization that is having a meeting or convention, please call for a promotional packet.

Bibliography/Sources

YOU'LL NOTICE that many of the books on this list are older books. One of the reasons for this is that many times older works have a depth and a classic approach that is not affected by time. Parenting and personal growth are like that. Another reason for the age of some of these books is that they are the resources that were most helpful to me in raising my family and in my own personal growth and development. They are the books that I have chosen to keep in my library because of the impact they have had on my life, so I choose to share them with you.

Bradshaw, Elma S. "Being An Effective Grandmother." N.p., n.d.

Campbell, Dr. Ross. *How to Really Love Your Child.* 1979. Wheaton, IL: Victor Books.

Campbell, Dr. Ross. *How to Really Love Your Teenager.* 1971. Wheaton, IL: Victor Books.

Caruba, Alan. Ten Secrets to Avoid Boredom. N.p., n.d.

Chapman, Gary. *The Five Love Languages.* 1992. Chicago: Northfield Publishing.

Covey, Stephen. *The Seven Habits of Highly Effective Families.* 1997. New York: Franklin Covey/Golden Books.

Dobson, James C. *Dare to Discipline.* 1997. New York: Bantam Books.

———. *Parenting Isn't for Cowards.* 1987. Dallas: Word Publishing.

Doherty, William J. *The Intentional Family.* 1997. Reading, MA: Addison Wesley Publishing.

Drescher, John. *If I Were Starting A Family Again.* 1979. Nashville: Abingdon Press.

Frost, Gerhard E. *Bless My Growing.* 1974. Minneapolis: Augsburg Publishing House.

Frankl, Victor. *Man's Search for Meaning.* 1984. New York: Washington Square Press.

Gibran, Kahlil. *The Prophet.* 1951. New York: Alfred A. Knopf.

Glanz, Barbara A. *CARE Packages for the Workplace—Dozens of Little Things You Can Do to Regenerate Spirit at Work.* 1996. New York: McGraw-Hill.

———. *The Creative Communicator—399 Ways to Make Your Business Communications More Meaningful and Inspiring.* 1993. New York. McGraw-Hill.

Halberstam, Yitta, and Leventhal, Judith. 1997. *Small Miracles—Extraordinary Coincidences from Everyday Life.* Holbrook, MA: Adams Media Corporation.

Howard, Linda. *Mothers Are People, Too.* 1976. Plainfield, NJ: Logos International.

Irion, Mary Jean. *Yes, World: A Mosaic of Meditation.* N.p., n.d.

Johnson, Barbara. *Fresh Elastic for Stretched-Out Moms.* 1986. Old Tappan, NJ: Fleming H. Revell Co.

———. *So, Stick a Geranium in Your Hat and Be Happy!* 1990. Dallas: Word Publishing.

———. *Splashes of Joy in the Cesspools of Life.* 1992. Dallas: Word Publishing.

Kerr, Barbara. "Happy Family Study." Presented to the American Psychological Association, August 1997. Tempe, AZ: Arizona State University.

Lair, Jess, Ph.D. *I Ain't Much, Baby, But I'm All I've Got.* 1972. Garden City, NY: Doubleday & Company, Inc.

Leider, Richard. "Till Travel Do Us Part." *Training and Development.* May 1991

Lindbergh, Anne Morrow. *Gift from the Sea.* 1975. New York: Pantheon.

Macaulay, Susan Schaeffer. *Something Beautiful from God.* 1980. Westchester, IL: Cornerstone Books.

Mandino, Og. *A Better Way to Live.* 1991. New York: Bantam Books.

Markova, Dawna, and Daphne Rose Kingma. *Random Acts of Kindness.* 1993 Berkeley, CA: Conari Press.

Mayhall, Carole. *Words That Hurt, Words That Heal.* 1986. Colorado Springs: Navpress.

McCauley, Barbara. *Where Are the Other Nine?* N.p., n.d.

———. *Friendship is an Art.* N.p., n.d.

McPherson, John. *Close to Home Unplugged.* 1997. Kansas City, MO: Andrews McMeel Publishing.

———. *Close to Home Revisited.* 1995. Kansas City, MO: Andrews McMeel Publishing.

Moore, Pat, and Charles Paul Conn. "Look Closer at Me." *Disguised: A True Story.* 1985. Dallas: Word Publishing.

Moran, Victoria. *Shelter for the Spirit. How to Make Your Home a Haven in a Hectic World.* 1997. New York: HarperCollins.

Powell, John. *Fully Human Fully Alive.* 1976. Niles, IL: Argus Communications.

Prather, Hugh. *The Quiet Answer.* 1982. New York: Doubleday.

Raines, Robert A. *To Kiss the Joy.* 1973. Waco, TX: Word Books.

Remen, Rachel Naomi, M.D. *Kitchen Table Wisdom—Stories That Heal.* 1996. New York: Riverhead Books.

Ryan, Michael. "How One Woman's Twelve Friends Became a Family." *Parade.* March 30, 1997.

Sallee, Lynn Kant. *To God from Mom.* 1975. Grand Rapids, MI: Baker Book House.

Sark. *Inspiration Sandwich—Stories to Inspire Our Creative Freedom.* 1992. Berkeley, CA: Celestial Arts.

———. *Living Juicy.* 1994. Berkeley, CA: Celestial Arts.

Selling Power, October 1997.

Smollin, Anne Bryan, CSJ, Ph.D. *Jiggle Your Heart and Tickle Your Soul.* 1994. Latham, NY: Canticle Press.

St. Michael's Lutheran Church. "Listen to the Children." Hamburg, PA. N.p., n.d.

Swindoll, Charles R. *Strengthening Your Grip.* 1982. Waco, TX: Word Books.

Trelease, Jim. *The Read Aloud Handbook.* 1982. (Updated 1995). New York: Penguin Books.

Unell, Barbara C., and Wycoft, Jerry L., Ph.D. *20 Teachable Virtues— Practical Ways to Pass on Lessons of Virtue and Character to Your Children.* 1995. New York: The Berkley Publishing Group.

Viorst, Judith. *Necessary Losses.* 1986. New York: Simon and Schuster.

Some Very Special Children's Books That Exemplify Spirit:

Bartone, Elisa, and Lewin, Ted. *Peppe, the Lamplighter*. 1993. New York: Lothrop.

Cannon, Janell. *Stellaluna*. 1993. San Diego: Harcourt Brace and Co.

Fleming, Virginia. *Be Good to Eddie Lee*. 1993. New York: Philomel Books.

Joyce, William. *Santa Calls*. 1993. New York: Harper Collins Juvenile Books.

MacLachlan, Patricia. *All the Places to Love*. 1994. New York: HarperCollins.

Miles, Bernard. *Favourite Tales from Shakespeare*. 1976. London: The Hamlyn Publishing Group Limited.

Pfister, Marcus. *The Rainbow Fish*. 1992. New York: North-South Books.

Rylant, Cynthia. *All I See*. 1988. New York: Orchard Books.

———. *An Angel for Solomon Singer*. 1992. New York: Orchard Books.

Spinelli, Eileen. *Somebody Loves You, Mr. Hatch*. 1991. New York: Bradbury Press.

Tazewell, Charles. *The Littlest Angel*. 1946. Nashville: Ideals Children's Books.

Viorst, Judith. *Alexander and the Terrible, Horrible, No Good, Very Bad Day*. 1992. New York: Atheneum.

Wojciechowski, Susan. *The Christmas Miracle of Jonathan Toomey*. 1995. Cambridge, MA: Candlewick Press.

Wood, Douglas. *The Old Turtle*. 1993. Duluth, MN: Pfeifer-Hamilton.